Surrender and Survival

SURRENDER
AND
SURVIVAL

The Experience of American
POWs in the Pacific
1941–1945

E. BARTLETT KERR

WILLIAM MORROW AND COMPANY, INC.
NEW YORK

Library of Congress Cataloging in Publication Data

Kerr, E. Bartlett.
   Surrender and survival.

   1. World War, 1939–1945—Prisoners and prisons, Japanese. 2. World War, 1939–1945—Atrocities. 3. Prisoners of war—United States. 4. Prisoners of war—Pacific Area. II. Title.
   D805.J3K43 1985   940.54'72'52   84–25586
   ISBN 0–688–04344–5

Printed in the United States of America

2 3 4 5 6 7 8 9 10

BOOK DESIGN BY ELLEN LO GIUDICE

To my father and the others
who did not return to tell
their stories

FOREWORD

Few Americans today are aware of the experience of over twenty-five thousand U.S. soldiers, sailors, airmen, and Marines who were prisoners of the Japanese during World War II. The valiant stand of the defenders of Wake Island, Bataan, and Corregidor, against impossible odds, held the national spotlight briefly in early 1942. With the fall of these U.S. outposts in the Pacific, a curtain of obscurity dropped over their defeated garrisons, the largest number of Americans ever to surrender to a foreign power. In the years that followed, these men, scattered in prison camps across East Asia, struggled for survival under conditions which at times were so horrible as to have few parallels in modern warfare.

In the United States, little was known of the fate of the American prisoners until January 1944, when President Roosevelt authorized the release of information brought back by men who had escaped from a POW camp in 1943. Newspapers headlined and grimly recounted the Japanese harsh and inhumane treatment of American prisoners. However, these stories were soon buried in the avalanche of events that eventually led to the end of World War II.

Among millions of other servicemen, the return of surviving POWs attracted little public notice. Some ex-POWs shared their experiences with families and friends, a few wrote about them, and still others were silent. With the meager information available from returning POWs and from the U.S. government, most families of those who died or were killed as POWs drew heavily on the atrocity stories briefly featured in the newspapers in early 1944. With such visions of endless horror it is not surprising that many of the next of kin were loath to probe further.

Such were my feelings in the fall of 1945 after I learned of my father's death as a prisoner of the Japanese. In the decades that followed, my curiosity was limited to reading one or two books by former POWs. But in the late Seventies after a trip to the Philippines, where I visited the sites of several of the larger POW camps, my interest in what these men had gone through became intense. My earliest focus was on the experiences of the men—my father was one of them—on the voyage of the Japanese ship *Oryoku Maru* in late 1944 and the ordeal of the survivors that followed the sinking of this ship. I researched and wrote an account of this journey, but even before I had completed it I realized that it was but a single episode in a much larger story. Nowhere was there a full account of the long struggle for survival of thousands of Americans suddenly thrust into the very center of an ideological and racial contest between two alien cultures.

The objective of this book is to provide this long-absent historical account. One that presents a broad mosaic of POW experiences—brutality, hunger, disease, overwork, and tedium; portrays individual reactions—courage and hope, fear and anguish, and, only rarely, joy and happiness; describes Japanese policies and regulations for war prisoners and the way prison camp commanders and guards carried them out; discloses the efforts of Allied relief agencies that brought hope and comfort to American POWs, and the actions of U.S. bombers and submarines that unknowingly brought an untimely death to many others; and, finally, tells of the victorious return of Allied forces and of the liberation of the Americans who made it till the end.

For those readers who lived through World War II and for others who have grown up since, it is my hope that what follows will illuminate a dark and little-understood chapter in the history of that great conflict.

—E. BARTLETT KERR

CONTENTS

CHRONOLOGY

1941

Dec • Japanese capture Americans—China, Guam, & Wake Island
     • Tojo establishes Prisoner of War Bureau

1942

Jan • Guam captives to Zentsuji, Japan
    • Wake & China captives to Shanghai, China
Mar • Japanese capture Americans—Java, USS *Houston*
    • General MacArthur to Australia. Vows return
Apr • Bataan falls. Death March to Camp O'Donnell
May • Corregidor surrenders. Captives to Bilibid Prison, Cabanatuan, & Tarlac
Jun • Americans transfer O'Donnell to Cabanatuan
    • 1,500 Americans die at O'Donnell
    • Bilibid becomes hospital & staging area
    • Tojo announces "No work—no food"
    • POW camp chiefs meet in Toyko
    • Japanese execute 10 Americans when one escapes. Threaten to carry out punishment in future escapes
    • Naval defeat at Midway halts Japanese advance
Jul • 800 die at Cabanatuan
Aug • American generals & colonels to Formosa
    • Guadalcanal. U.S. forces take the offensive in S. Pacific
Oct • 1,931 Philippine Islands (PI) POWs on *Tottori Maru* to Manchuria & Japan to work in industry
    • 890 POWs from Java to Malaya, Japan & Burma
    • Work begins on Burma–Thailand railroad
    • War Ministry publishes "Basic Food Allowances for POW"
Nov • 1,000 POWs move Luzon to Davao Penal Colony
    • 1,500 PI POWs to Osaka, Japan, on *Nagato Maru*

11

- 1,800 POWs work on airfields—Nichols, Nielson, Clark, Palawan
- 400 load ships in Manila

Dec
- Red Cross supplies & mail reach POWs at Cabanatuan, Bilibid, Shanghai, & Japan
- Mortality rate at Cabanatuan drops after total deaths reach 2,545
- Japanese transmit names of POWs in PI to the U.S.

1943

Jan
- PI POWs write first postcards home
- U.S. forces begin drive on New Guinea

Feb
- Utinsky & Phillips begin smuggling money & food to POWs at Cabanatuan & Manila
- Japanese make Zentsuji an officers' camp

Mar
- More than 500 Americans die during winter at Osaka, Mukden, & Pusan

Apr
- Shinagawa, near Tokyo, functions as a POW hospital & postal center
- McCoy, Mellnik, Dyess, & 7 others escape from Davao Penal Colony

Jul
- Davao escapees reach freedom in Australia

Aug
- 500 PI POWs to mining camp Kyushu, Japan

Sep
- Over 800 POWs work on airfields at Lipa, Las Piñas

Oct
- 96 American construction workers executed on Wake Island
- 800 more PI POWs to Japan work force

Nov
- Burma–Thailand railroad completed. 20 percent of Americans die

Dec
- Second shipment of Red Cross supplies reaches some Luzon, China, & Japan camps. (Other camps later)
- Americans take Tarawa. Begin offensive in the Central Pacific

1944

Jan
- U.S. releases Davao escapees' accounts of Japanese atrocities

Mar
- Japanese decide to move POWs out of PI
- Two shipments totaling 500 men leave for Japan

May
- Japanese arrest black market participants at Cabanatuan & Manila. Some are executed

Jun
- Allied forces invade France

- U.S. Navy victor in Battle of the Philippine Sea
- 1,200 POWs moved from Davao to Luzon

Jul
- Roosevelt approves attack on Philippines next
- More than 2,500 men leave PI on *Canadian Inventor* & *Nissyo Maru* to Japanese industrial & mining camps
- U.S. forces seize Saipan & Guam for bombing Japan

Aug
- 985 more POWs leave the PI for Japan aboard *Noto Maru*

Sep
- U.S. submarine sinks *Shinyo Maru* carrying last POWs from Mindanao. 668 lost; 82 survivors rescued by guerrillas, reach Australia by submarine
- U.S. forces take Moratai, 300 miles south of PI
- Navy carriers bomb Manila harbor

Oct
- 1,100 men PI to Formosa on *Haru Maru*. 39 die in transit
- About 1,800 POWs from PI on *Arisan Maru* en route Japan torpedoed by U.S. submarine. Five reach China & freedom. Four recaptured. Others perish
- U.S. Army lands on Leyte, PI. MacArthur returns

Nov
- *Hakusan Maru* carries Red Cross supplies from Siberia to Japan & Korea. Bulk remains in storage
- B-29's from Saipan bomb Tokyo
- Generals & colonels moved from Formosa to N. Manchuria

Dec
- U.S. bombs kill 19 POWs, wound 35 at Mukden, Manchuria
- Japanese guards massacre Americans on Palawan; 11 of 150 survive
- U.S. carrier planes sink *Oryoku Maru* with 1,619 POWs aboard; nearly 300 die. Survivors continue north aboard *Enoura Maru* & *Brazil Maru*

1945

Jan
- MacArthur's forces land on Luzon
- *Enoura Maru* bombed at Takao, Formosa, killing more than 290 POWs
- *Brazil Maru* reaches Japan with about 500 survivors

Feb
- U.S. Rangers liberate 516 POWs at Cabanatuan
- Sixth Army frees 828 POWs at Bilibid Prison

Mar
- B-29 incendiary raids begin. 80,000 killed in Tokyo
- Japanese order POWs moved from areas threatened by Allied attack

Apr
- U.S. submarine sinks *Awa Maru* after U.S. guarantees safe passage
- U.S. forces invade Okinawa

May
- Shanghai POWs move near Peking. (Later to Hokkaido, Japan)

- Japanese move POWs out of some Osaka camps
- Japanese capture increasing number of downed U.S. fliers
- 60 U.S. fliers burn to death in Tokyo jail during firebombing

Jun–Jul
- Allies issue Potsdam Declaration. Promise stern justice for war criminals
- Executions of downed airmen exceed 200

Aug
- Atomic bombs released over Hiroshima & Nagasaki; 135,000 Japanese die
- Russia declares war on Japan
- Emperor announces Japanese surrender
- 16 American fliers executed
- War Ministry orders military documents burned. Advises personnel who mistreated POWs to flee
- Russian troops liberate POWs at Mukden, Manchuria
- B-29's drop food & clothing to POW camps

Sep
- U.S. troops land on Honshu
- Japanese sign surrender documents on battleship *Missouri*
- U.S. rescue teams free over 13,400 Americans from Japan, Manchuria, Korea, Thailand & the Celebes

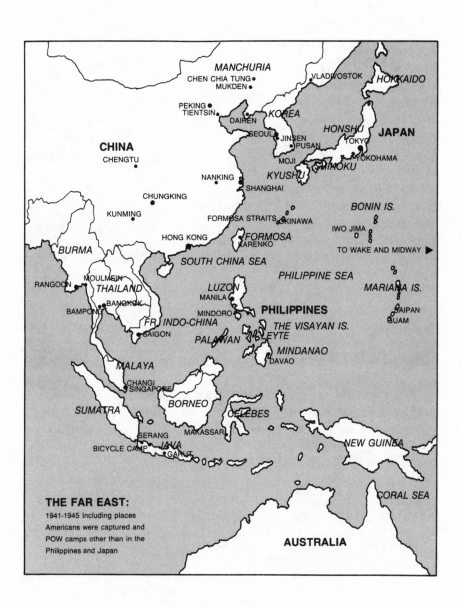

THE FAR EAST:

1941-1945 Including places
Americans were captured and
POW camps other than in the
Philippines and Japan

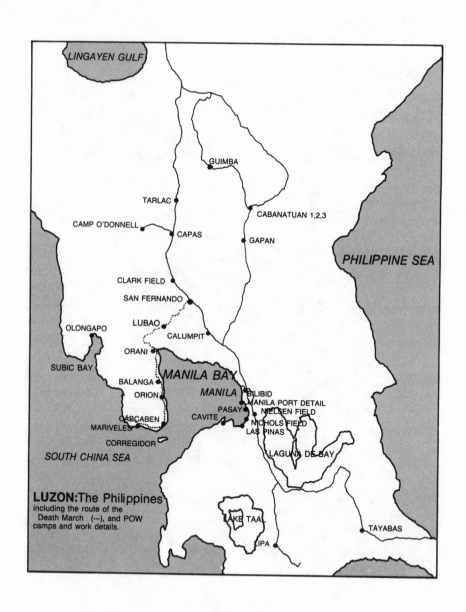

LINGAYEN GULF

GUIMBA

TARLAC

CABANATUAN 1,2,3

CAMP O'DONNELL

CAPAS

GAPAN

PHILIPPINE SEA

CLARK FIELD

SAN FERNANDO

LUBAO

OLONGAPO

CALUMPIT

ORANI

SUBIC BAY

MANILA BAY

BALANGA

ORION

MANILA

BILIBID

MANILA PORT DETAIL

PASAY

NIELSEN FIELD

CAVITE

NICHOLS FIELD

CABCABEN

LAS PINAS

MARIVELES

CORREGIDOR

SOUTH CHINA SEA

LAGUNA DE BAY

LUZON: The Philippines
including the route of the
Death March (---), and POW
camps and work details.

LAKE TAAL

LIPA

TAYABAS

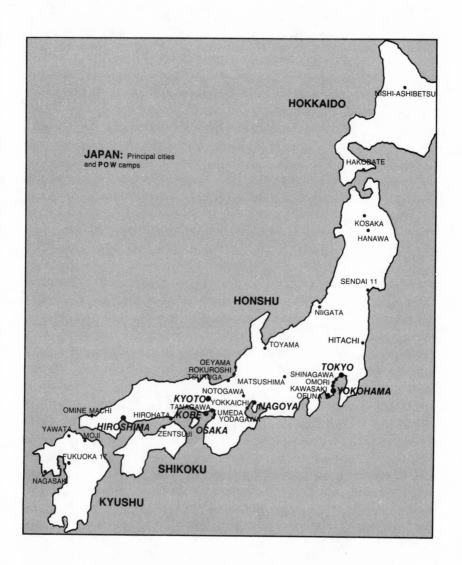

JAPAN: Principal cities and P O W camps

HOKKAIDO

NISHI-ASHIBETSU

HAKODATE

KOSAKA
HANAWA

SENDAI 11

HONSHU

NIIGATA

HITACHI

TOYAMA

OEYAMA
ROKUROSHI
TSURUGA

MATSUSHIMA

TOKYO
SHINAGAWA
OMORI
KAWASAKI
OFUNA
YOKOHAMA

NOTOGAWA

KYOTO
YOKKAICHI
TANAGAWA
NAGOYA

OMINE MACHI
HIROHATA
KOBE
UMEDA
YODAGAWA

YAWATA
HIROSHIMA
OSAKA

MOJI
ZENTSUJI

FUKUOKA 17

SHIKOKU

NAGASAKI

KYUSHU

Surrender and Survival

PROLOGUE

★ ★ ★ 1 ★ ★ ★

In the spring of 1941, England stood alone against Nazi Germany, which had conquered all of Europe and had a nonaggression pact with Soviet Russia. In Southeast Asia, Japanese military expansionism threatened American, British, and Dutch interests. In March the U.S. Secretary of State Cordell Hull and a new ambassador from Japan, Admiral Kichisaburo Nomura, had begun negotiations to ease the tension between their two countries. Talks bogged down early. By May, Hull was very discouraged and visitors to his office were apt to hear him say "everything is going hellward."

In that same month the United States and Great Britain agreed upon what would later become known as the "Europe First" strategy, the core of a plan called "Rainbow-5" by military planners. This strategy called for a massive buildup and defensive to defeat Germany while maintaining a purely defensive posture against a possible attack by the Japanese.

The American plan for defending the Philippines was called "War Plan Orange-3" (orange was a color code for Japan; other potential enemies had different colors). The plan assumed a Japanese surprise attack on Luzon, the principal island of the Philippine group, with the major objective of seizing the port city of Manila with its modern and strategically located harbor. The U.S. plan, recognizing Japanese superior military strength, envisioned abandoning the city of Manila to the enemy and withdrawing to defensive lines on the Bataan Peninsula, a heavily jungled, mountainous landmass which juts like a huge thumb down the west side of Manila Bay. The troops on Bataan would provide land protection to nearby Corregidor and the three other heavily fortified islands whose big guns dominated the sea approaches to Manila Bay and its harbor facilities. The plan called for Bataan and Corregidor to be defended to "the last extremity." Ideally, this would buy enough time to permit a powerful American fleet to steam out of Pearl Harbor, meet and defeat the Japanese fleet, and then proceed to the relief of the Philippine defense forces.

Actually, few military officers believed in the plan. Naval officers estimated that the U.S. fleet would take a year or more to fight its way across the Pacific. As for the ground forces, after years of War Department refusal to send more troops and equipment to the Philippines, realistic Army planners saw little chance for the Philippine defenders to hold out for more than six months. Finally, the plan was silent on the size and nature of the relief force to be sent to the Philippines, a reflection of the underequipped and undermanned U.S. Army prior to 1941.

Other U.S. possessions in the Pacific were equally ill prepared. In 1938 the Navy had strongly recommended the fortification of the islands of Guam, Wake, and Midway to serve as advance naval and air bases in the western Pacific. The bases were intended to strengthen the defense of Hawaii to help keep the sea-lanes to the Philippines open. Congress turned down the recommendations on Guam for fear of offending the Japanese, who were themselves busily fortifying Guam's neighboring island Saipan. The development of Wake Island as an advance air base was approved, but funds would not be provided until 1940. With the failure to fortify Guam and no action to strengthen the forces in the Philippines, a successful defense in the western Pacific was virtually impossible.

In July 1941, just a few days after Germany launched a massive attack against Russia, in a rapid turnabout the United States suddenly decided to make a serious effort to hold the Philippines. First indications of this came when President Franklin D. Roosevelt created a new command in the Philippines and appointed then Lt. Gen. Douglas MacArthur to head it. MacArthur, formerly Army Chief of Staff, had since his retirement in 1936 served as the military advisor to the Philippine government and helped it to develop its own defense force. His new command would include both American forces and the partially trained and equipped Philippine Army, which was called into the service of the United States at this time. Soon after MacArthur's appointment, Gen. George C. Marshall, the Army Chief of Staff, announced to his top subordinates that it was now the policy of the United States to defend the Philippines and that reinforcements must be sent there as rapidly as possible. A key part of the reinforcement effort would be the establishment of a formidable force of B-17 heavy bombers—the country's newest and best—in the Philippines to deter Japanese attack. This strategic concept, which appeared seemingly out of thin air, may have been the driving force behind the abrupt change in Washington's attitude toward defending the Far East. So, beginning in August, the War Department made hurried and often chaotic efforts to rush men, guns, and planes to the Philippines. Unfortunately, thousands of men and tons of equipment were still to be on West Coast piers or on the high seas when the hostilities began.

By the first of October, as reinforcements began reaching the Philippines, General MacArthur, highly optimistic, informed Washington that the War Plan Orange-3 concept of defending Manila Bay was not enough. He asked for and obtained approval to enlarge his mission to include the defense of all the Philippine islands. This decision was predicated on his deeply held conviction that the Japanese attack would not come until April 1942. But with their oil supplies denied them by the United States, the British, and the Dutch, the Japanese were wasting no time and were already hard at work on detailed planning for the conquest of the Philippines, Malaya, Java, Borneo, and the Netherlands Indies as, in mid-October, Gen. Hideki Tojo took office as premier. As December began, negotiations between the United States and Japan in Washington had broken down completely, and Imperial Japanese Army and Navy units were moving into positions to attack Allied possessions throughout the Pacific area.

The forces General MacArthur had to meet this onslaught numbered about 120,000 men on paper, an impressive number until examined carefully. Most of the force was made up of untrained Filipino soldiers—many had not yet fired their rifles—assigned to ten reserve Army divisions which had been only partially mobilized. About 23,000 American officers and men had arrived in the Philippines by early December. Some of the larger units or groups to which these men were assigned were:

GROUND FORCES

59th and 60th Coast Artillery. These two units on Corregidor and its neighboring small islands had the responsibility for the sea and air defenses at the entrance to Manila Bay.

31st Infantry Regiment. This was the only Army infantry regiment in the Philippines and had been assigned there for many years. It was part of the Philippine Division, the remainder of which consisted of well-trained and -equipped Filipino soldiers assigned to infantry and artillery units under American officers.

200th Coast Artillery (Anti-Aircraft). A National Guard unit, the 200th was hurriedly called up and rushed to the Philippines in the fall of 1941. Most of the men in the unit were from the state of New Mexico.

192nd and 194th Tank Battalions. These battalions were an amalgamation of National Guard units from across the United States—Illinois, Ohio, Kentucky, Wisconsin, Minnesota, and California. The men in the individual companies of the two battalions usually came from the same town or city.

AIR FORCES

19th Bomb Group. This unit was equipped with thirty-five B-17 bombers, the largest concentration of American heavy bombers in one place in the world at this time.

27th Bomb Group. The fifty-four A-24 medium bombers which were to catch up with the recently arrived pilots and ground crews of this unit left the United States but had gotten no farther than the docks at Brisbane, Australia, when the war broke out.

24th Pursuit Group. This group was more fortunate. Its sixty modern P-40 fighter aircraft arrived in September.

NAVAL FORCES

Navy personnel were assigned to submarines, gunboats, submarine tenders, minesweepers, and miscellaneous other ships as well as to facilities at the Cavite Navy Yard. The last major unit to joint the Philippine defense forces was the Fourth Marine Regiment, which arrived from its station in China on December 1.

SERVICE FORCES

In addition to the organizations with combat missions, a large number of Americans were assigned to a variety of service and supply units.

At the other Pacific outposts, a small detachment of Marines and native troops had the responsibility of defending Guam. Wake Island was a little better off. During the fall of 1941 the Navy Department had sent elements of the First Marine Defense Battalion to this remote island. The men there were equipped with coast defense and antiaircraft artillery pieces, and at the very last twelve obsolete fighter aircraft arrived. The only units west of Guam (outside of the Philippines) were two detachments of Marines stationed at Peking and Tientsin in China.

While the high commands in Washington and in the Philippines knew that war was inevitable and hoped for more time, many Americans in the Pacific still found it hard to believe that war—brutal and unrelenting—would come soon to the tranquil, palm-covered islands which they were assigned to defend. Feeding this feeling was the doubt, or perhaps the hope, that despite all the bluster and saber-rattling, little Japan would not dare take on the most powerful nation on earth.

★ ★ ★ **2** ★ ★ ★

The military confrontation between the United States and Japan was the culmination of years of mistrust and misunderstanding between the two countries. The first issue to arise was one of racial bias. In 1907 the San Francisco school board voted to exclude Orientals from city schools. The Japanese government, indignant at this insult to their race, protested. President Theodore Roosevelt was drawn into what soon became no longer a local issue. He got the board to rescind its order only after he had taken action at the federal level to reduce the influx of Japanese laborers into the United States. Roosevelt took the attitude of the Japanese seriously enough to request his top-ranking military officers to give him recommendations on actions to be taken in the event Japan made any military moves against the United States. His military advisors responded with a plan for a holding action in the Philippines until our fleet could get there with reinforcements. Thus the basic concept of what would later become War Plan Orange was born. Fortunately, Japanese feelings cooled and the San Francisco school board crisis passed without further incident.

But American concerns and negative feelings about the Japanese persisted. Books and articles appeared predicting a Japanese invasion of the United States. But by far the most pervasive writing on the Japanese in these times was by Wallace Irwin, a San Francisco newspaperman. Irwin created a character named Hashimura Togo, a Japanese who spoke pidgin English and worked as a houseboy for an American family. He was pictured as a buck-toothed, ever-smiling, ultra-polite, but crafty little man. Irwin's articles were in the major periodicals of the time—*Colliers*, *The New York Times*, and *Good Housekeeping*. Later they were published in book form and introduced to millions more Americans. Irwin's writings created a stereotypical Japanese image which was to be frequently used by American cartoonists for many years.

In World War I, Japan declared war on Germany but did not fight in Europe. The Japanese delegation to the Paris Peace Conference asked to retain the German territories in the Pacific that the Japanese had occupied in 1914. They also requested that a statement of "world racial equality" be included in the Covenant of the League of Nations. They did not get the statement of equality but did gain political control over the Mariana, Marshall, and Caroline island groups in the western Pacific. These islands, covering an expanse of the Pacific greater than the area of the United States, had great strategic significance since they lay athwart the sea-lanes from the United States and Hawaii to the Philippines. In 1922 Japan met with the United States and other sea powers to discuss their respective naval forces and bases in the Pacific. At this conference Japan agreed to restrict the size of its fleet and the United States promised not to increase fortifications in the Philippines, Guam, and other islands west of Hawaii.

A few years later the racial issue, which had never really died after Roosevelt's intervention in the San Francisco school board crisis, reached its peak. The problem this time was the California growers' resentment of the low-cost competition by Japanese farmers in their state. Previous legislation had curtailed Chinese laborers' entering the country. Now California agricultural interests influenced Congress to pass the so-called Exclusion Act of 1924, which banned all further immigration by Orientals—notably the Japanese. Repercussions were immediate. The American ambassador to Japan resigned, and upon his return to the United States he denounced the act. The Japanese government declared the act's effective date to be observed in that country as "Humiliation Day." Among the citizens protesting was a Japanese man who committed harakiri (ritual suicide) near the American Embassy in Tokyo. In Washington the first formal version of War Plan Orange was prepared, but once again the Japanese indignation subsided.

In 1929 representatives from forty-seven nations including the United States and Japan met in Geneva, Switzerland, to amplify and clarify principles and rules regarding the treatment of POWs which had emerged from another international conference held at The Hague, Netherlands, in 1907. The Hague Conference had established guiding principles for the humane treatment of POWs. Under these guidelines prisoners' personal belongings, except arms and ammunition, would remain their private property. They could be interned or restrained but could be kept in solitary confinement only under the most extreme circumstances. Prisoner labor could be utilized, except for officers, in nonmilitary work activities. Work could not be excessive and should be paid for at the same rate as that of soldiers of the nation holding the prisoners. The earnings of prisoners should go toward their own benefit and any balance paid to them upon their release. The government holding prisoners of war would be bound to maintain and protect them against acts of violence, insults, and public curiosity. Escaped prisoners, if captured, would be liable to disciplinary punishment. Bureaus of information should be set up in each

belligerent state to answer inquiries concerning the fate of captured men. Relief societies for prisoners would receive full
cooperation. Prisoners would be allowed freedom of religious
worship. Sick and wounded would be properly cared for.
The captor nation should send to the government of the captured men identification of those held as well as those sick,
wounded, and dead.

The Japanese had participated in the Hague Conference,
had signed the Conference document, and were committed
to its provisions. But after months of work alongside the other
conferees at Geneva, the Japanese found themselves faced with
a set of rules for the treatment of prisoners of war which went
far beyond, in scope and in detail, the principles to which they
had previously agreed at the Hague Conference. The Japanese
delegation—it was the only one which had in it both an army
and a navy officer in addition to the chief delegate, a civilian—
heavily influenced by the views of the military in Tokyo, took
a hard look and found the new provisions highly objectionable.
The overriding objection of the Japanese was that for them
the rules as a whole were unilateral, not reciprocal. This major
reservation stemmed from their military doctrine that did not
recognize or permit a Japanese soldier or sailor to become
a prisoner of war. When faced by overwhelming enemy
strength, the only acceptable outcome for a Japanese member
of the armed forces was to be killed in action or, if he were
captured, to commit suicide. Surrender under Japanese military law was a punishable offense. Moreover, a soldier who
surrendered would be completely disgraced in the eyes of his
family and his friends. The Japanese military raised other ob-
jections. One was that the Convention's provisions for punishment were more lenient than those of the Japanese Army code
of military justice, making revision of the latter necessary if
the Japanese adopted the Geneva Convention, thus weakening
discipline in the armed forces. Despite these reservations, the
Japanese chief delegate signed the Geneva Convention Relating to the Treatment of Prisoners of War. (A listing of its
most significant articles is found in Appendix A.) He was aware
that it required ratification by his government before it was
legally binding. The United States also signed and three years
later ratified the Convention. The Japanese government never
did. However, Japan was a signatory to and later ratified the

Geneva Red Cross Convention, which was promulgated at the same time as the Prisoner of War Convention and dealt with the treatment of the wounded, sick, and dead in time of war.

★ ★ ★ **3** ★ ★ ★

By 1931 the military-industrial factions were rapidly gaining power in Japanese politics. In that year, through a contrived incident, the Japanese Army seized control of Manchuria, a large land area with great economic potential, from China. From that time on, with only a few pauses, Japanese military expansionism continued unabated. But few Americans felt any real concern about the Manchurian land grab. It was in a strange and remote land far removed from the immediate and growing problems of the Great Depression, which had recently begun. This economic cataclysm increasingly kept Americans' attention directed inward.

But not the Japanese's. The League of Nations condemnation of the Manchurian occupation caused the Japanese delegation to march out of the League permanently and solidified that country's public opinion against the presumed deliberate interference of other nations in Japan's affairs. The peoples' nationalistic feelings were fostered and encouraged by a military-dominated political regime which exerted its influence through state-controlled schools and communications media.

The politicians had a strong foundation upon which to build. Loyalty and patriotism were an integral part of the Japanese way of life. Under the state religion, Shintoism, the emperor, a direct descendant of the sun goddess, the country's creator, was himself considered a god. To a lesser extent, all of the people were part of this godlike family. As the head of this family and the nation, the emperor's decrees on any matter, public or private, were revered and obeyed without question. Most Japanese (with the exception of a small number of intellectuals and the wealthy) were docile, law-abiding, and long-suffering. Increasing numbers of Japanese came to believe in and support an emerging national policy which emphasized Japanese racial superiority, military invincibility, and a destiny to rule the Far East.

In the summer of 1937, from its new base in Manchuria, Japan launched a major military effort to conquer China. The first thrust was at Nanking, then the capital of China. The Japanese Army entered that city in December 1937. The orgy of murder, rape, and pillage which followed has few parallels in modern times. Soldiers were let loose to desecrate the city. Indiscriminate killing of civilians—men, women, and children—was common. Soldiers took what they wanted from individuals, private houses, and stores. The Japanese rounded up and executed large numbers of Chinese men who they suspected were soldiers who had shed their uniforms. By the end of six weeks more than 200,000 Chinese had died.

Nor was Japanese militancy confined to the Chinese. On the Yangtze River north of Nanking, the Japanese bombed and sank an American gunboat, the *Panay*, and destroyed three oil tankers. In the face of strong protests from the United States, Japan apologized for the incident and sent compensation to the victims.

Despite strained relationships, U.S. trade with Japan increased. Among other things, Japan bought increasing amounts of scrap iron and steel. A *Washington Post* article at the time headlined "AMERICAN SCRAP IRON PLAYS GRIM ROLE IN FAR EASTERN WAR . . . Japanese rain death with one-time junk. Guns, bombs and battleships, all made from old metal shipped across the Pacific in growing amounts." The media helped arouse American feelings against the Japanese and for the Chinese. *The Good Earth,* a book read and as a movie seen by millions of Americans, depicted the Chinese as a polite, diligent, and hardworking people, while newsreels showed Japanese bombers pouring death and destruction down on Chinese cities. Even before the "Rape of Nanking" was described in Western newspapers, American public opinion had made a major shift. In a Gallup poll taken in 1937, 55 percent of the Americans polled said that they had no sympathy for either side. By October of that same year, the polls showed that 59 percent sympathized with China. But the United States was still gripped by the Great Depression, and the average American's greatest concern was about when the nation was going to recover from its economic doldrums. The prevailing feeling was that this country should not get involved in international controversies. However, with the war in China still at center stage and despite their strong isolationist feelings, many Americans read about and viewed with indignation the Japanese Army's destruction—with no apology—of foreign businesses, schools, and church properties. Some satisfaction was drawn from the fact that after more than a year, despite local victories, Japan was apparently enmeshed in a long and costly war with China.

As American emotions rose, some of the old misconceptions and a number of new ones regarding the Japanese cropped up. Underlying these was a continuing tendency to belittle the Japanese. The basis for this attitude was probably a combination of American pride and a psychological desire to play down the increasing threat posed by an adversary of long standing. As national relationships worsened, many stories of ineptness and stupidity circulated: the Japanese Army was slovenly and ill disciplined and could barely succeed against the untrained and underequipped Chinese; the Japanese possessed poor eyesight, which made them poor aviators; they built topheavy warships which capsized at launching; mechanically inept, their airplanes were poor copies of Western models; their .25-caliber rifle cartridges wouldn't stop a Caucasian; and more.

These views of Japanese inferiority were not confined to the general public and the press. U.S. military intelligence agencies, though remarkably successful in some respects—they broke the Japanese military code early in the war, making much of the enemy's secret communications available to American commanders—obtained very little information before 1941 on the actual combat capability of the Japanese Army and Navy. Lacking this information, top-ranking American officers felt the same as the public. The Japanese Army and Navy, they thought, would have a tough time of it if they had to face an American or European military force. In taking this view, they had overlooked one of the fundamentals in war: know your enemy.

The relatively few Western observers of the Japanese Army and Navy in training and in combat provided a much different and largely ignored picture. They found the Japanese soldier to be a trained, disciplined, tenacious, and seemingly fearless fighter—and well he should be. Most recruits entered the military services already imbued by tradition, religion, and education with the feeling that they were instruments of the emperor and the state. No service was more honorable than becoming a member of the Imperial Japanese Army or Navy and, if need be, dying in the emperor's service. The tough training that they received built on this. In the Army long forced marches were frequent. The military ration was frugal but adequate. Troop movement by train and ship was designed to get the most to the destination with the minimum expenditure of equipment. As a consequence, crowding and other conditions were usually bad by Western standards. Physical punishment was forbidden but common. It was routine for a superior to strike or beat a subordinate for minor infractions. Mass punishment was not unusual. A noncommissioned officer would not hesitate to slap everyone in his squad or stand everyone at attention for an hour if he could not place the responsibility for an offense with a single individual.

Japanese military training and discipline, while much harsher physically than that of most Western armies, went considerably further. Its psychological component, which bordered on the spiritual, distinguished it from other nations, including Nazi Germany. For most Japanese soldiers and sailors, their allegiance to the emperor and the state was reaffirmed on a daily or weekly basis when they faced in the direction of the Imperial Palace in Tokyo and recited portions of the "Imperial Rescript to Soldiers and Sailors" proclaimed by Emperor Meiji in 1875. The "Rescript," virtually the Bible for the armed forces after militarism in Japan became preeminent, consisted of five separate precepts. The first revealed much about what was expected of the Japanese serviceman: "The soldier and sailor should consider loyalty their essential duty . . . and bear in mind that duty is weightier than a mountain, while death is lighter than a feather. Never by failing in moral principle fall into disgrace and bring dishonor to your name." The remaining precepts, with some indirection and ambiguity for the Western reader, emphasized obedience to orders, bravery, faithful performance of duty, and finally avoidance of frivolity and extravagance. The "Imperial Rescript" held in it the essence of the Code of Bushido—honor, obedience, and valor— formerly applicable only to the samurai, the warriors who with their masters the feudal barons held sway over the common people until the abolition of the feudal system in 1871.

The principles of the "Imperial Rescript" were augmented and romanticized by the literature of the time: the classic story and play *The Tale of the Forty-Seven Ronin,* about a group

of samurai who committed mass suicide after avenging the
death of their master and thus became heroes; the purported
true account of Lt. Jiro Usairoku, who, after making a mistake
in reading the "Imperial Rescript" to his troops, felt such shame
and remorse that he committed suicide so as to "live again
in righteousness"; the legendary "Three Human Bombs" who
during the fighting in China supposedly blew themselves
up in a field of barbed wire to make an opening for their comrades to attack and seize an enemy position; heroes all, in Japanese eyes.

Based on his own values and standards, the Japanese soldier,
influenced by domestic newspapers and American movies,
looked upon Americans as pleasure-seeking, soft, and material-
istic. As to the fighting ability of the U.S. military forces, little
doubt existed in the Japanese mind—the Imperial Japanese
Army and Navy would prevail. The gods and history could
not be wrong. Japan had never lost a war, the difficulties in
China notwithstanding.

Initially the gods were right. Within six months virtually
all the Americans defending the Pacific outposts would be dead
or captured. Out of millions of their countrymen, these Americans would reap the bitter harvest of years of misunderstanding
between the United States and Japan. Whatever their former
roles in life—general, doctor, farmer, banker, garage me-
chanic—they would as prisoners drop to the lowest level in
the Japanese social system. Here they would be forced to contend daily with the myriad differences and deep-seated animos-
ities existing between them and their new and absolute masters.
For most, their toughest battle would begin after the guns were
still.

PART I

Surrender and Survival

December 1941– December 1942

1

FIRST CAPTIVES

December 1941–March 1942
China—Guam—Wake—Japan—
Java—Celebes

★ ★ ★ 1 ★ ★ ★

In the predawn hours of December 8, China time, two river gunboats floated peacefully at their moorings in the Whangpoo River along the waterfront at Shanghai. The HMS *Petrel* was British. The USS *Wake* was American. The *Wake* and another gunboat, the *Tutuila,* anchored up the Yangtze River at Chungking, were the last of the U.S. Navy's Yangtze River Boat Flotilla left in China. The other gunboats had sailed for the Philippines that fall, leaving the *Wake* stripped and rigged for demolition with only a skeleton crew aboard.

At about four that morning the Japanese, who controlled Shanghai, sent boarding parties to both vessels demanding surrender. The skipper of the *Petrel* refused. The Japanese, unperturbed, returned to shore, and soon afterward shore batteries shelled and sank the *Petrel*. Most of its crew were able to swim to shore or were picked up by Chinese in sampans.

On the *Wake,* the senior man (the ship commander C. D. Smith was ashore), surprised before he could blow up the ship, surrendered it. The Japanese took the crewmen, the first American POWs of World War II, to a former Chinese hospital and confined them there along with the survivors from the *Petrel*.

The Japanese Navy, who ran this temporary camp for about one hundred captured U.S. and Allied Navy and merchant seamen, treated their new charges reasonably well. At first a few of the guards slapped some of the seamen. But after an officer reported this to the camp commander the slappings ceased and thereafter the guards were courteous. Conscious of rank, the Japanese commander assigned the former commanding officers of the *Wake* and *Petrel* each to a private room. Less senior officers slept on hospital beds with mattresses, four to a room, while the rest of the men occupied one large room, dormitory style. Meals were drab but nutritionally adequate: porridge and soybean coffee for breakfast; and boiled fish, vegetable, or sometimes meat stew for lunch and dinner. Shared American food—the *Wake* men had brought with them as much as they could grab and carry as they left their ship—helped add variety to the diet. This along with daily hot baths, modern plumbing, and ten cigarettes a day made life, if not pleasant, at least bearable.

All in all, except for forcing each man to sign a statement that he would not attempt escape, the Japanese commander ran this camp in accordance with the Geneva Convention. Those held at the Shanghai Naval Prisoners Camp would be among the few to receive such treatment.

Other Americans who made the abrupt change from freedom to captivity with little physical hardship were the 204 Marines stationed at Peking and Tientsin. At both cities the commanders reluctantly surrendered without opposition to Japanese officers who dealt with them sternly but courteously. The Japanese let them remain, under guard in their barracks, and agreed to consider whether the members of the two detachments would be eligible for repatriation under an obscure provision of the "Boxer Protocol of 1901."* Even with this prospect, passively turning over their rifles, pistols, and ammunition to enemy soldiers and hauling down the American flag came hard for the few Marines involved. One of these was Capt. John A. White, executive officer at Tientsin, who summed up Pearl Harbor Day there as marked by "No shooting, no

---

* Actually no such provision existed. The senior Marine officers had heard it from a State Department man. When repatriation of diplomatic personnel did occur six months later, no Tientsin or Peking detachment Marines were included.

heroics nor great drama, only sorrow and frustration." A professional officer, he had trained for ten years to defend his country, and it was all over in one day.

★ ★ ★ **2** ★ ★ ★

It was over quickly at Guam, too. On December 10 a Japanese force of about five thousand men overwhelmed the small garrison of this island outpost after brief but spirited resistance in which seventeen Americans and Guamanians were killed. Seeing that further resistance was futile, G. J. McMillan, U.S.N., the island governor, signed a surrender agreement after being assured that the rights of the Navy population would be respected and that military personnel would be treated humanely in accordance with rules and customs of war.

The Americans soon learned what "humanely" meant to the Japanese. Shortly after the surrender, members of the Japanese landing force began assembling their captives in the plaza of Agana, the island's major town. Marine John Podelesny was among a group of about forty Americans whom the Japanese lined up to be searched. The Japanese used sign language and the point of their bayonets to order the men to remove their shirts, trousers, and shoes. As Podelesny began removing his clothing, he noticed that the Marine on his left was not doing so. Whether his companion's action was one of defiance or slowness, Podelesny was not sure. Suddenly the Japanese guard nearest the two men leaped forward and with a single thrust ran his bayonet through the man, who, without a sound, crumpled to the ground and died. Horror-stricken, Podelesny hastened to comply with the order as he watched the Japanese drag the body away. Later the Japanese marched the men to a nearby church where they, along with other American captives, were confined for a month of uncertainty and discomfort.

The Japanese had to fight hard to take Wake Island. After several unsuccessful attempts, and against fierce resistance by the force of U.S. Marines, construction workers, and Navy personnel, they finally took the island on December 23, capturing about 470 military and 1,146 civilian prisoners. This time there was no pretense of a written surrender agreement. Comdr. W. C. Cunningham, U.S. Navy, and Maj. James P. S. Devereux, U.S. Marine Corps, had to accept terms that were unwritten and simple—unconditional surrender.

All the officers were confined in one building and the Japanese treated them fairly well. For the enlisted men and civilians, it was another story. They were ordered to strip down to their underwear. Their hands were bound behind them with telephone wire and pulled high up on their backs. One end of the wire was tied around their necks so that they would choke if they tried to free themselves. In this condition they were crowded along with the sick and wounded, some trussed like the well men, into hospital dugouts. Packed to the point of suffocation, they were held in the dugouts for what to most of them seemed an eternity. Finally one of the men and a doctor prevailed on the Japanese to let some of the prisoners out, which helped to relieve the terrible conditions in the dugout. Later the whole group was moved to the airstrip on the island and put to work clearing it. The Japanese gave them little food, and the water they drank came from recently emptied gasoline drums. On the day after Christmas one of the enlisted men bringing food to the officers passed a note to Major Devereux informing him of the conditions at the airstrip. Major Devereux wrote a letter of protest to the Japanese commanding officer. He never received an answer to his letter, but it had its effect. Shortly thereafter the men were moved into barracks and were given more food.

Soon after the outbreak of hostilities, the Swiss government had assumed responsibility as "protective power" for U.S. interests (including prisoners of war) in Japan and territories occupied by that country. During the last week in December, by imperial order, Gen. Hideki Tojo, prime minister and also minister of war, assumed the overall responsibility for all POW camps. Another imperial order established in the War Ministry, under Gen. Seitaro Uemura, a Prisoner of War Information Bureau as called for by Article 77 of the Geneva Convention for prisoners of war. This bureau was supposed to compile and maintain records on POWs, investigate and communicate information on their condition, and prepare replies to inquiries about them sent through the appropriate international channels, usually the Swiss government or the International Red Cross, headquartered in Geneva, Switzerland.

Within a few days the War and Foreign ministries had an important issue to face. The United States, using the Swiss as intermediary, asked the Japanese government whether it intended to abide by the Geneva POW Convention of 1929. This question would take the Japanese over a month to answer.

★ ★ ★ **3** ★ ★ ★

Even while it was grappling with the Geneva Convention issue, the War Ministry ordered American captives from Guam and Wake Island moved to new locations.

On January 10, 1942, one month after the Japanese had taken Guam, Navyman Hugh Meyers and over four hundred other Americans loaded on a Japanese passenger-freighter, the *Argentina Maru*. Aboard, Meyers found himself in the hold of the ship, a bare room but with adequate space for him and his companions. Twice a day a guard at the top of the ladder leading down to the hold would lower buckets of fish and wormy rice to the men below. He also filled and lowered a water bucket, as needed. The men were allowed to climb the ladder and use a toilet nearby. Initially some men complained that the distribution of food from the buckets was unequal. Then three of the Navy chief boatswain's mates took charge of rationing and this problem ceased. For Meyers and the others the days in the hold were monotonous but bearable. What concerned them most was where they were headed.

Six days later they had their answer when the ship anchored in the Inland Sea, off the northern coast of the island of Shikoku, the smallest of the Japanese main islands. After spending a very uncomfortable day in the hold—the Japanese had turned off the heat that morning—in the evening they finally were taken on barges to the shore, the first American POWs to reach the Japanese home islands.

After a short ride by streetcar, they arrived at Zentsuji, a large military installation which had been used in 1904–1905 to house Russian prisoners. Here, in a compound surrounded by high board walls topped by barbed wire, they were counted off, divided into groups, and assigned forty to a room in two-story barracks. Chilled and tired, Meyers entered the room assigned to his group and found rice straw neatly strewn on the floor and forty pillows filled with rice hulls (very hard), blankets (few and thin), an aluminum dish, and a spoon, all of the items aligned with military precision.

The Japanese sergeant in charge of the group spoke and understood English quite well and seemed to enjoy the opportunity to use this ability. After all of the men had been assigned to their places, he called for a detail which returned shortly thereafter with hot cabbage soup, enough for a fair-size portion for each man. The weary Americans were much impressed by the sergeant's considerate act.

The Japanese in charge of moving the Wake Island captives were a much different sort. On the day before they were to leave the following notice was posted.

COMMANDER OF THE PRISONER ESCORT
Navy of the Great Japanese Empire

REGULATIONS FOR PRISONERS

1. The prisoners disobeying the following orders will be punished with immediate death:

    (a) Those disobeying orders and instructions.

    (b) Those showing a motion of antagonism and raising a sign of opposition.

    (c) Those disordering the regulations by individualism, egoism, thinking only about yourself, rushing for your own goods.

    (d) Those talking without permission and raising loud voices.

    (e) Those walking and moving without order.

    (f) Those carrying unnecessary baggage in embarking.

    (g) Those resisting mutually.

    (h) Those touching the boat's materials, wires, electric lights, tools, switches, etc.

(i) Those climbing ladder without order.

(j) Those showing acton of running away from the room or boat.

(k) Those trying to take more meal than given to them.

(l) Those using more than two blankets.

Following this list of major crimes were more detailed instructions on prisoner conduct aboard the ship.

Despite the outlandish nature of these regulations, Cunningham and other officers reading them had to take them seriously. The one that bothered them the most referred to "unnecessary baggage." "What does this mean?" they asked "Garters," a friendly guard they had nicknamed thus because he wore socks and garters with his shorts. Garters replied that he didn't know. "Well, does it mean one bag or two?"

"I don't know," said Garters.

"Will you find out?"

"No, I can't find out."

The prisoners then decided among themselves that to be on the safe side they would restrict themselves to one bag.

On the morning of January 12 the Americans began their trip to Japan aboard the *Nitta Maru*, a liner which had been converted into a prison ship. They left behind 400 civilian construction workers along with the seriously wounded. Over 300 of these civilians and the surviving wounded were later shipped to Japan. About 100 civilians remained on a work detail for the Japanese.

Aboard the *Nitta Maru*, the officers were confined in a crowded compartment directly over the engine room. The enlisted men and civilians were held in cargo spaces in the forward part of the ship. Generally the physical conditions for the prisoners on board the *Nitta Maru* were similar to those of their predecessors on the *Argentina Maru*.

Each evening Capt. Toshio Saito, the guard commander, required the officers to seat themselves in rows for inspection by one of the Japanese guards. Any delay in carrying out an order meant a resounding slap on the face, and since orders were not always understood, there was much slapping. The Japanese kept the lights burning all the time and a guard stood at the door to see that no one talked, even whispered, to anyone else. Once one officer was accused of whispering and a guard entered and beat him severely with a stick. None of the other officers interfered since they feared it might lead to some form of extreme punishment, possibly execution.

Six days later the *Nitta Maru* arrived in the harbor of Yokohama, Japan. Here a group of officers, including Cunningham and Devereux, were ordered to clean up and report to an upper deck room, which they found swarming with Japanese newspapermen and cameramen. Their captors seemed anxious to have the outside world believe that they treated their prisoners well. The pictures taken that day of the officers smiling turned up later in English-language magazines published in the world press. Possibly as compensation for the picture-taking, Cunningham and several others were allowed to send radiograms to their next of kin. After two days in port, the *Nitta Maru* sailed for Shanghai, China.

It was on this leg of the journey that Captain Saito carried out the threats of death expressed in the regulations for prisoners. Soon after leaving Yokohama, five Americans were taken from the hold under guard. When they returned, they told one of their companions that they had been accused of lying in answer to questions about their naval experience and had been warned that they would be punished. Later the guards returned and took the five men from the hold, blindfolded with their hands tied behind their backs. On the upper deck members of the guard detail and the ship's company were gathered in a semicircle around Captain Saito, who was standing on a box. When the five men were lined up in front of Saito, he drew his sword and read an order of execution in Japanese. Then one of the Americans was forced to kneel on a small mat in ritual fashion and a guard stepped forward and beheaded him with his sword. Other guards previously designated by Saito then stepped forward and in turn executed the remaining four Americans. After the ceremony was completed, the spectators dispersed and the bodies were thrown overboard. The POWs were not told of the executions, and though the victims were later recorded as missing, their comrades did not learn their fate until after the war.

After arrival at Shanghai the ship moved to the nearby port of Woosung. Here the Navy turned the POWs over to an army guard detail and they marched five miles to a former cavalry camp—seven old wooden, unheated barracks, now surrounded by two electrically charged fences. Settling into their bleak surroundings, within a week they were joined by the Marines from Peking and Tientsin. The total number of Americans at Woosung stood at about fourteen hundred.

Meanwhile, on February 4, 1942, the Swiss government in Bern relayed the following telegram from their minister in Tokyo: JAPANESE GOVERNMENT HAS INFORMED ME: FIRST, JAPAN IS STRICTLY OBSERVING GENEVA RED CROSS CONVENTION AS A SIGNATORY STATE. SECOND, ALTHOUGH NOT BOUND BY THE CONVENTION RELATIVE TREATMENT PRISONERS OF WAR JAPAN WILL APPLY MUTATIS MUTANDIS PROVISIONS OF THAT CONVENTION TO AMERICAN PRISONERS OF WAR IN ITS POWER.

By "mutatis mutandis" the Japanese meant that the Convention would be observed when it did not conflict with their existing laws, policies, and regulations. A set of regulations for the treatment of prisoners of war did exist (Appendix B). Issued in 1904 during the Russo-Japanese War, the regulations called for fair treatment, freedom of religion, and respect for personal possessions, and included many other provisions which were in accord with generally accepted humane principles. It was this set of regulations, with a few minor revisions, that was in force at the beginning of the war.

Then on March 2 Japanese foreign minister Togo wrote the Swiss government:

> ***I desire to inform your Excellency that the Imperial Government intends to take into consideration, with regard to provisions and clothing to be distributed, the national and racial customs of American war prisoners and civilian internees placed under Japanese power.
>
> Asking you to kindly inform the American Government of the United States of America of the above,
>
> I am, yours truly,
>
> *Togo*
> Minister of Foreign Affairs

On paper, at least, it didn't look too bad for Americans captured by the Japanese.

★ ★ ★ 4 ★ ★ ★

Early in March, around or on the Dutch-governed island of Java, the Japanese captured about 1,100 Americans. This occurred only two weeks after the fall of Singapore, Britain's vaunted bastion in the Far East, where thousands of British, Australian, and native troops surrendered to the Imperial Japanese Army.

The first of three American ships to fall prey to the Japanese Navy off the coast of Java was the USS *Houston,* sunk on the night of February 28. Many of the about 350 oil-soaked survivors of the *Houston* were picked up by Japanese ships and taken to shore and then to Serang, a town near the western end of Java. Others made it to the beach on rafts and floats. The freedom of these men was short-lived. Javanese natives, reflecting their dislike of the Dutch and Occidentals in general, turned the weary Americans over to the Japanese and they, too, ended up in Serang—some in the town jail and others in a theater. At both locations the men were crowded, stifling hot, dirty, and thirsty.

Northeast of Java at the city of Makassar, on the island of Celebes, the Japanese had assembled over 3,000 Allied prisoners—Dutch, British, native troops, and about 200 survivors of a scuttled American submarine, the USS *Perch,* and a sunken destroyer, the USS *Pope.*

On March 8, over 500 Americans, members of a Texas National Guard unit—the 2nd Battalion, 131st Field Artillery, which had been originally destined for the Philippine Islands but had only gotten as far as Java—received word that the Dutch commander of the island had surrendered all Allied troops to the Japanese. Most of the artillerymen, who had seen little or no action against the Japanese, set up camp at a racetrack near the town of Garut. Surprisingly, the Japanese left them alone, but many of the Americans were still apprehensive about the progress of the war and what their ultimate fate would be.

★ ★ ★ 5 ★ ★ ★

Meanwhile, five of the men at the Woosung camp in China decided to take fate in their own hands and attempt escape. Comdr. C. D. Smith, former skipper of the captured USS *Wake* and an old China hand, conceived and planned the escape. Four others were in on the plot: Commander Cunningham; Comdr. John B. Woolley, the senior British naval officer present in Shanghai when the war began and a stout fellow in the classic British tradition; Dan Teters, the former head of the construction project on Wake Island and a big, husky, level-headed man; and a Chinese youth named Loo, who had worked as a cabin boy on the USS *Wake* and would serve as interpreter.

Smith was convinced that the Chinese troops then fighting the Japanese were in control of the town of Pootung, across the Yangtze River from the prison camp. If these troops could be reached, the path to freedom would be open. Smith's plan was to assemble at night at one of the empty barracks, cross an open field to the electrified fence enclosing the camp area, trench under it, climb over the barbed-wire fence beyond, and head for the Yangtze.

It took nearly two weeks to complete preparations, but finally, on the night of March 11, led by the doughty Commander Woolley, the five men made good their escape and headed north. After proceeding about five miles they reached the banks of the Yangtze, where they began a vain search for a sampan to take them across. When they finally spotted one, the Chinese crewmen refused all offers and disappeared into the fog. At dawn, huddled in a deserted building, they heard a Japanese bugle sounding reveille and realized that they had moved in the wrong direction and were too close to their captors. Reversing direction, they walked, now in daylight, until they saw a farmer coming out of his house. Deciding that they must hide themselves, they sent Loo to ask the farmer's help. The farmer agreed to let them hide in a shed near his house and to arrange for a sampan to cross the river after dark. They remained in the shed all day, still optimistic about their chances. "With any luck we'll be in Pootung tonight," said Smith.

These hopes were shattered when late that afternoon a platoon of soldiers surrounded the shed. Moments later, an officer, sword in hand, entered and ordered them out. The soldiers, Chinese, but part of the puppet government under the Japanese, took them to a nearby town jail. Soon a detachment of the Kempeitai, the Japanese secret military police, arrived and moved them to the Woosung jail. The police interrogated them there about their escape. After this they were taken back to the Woosung POW camp, where, in the presence of a humiliated camp commandant, Colonel Yuse, and the camp guard detachment as well as some of their assembled fellow prisoners, they were forced to reenact their escape in detail. Then they were loaded back into cars and driven to the Bridge House jail in Shanghai. Two months later, after two trials at which they had no opportunity for defense, they learned that they were guilty of desertion. Commanders Cunningham, Woolley, and Smith were sentenced to ten years' imprisonment, Teters to two years, and Loo to one year. The three military men breathed a sigh of relief. In the U.S. and European armies the penalty for desertion in time of war is usually death. Soon after the Smith group's attempt, four Marines escaped from Woosung and evaded capture for several weeks before being apprehended and sentenced to four years in prison.

★ ★ ★ 6 ★ ★ ★

In March the War Ministry, after over three months of spectacular military successes, found itself unprepared for a mounting number of decisions concerning the tens of thousands of Allied military prisoners and civilian internees in scores of locations across East Asia. The existing 1904 regulations for treatment of prisoners of war assigned certain responsibilities to army commanders in the field. At this time the major commands were in China, Manchuria, the Southern Area (Java, Sumatra, Malaya, etc.), and the Philippines. The responsibilities included sheltering and feeding captured military personnel, interrogating them, preparing rosters of them, and arranging for their movement to permanent prisoner-of-war camps. It fell to the War Ministry to decide where the permanent camps were to be.

The disposition of the first American captives illustrates the War Ministry's delay and confusion in making such decisions. Movement of the men from Guam to Zentsuji in Japan was easy. Tokyo military officials knew they already had a POW camp there and just followed precedent. The reason for sending the Wake captives to Shanghai is nowhere documented. Seemingly, the high command did not want to bring any more prisoners to Japan at the time, and space was available in nearby Shanghai. The Americans in Java, a small part of the total captured there, were to remain in a temporary status on the island for over six months until the Japanese decided what to do with them. Most of the Americans, along with other Allied captives, held at Makassar remained there until the end of the war. For undisclosed reasons, this camp was never declared an official permanent camp and the Japanese did not report the men in it as prisoners of war. As a result they were listed as "missing in action" on American rolls until the end of the war.

But the problems concerning permanent camps were only part of a number of other administrative matters with which the War Ministry had to contend. Food, clothing, housing, discipline, transportation for POWs all required more specific instructions than were contained in the general language of the 1904 regulations. So on March 30, 1942, the War Ministry established the Prisoner of War Administration Division, with responsibility for "all affairs relative to the treatment of prisoners of war and civilian internees." General Uemura, the chief of the earlier established Prisoner of War Information Bureau, was named to head the division. The small staff of officers and clerks assigned to the information bureau served as the staff for both the bureau and the division. This somewhat unusual organizational arrangement, apparently intended to preserve the independent international identification of the information bureau, continued through the war. (Hereafter both the information bureau and the administration division will be referred to by the single title "Prisoner of War Bureau.")

As March ended, only one isolated pocket of resistance to Japan's total domination of Southeast Asia remained, the Americans defending the Philippines on Bataan and Corregidor.

2

BATAAN TO O'DONNELL

April–May 1942
The Philippines

★ ★ ★ 1 ★ ★ ★

Early on the evening of April 8, Lt. John Gamble, an antiaircraft battery commander, was dismayed by the order to disarm his guns and move with his men to the rear. Now, along a jungle trail on Bataan, he sensed the earth heaving beneath his feet. Gamble felt as if he were standing on a mammoth monster that was sluggishly moving in its sleep. Big banyan trees swayed menacingly. A monkey screamed. In a minute the earthquake was over, leaving Gamble with a sense of foreboding.

At 2 A.M. the following morning, April 9, the ground shook again. This time the tremors were man-made. The sky lit up like an immense Independence Day fireworks display. The Army had just blown up its main ammunition dump, signaling to all those within sight or hearing that the defense of Bataan Peninsula was ending.

Just two days earlier the Japanese 14th Army under Gen. Masaharu Homma had launched a powerful thrust against the American and Filipino defenders. In January General MacArthur had ordered a withdrawal to the peninsula in accordance with War Plan Orange-3. From successive defensive positions, American and Filipino units had blunted all previous

Japanese attempts to seize this important landmass, which with the island of Corregidor dominates the approaches to the strategic port of Manila. This time Homma's all-out attack (he was under great pressure from Tokyo to eliminate this last vestige of Allied power remaining in the Far East) broke through the final defense line, driving the mostly shattered and disorganized units into the southern tip of the peninsula.

The over 76,000 defeated troops—about 11,500 Americans and 65,000 Filipinos—were in a deplorable state. Enemy guns and bombs had taken a toll in dead and wounded, but malnutrition and malaria had a worse affect.

From the beginning the Americans and Filipinos had been issued a steadily diminishing and, for the Americans, an unbalanced allowance of food. On half rations since January, the troops found their rations for February below that. Instead of flour, which was no longer available, the Americans were introduced to rice as a staple in their diet. The balance of the daily ration consisted of small quantities of canned meat or fish, carabao (a native water buffalo), and salt, sugar, and sometimes canned milk. As they gazed at the meager portion in their mess kit, many Americans at the time recalled wistfully the generous helpings of prewar days.

As the campaign wore on, inequities in the distribution of food increased. Some units exaggerated their numbers to obtain more; others missed an issue when the unit moved; individuals or groups hijacked and hoarded; the quartermaster made errors in distribution. While such occurrences were common in many war situations, on Bataan they had a critical impact. Gnawing hunger, with accompanying vitamin deficiencies, steadily dampened the spirits and weakened the bodies of the vast majority of the men on Bataan.

The effects of malaria were equally serious. In March the supply of quinine, a preventive for malaria, ran out. Thereafter the incidence of this debilitating disease soared. By the end of March admissions for malaria to the two American hospitals located on the southern end of Bataan numbered nearly one thousand a day. But as the men fought on, it became more and more difficult for medical officers to determine whether their gaunt patients were victims of disease or mental or physical exhaustion, or a combination of all three.

The defenders' morale, high in the first two months, gradually crumbled thereafter. The worst blow came on March 11. On that day General MacArthur, under presidential orders, left Corregidor for Australia. Nine days later Gen. Jonathan M. Wainwright, formerly a corps commander on Bataan, assumed MacArthur's old command. Despite MacArthur's statement when he arrived in Australia, "I shall return," most Americans had by that time given up hope that reinforcements would reach them.

★ ★ ★ **2** ★ ★ ★

At 9 o'clock on the morning of April 9 Gen. Edward P. King, the stocky, soft-spoken commander of the forces on Bataan, put on a fresh uniform, climbed into a Jeep, and with some members of his staff drove north to the town of Lamao to surrender. General Homma had sent Col. Motoo Nakayama, his senior operations officer, to represent him. Nakayama expressed displeasure that General Wainwright was not there and initially refused to accept any surrender that did not include all forces in the Philippines. The stern-faced colonel was unreceptive to King's request that he be permitted to organize and conduct the movement of his own troops out of the peninsula to a place designated by the Japanese, using American vehicles for those unable to make the march. King, realizing he was getting nowhere, finally agreed to unconditional surrender. Nakayama asked King for his saber but, since the general had none, accepted his pistol instead. The meeting over, King and his officers passed into captivity.

The reason that Nakayama was uninterested in King's proposal for evacuating the troops from Bataan was that General Homma had already approved a plan for doing so. Maj. Gen. Yoshikata Kawane was in charge of the operation, which the Japanese had divided into two phases. In the first, all captured troops were to move on foot to Balanga, a little over halfway up the narrow blacktop road running along the east coast of the peninsula. From the town of Mariveles, where the troops defending the western side of the peninsula were to start, to Balanga was twenty-eight miles; from the Cabcaben airfield, where the east-sector men were to begin en route to Balanga, the distance was nineteen miles, the latter distance somewhat under a normal day's march for American infantry. The second phase of the movement, from Balanga through Orani and out of the peninsula to the railhead at San Fernando, was the longest—thirty-five miles. The plan envisioned the use of available trucks to shuttle captives to San Fernando with two medical stations and four food stops along the way. For men assembled at Mariveles the route covered sixty-three miles; for those starting at Cabcaben, fifty-four miles. At San Fernando freight trains would haul the men thirty miles north to the town of Capas. From there the men would walk seven miles to an abandoned Philippine army training camp, Camp O'Donnell.

The plan was riddled with faulty assumptions. Fourteenth Army medical and transport services were barely adequate for the Japanese troops, whose movement south for the assault on Corregidor had overriding priorities. General Homma's staff had greatly underestimated the number of men to be captured. General Kawane had inspected Camp O'Donnell and reported it suitable for as many as thirty thousand men. Nearly twice that number were eventually to arrive there. Homma and Kawane were either unaware of or gave little weight to the weak and disease-ridden condition of the Americans and Filipinos which rendered them unfit for sustained physical effort. Both the plan and its execution were to be dismal failures, earning the evacuation the well-deserved title the Bataan Death March.

★ ★ ★ 3 ★ ★ ★

Gamble and a minority of captive Americans escaped the March altogether. At the time of King's surrender he and hundreds of other men of the 200th and 515th Anti-Aircraft regiments were on a knoll near the Cabcaben airfield. Soon elements of a Japanese motorized division moved in, set up artillery, and began firing on Corregidor. Return fire wounded a few Japanese and Americans. Meanwhile, the Japanese were inspecting, counting, and organizing the men in Gamble's group. During the inspection some Japanese soldiers helped themselves to the possessions of their captives. Gamble had to give up seven hundred dollars in Filipino pesos, his wristwatch, and a pair of gold-framed glasses. Choking with indignation, he watched as the Japanese soldier knocked out the lenses and kept the frames.

Searching newly captured enemy soldiers is a common military practice. Such searches have two generally accepted purposes: to be sure the captives are disarmed and to acquire combat intelligence. In addition, victorious forces often take personal possessions from the vanquished, a forbidden but seldom punished action in most armies of the world. Not surprisingly, Japanese searches and inspections were to include much of this. To the Japanese soldier, the high-quality wristwatches, cigarette lighters, and fountain pens, along with gold rings, were extremely tempting. Filipino currency was somewhat attractive but American dollars much less so because the average Japanese had no way to exchange them. The thoroughness of Japanese inspections depended upon the time available. Most were rushed and missed some of the men, particularly those in large groups. In some cases officers did not permit the taking of personal items. In other situations a person might be able to hide his money or other valuables. So despite the searches a number of Americans retained personal items and American and Filipino currency as well. Possession of the latter, though most Americans did not realize it at the time, was to make a big difference in their life, or death, as prisoners of war.

About dusk a line of trucks arrived, and Gamble and others in his group rode that night to Orani, the last town on the coast before leaving the peninsula. The following morning they were fed rice and searched. Luckily this time Gamble kept his fountain pen. They again boarded trucks and at three that afternoon, April 10, they unloaded at the abandoned Philippine army training camp, Camp O'Donnell. The trip had taken about twenty hours. For those that followed, the trip would be far tougher.

On the same day as Gamble arrived at Camp O'Donnell, Capt. William E. "Ed" Dyess, a fighter pilot turned infantryman on Bataan, began a five-day trek to the same destination.

It began when Dyess, along with about one hundred men of his Air Corps squadron and some five hundred other Americans and Filipinos, was subjected to an inspection and some confiscation of personal items on the airstrip at Mariveles.

Word had been passed on the way to the strip: "Get rid of your Japanese stuff." Dyess saw an Air Corps officer who, it was said, had not and was beheaded. This was the first of a number of times that men were executed after Americans saw guards discover Japanese money or other Japanese articles on them. Most Americans believed the then prevalent story that—despite their own actions toward captives—the Japanese considered robbing dead soldiers (no Japanese surrendered) a capital offense.

Soon the guards ordered them on their way. They struggled up a zigzag road that rose steeply for about a mile. Then, gasping for breath, they continued east until the road became jammed with Japanese trucks and soldiers and traffic headed in the opposite direction. Amidst barked harsh orders, grinding gears, and general confusion, the guards herded their charges off the road, where they waited, baking in the sun, for the Japanese troops to pass. Back on the road again they encountered a crushed body in the road—nationality unknown—which had been passed over countless times by trucks and other vehicular traffic. On the Japanese military priority list, getting men and guns in position for the forthcoming attack on Corregidor had top priority. Captives were at the bottom of the list.

It was dark when they arrived at Cabcaben Airfield (Gamble's departure point), where they expected to stop for the night. By now they had covered only about nine miles, less than a Boy Scout qualification march, but nearly all were exhausted.

Respite was not to be theirs. Some had just fallen asleep when they were shouted and kicked onto the road again. They trudged another two hours. Then to their dismay the Japanese turned them around. The weary men walked back to Cabcaben, where they arrived about midnight, and slept until dawn, when they started north again. The next day, with the greenish-blue waters of Manila Bay often visible on their right and dust-covered banana palms and bamboo groves on their left, they labored each mile. Every ounce of extra weight became a burden. By now most of those who had started with them had discarded packs, blankets, and steel helmets, retaining only a belt and canteen and a few toilet articles. Headgear, vital for protection against the burning sun, varied widely. Some had none. Others had handkerchiefs or towels over their heads while still others had cotton caps, some with bills on them. The most fortunate wore military sun helmets.

It was still stop and go. When the road became too congested, the guards with fixed bayonets would wave and shout them to the side. Then truckloads of Japanese soldiers, towed artillery, and supply vehicles would roll by. Occasionally some of the Japanese riding in the vehicles would lean over the sides and knock the hats off the Americans and Filipinos with sticks or poles. By sundown, after nineteen miles of walking, the weary column reached Balanga—the town from which, according to the 14th Army plan, the men were to be trucked to San Fernando.

It was also the location of the headquarters of the 14th Army commander, General Homma. On occasion, either here or at his forward command post at Lamao to the south, Homma would watch the prisoners moving north up the coast road. He would later claim that he saw nothing "extraordinary" and that no atrocities were reported to him.

Extraordinary things continued to happen to Dyess and his group. Just as they were settling down in the Balanga prison enclosure, they were ordered out again. This time the word was that the Japanese had caught three Americans with weapons. Whatever the reason, the guards quickened the pace. Now marching in the dark, Dyess was able to make out some men dropping out in twos and threes and was puzzled that the guards nearby did nothing. The explanation came soon. Rifles cracked at the rear of the column. A shocked Dyess and companions walked on, arriving at the barbed-wire compound at Orani just before dawn.

They spent that day and night there, got a little water and rice, tried to rest in the hot, crowded compound, and departed the following evening.

Dyess recalls that they walked all night with the Japanese "cleanup squad" again bringing up to the rear and performing its grim work. At sunup the following morning, the column moved past a bubbling artesian well. Its clear waters glistened in the morning sun. A Filipino soldier darted from the ranks and ran toward the well, followed by five other Filipinos. The guards raised their rifles and fired when the six reached a grassy ditch. Most of the Filipinos fell at the first volley but two of them, desperately wounded, kept crawling toward the water. The Japanese fired again, killing all six. Dyess had been aware of the men being killed behind him all through the night but these actions had been veiled by darkness. The wanton execution of the six men in broad daylight left Dyess and his companions disheartened, as did the sight later of a disemboweled Filipino soldier hanging on a barbed-wire fence. Then, just outside San Fernando, Dyess saw an American colonel help two exhausted American soldiers into a Filipino pony cart. When they were soon discovered, a Japanese whipped the three, as well as the Filipino cart driver, unmercifully as Dyess and the others looked back helplessly.

Finally, five days after leaving Mariveles, they arrived in San Fernando. The night spent in a prison pen there was miserable. The rice ran out before Dyess got any, and more men were becoming ill with dysentery, filling the entire area with a terrible stench. The next day the Japanese loaded Dyess and a large group of other Americans into boxcars for a hot and uncomfortable ride to the town of Capas. Then they walked seven miles to Camp O'Donnell. Dehydrated from the closed train ride, Dyess and many of the men successfully sneaked water from pails left along the road by sympathetic Filipino villagers.

Sgt. Earl Dodson, a member of a sixty-man Marine guard detail at General King's headquarters, like Dyess, saw death and hardship on the long walk to San Fernando. But for him the greatest hardship of all was the lack of water.

Dodson and the men in his detachment, never in combat and relatively well fed, began the movement in better physical shape than most. The Japanese didn't order the Marines out of their area for several days. When they did start, they moved under their own lieutenant as a unit with military packs on their backs. In his pack Dodson carried a blanket, towel, toilet articles, and a sack full of rice and cracked wheat. Hanging from his belt was a canteen full of water.

Dodson did not find the first day particularly trying. He had expected the worst, having just come from China and knowing firsthand of Japanese atrocities there. The shakedown at Cabcaben didn't bother him. He had no valuables. The Marines shared food and water and as a unit felt some sense of security. The most disturbing thing for the Marines was their first sight of bodies along the road. Though the Japanese gave them no food or water that day, Dodson and the others were still able to get by with what they had.

The next day was different. Dodson's canteen and many others were empty. The pace was rapid and in Dodson's part of the long column no stops were permitted. By midmorning just about everyone's canteen was empty. Dodson, tiring, along with others threw away his pack. He had never been so thirsty in his life.

At the next village some of the men in Dodson's group ran for a water pump but Dodson couldn't make it. Later he offered to help two of the lucky ones carry their large can of water if he could just have a swallow. Their answer was a flat no. By this time Dodson was determined to get water whatever the risk. After narrowly escaping a guard's bayonet in his first attempt, at the next opportunity he was seventh in line and got a half canteen of water. Later he ran into a field and broke off a stalk of sugarcane, which gave him a temporary shot of energy. At the halts and scrambles for water or sugarcane, the Marines got mixed up with others in the column. As the day wore on, it became more and more a matter of every man for himself.

That night the guards herded them into what looked like a mission courtyard. Dodson, giving little thought to sleep, immediately fell in a line of over two hundred men waiting to get to one slow spigot. An Army captain, too exhausted to join the line, offered to share a can of salmon with Dodson if he would fill the captain's canteen. Dodson agreed. Hours later Dodson returned and the captain kept his word. After wolfing down the salmon, Dodson slipped his own full canteen under his head—he was now among strangers—and fell asleep. The next morning the canteen was gone.

When the column formed the next morning some of the men, exhausted or dying, could not or would not join their departing comrades. Words of encouragement did little good. So Dodson and the others, convinced that those left behind were done for, quickly turned their minds to their own survival.

With the tropical sun soon ablaze, Dodson was desperate. He had no water and no container for it. As his column began to pass through populated areas outside of San Fernando, Filipi-

nos appeared along the road selling food to men in the column.
Dodson had no money but a Filipino gave him some sugar
anyway. This gave him some quick energy. A little later he
spotted a can to use as a water container. Things were looking
up a bit.

Entering San Fernando that evening, Dodson found himself
in a large schoolyard with what he estimated to be over a thousand Americans and Filipinos. The water line here, winding
like a serpent around the schoolyard to a single faucet, was
the longest ever—seemingly endless. After most of the night
in the line, Dodson, utterly exhausted, crawled on all fours
the last hour and finally got his water. This time he drank it
all before going to sleep.

The next day a Japanese sergeant came in and selected sixty
Americans, including Dodson, and loaded them into two trucks,
which immediately headed south. In just a few hours Dodson
was back almost to Cabcaben, where the whole ordeal had
started. The Japanese put him and the others to work repairing
roads and small bridges. With three meals of rice per day
and food off the trees, Dodson regained some of his strength.

Lt. Col. David L. Hardee, fifty-one years old and no stranger
to war, had fought as an infantry officer in France during World
War I. On Bataan he was second in command of the Provisional
Air Corps Regiment, a unit of aviators and mechanics hastily
converted to ground troops. Hardee would be in one of the
last large groups to walk out of Bataan.

At the time of surrender he was at his corps headquarters.
The arriving Japanese kept everyone there for six days. It
was not until April 16 that they started north.

Hardee's group, seventy Americans, mostly senior officers,
was treated better than most. This might have been because
of their age and rank. More likely it was because the Japanese
felt less urgency in moving them since the bulk of the captives
were off the peninsula and the heavy road congestion had eased.

At Balanga and Orani, Hardee and the other officers saw
and smelled the evidence of thousands who had gone before
them. Human waste, debris, and filth were everywhere in
the prison enclosures. Crude burial grounds nearby attested
to the fate of some who had stopped there.

The last leg of their journey was particularly wearing for

the officer group. It would have been worse but for the Japanese sergeant in charge of the guard detail for part of that day. He spoke good English and agreed to a request that the pace be slowed and halts be more frequent. Appreciative, Hardee and others tried to reward him with money and a wristwatch. He refused, saying he was a professional soldier and "a gentleman like yourselves."

From just outside Lubao to San Fernando the dead bodies in the ditches became more numerous. Hardee counted over seventy-five in one short stretch and then stopped. It was too discouraging.

At San Fernando the Japanese separated Americans and Filipinos. The Americans went to a schoolyard where they stayed for several days. While there the Japanese permitted burial details to leave the prison compound under guard to perform their assigned tasks. Often men on these details returned with purchased food. It was hardly ever shared. Though at the time he found such conduct unpardonable, Hardee later learned to accept it as common in a prisoner's life.

On April 26 Hardee's group reached O'Donnell. They had fared well. They hadn't lost a man.

Few groups were as lucky as Hardee's. Men on the Death March died from a variety of causes. Some succumbed to exhaustion, disease, and heatstroke; others were bayoneted, shot or beheaded. Whether a man lived or died depended upon a combination of factors: his physical condition at the start; how he cared for himself or was assisted en route; his will to survive; and the attitude of the Japanese guarding his particular group.

While the causes and reasons for deaths on the movement out of Bataan can be identified, the actual number has never been established. Estimates over the years have been, at their worst, wild guesses; at their best, careful approximations. Though the number of Americans who arrived at Camp O'Donnell was recorded, it was virtually impossible for the U.S. Army command to record at that time or later the number of men who began the movement from Bataan. To calculate this figure today with any degree of accuracy would require reasonably accurate figures on the following:

—the number of men on Bataan before the last Japanese offensive

—the number of men killed in action in the last offensive

—the number of men remaining in the two American hospitals on Bataan until after the Death March had concluded

—the number of men who evaded capture on Bataan

—the number of men who escaped to Corregidor

—the number of men whom the Japanese kept on work details on Bataan and who did not make the March

Such numerical data either do not exist or are of questionable reliability.

It is probable that American deaths on the March numbered in the hundreds. For the much larger number of Filipino participants the toll may have ranged into the thousands.

Though the number of men who died on the Death March is unknown, the effect of the March on the Americans who lived through it is clear. Denied adequate water, food, and sanitation and pushed to the limits of their endurance, hundreds of the men reaching O'Donnell after the grueling journey were just a few steps away from death. For them the March would continue, and this time its grim toll would be recorded.

★ ★ ★ 4 ★ ★ ★

The commandant at Camp O'Donnell was Capt. Yoshio Tsuneyoshi. A reserve officer recalled to active duty in 1937, he was, at fifty, far overage for his rank. Most of his classmates at the imperial military academy were colonels. General Kawane had hurriedly sent him to command Camp O'Donnell—a most undesirable assignment in the Japanese Army—just a week before the first men arrived. But instead of the 20,000 to 30,000 men he was told to expect, over 60,000 arrived, 9,300 of them Americans. With the three officers, about a dozen noncommissioned officers, and a guard platoon assigned to him by Kawane, the new commandant was responsible for a population the size of Topeka, Kansas. It would be hard to judge who was less prepared for the days ahead—captor or captives.

For most of the new arrivals, life at O'Donnell began with a greeting by the commandant. Bone-tired, sick, and vulnerable, few listeners would ever forget the experience.

After standing in formation, often for an hour or more, the men would watch as Tsuneyoshi, clad in a short-sleeved shirt, long baggy shorts, and riding boots, climbed on a box and began his oration. His words, translated into English by a Filipino interpreter by his side, varied somewhat from group to group but the message was unchanging. American domination of the Orient was over. Japan was now ready to take over the entire area of East Asia. He could destroy them all but the spirit of Bushido forbade such action. The slightest violation of any order would result in instant execution. As the speech continued, the Japanese captain became overwrought, waving his arms and shouting for emphasis. On one occasion he climaxed his speech by screaming at his shocked and disbelieving audience, "You are our enemies and we will fight you and fight you and fight you for a hundred years."

Following this tirade, Tsuneyoshi would leave and the guards would require the assembled men to display all of their possessions on the dusty ground before them. It was during these inspections that seven men, mostly officers, were summarily taken to the camp guardhouse. Inquiries as to what happened to them yielded nothing. None returned.

The Japanese assigned Americans and Filipinos to separate parts of the former Philippine army training camp. For the ever-hopeful Americans, located in the northern section, the barracks and surroundings were disappointing and depressing. The "barracks" were really line upon line of low huts built of bamboo with native grass roofs, some not finished. A man's bed was the bare bamboo floor unless he was fortunate enough to have a blanket or a raincoat to fold and lie on. Plumbing was nonexistent. Water was scarce. Sitting around their huts on a treeless, rolling plain surrounded by barbed wire and beyond it a vast expanse of tall brown cogongrass, many lonely Americans concluded that somehow fate had delivered them to the middle of nowhere.

But disease and death had followed them there. Men harbored malaria parasites in their bloodstreams. Weakened, they had little resistance to the dysentery organisms which, because of the awful sanitary conditions and poor or nonexistent personal hygiene, were soon spreading throughout the camp. The prime carriers of the dysentery organisms, the giant bluebottle flies, multiplied by the millions. At mealtimes the flies swarmed the short distance from open latrines to the glob of rice in the men's mess kits. Impossible to keep off the food, the flies were also a source of constant aggravation to the taut-nerved Americans.

Soap, razors, and towels were extremely scarce. Worse, the water supply was barely adequate for drinking and none was allowed for washing purposes. As one medical officer observed, finding an adequate substitute for water to keep clean was beyond any man's ability to improvise.

In just a few weeks five of the larger buildings designated as a hospital and staffed by American medical officers and corpsmen were full, but little could be done for the sufferers. The scant supplies of quinine for malaria and sulfa (sulfathiazole) pills for dysentery, which some medical officers had been able to get through the inspections, soon ran out. The medicines provided by the Japanese helped little. The amount of quinine would permit five grams for each person with the disease—a useless dose. Some medical officers decided to give a sufficient dosage to effect remission to the worst cases. Others decided who got the dosage by lottery. Often this was a decision which meant life or death.

For dysentery the situation was even worse. The only drug supplied by the Japanese was a small quantity of an anti-dysentery serum (unknown to American doctors) which was quickly exhausted and showed no positive results. In desperation the Americans turned to a native remedy—boiled leaves from a guava tree. The Japanese permitted some American details under guard out of the camp to pick the leaves. The potion did nothing to quell the disease. Finally dysentery became so bad that the most severe cases were isolated in one building. Here the naked, dying men wallowed in their own bloody excrement. Corpsmen had to minister to them without urinals, bedpans, toilet paper, mops, or buckets. Deaths became more and more frequent, and the dreaded building became known as "St. Peter's Ward."

Outside the hospital other Americans lounged, talked, worried, slept, and ate rice. Three times a day they lined up for small steamed portions of the Oriental staple along with some thin, watery vegetable soup. A few times the soup had tiny pieces of carabao meat in it. One medical officer estimated that the diet furnished about 1,500 calories—60 percent of the minimum daily requirement for a deskbound office worker and grossly deficient in protein and vitamins. Fortunately, except for men on work details, life at O'Donnell demanded little physical exertion and most of the famished Americans adapted to their new diet. Some dispirited men found it difficult to eat the bland, tasteless portion day after day. They were among the first to develop the vitamin-deficiency diseases, beriberi and pellagra, which would soon begin to take many lives.

Attempts by General King and members of his staff to obtain more food and medicines were unsuccessful. In response to their pleas, Tsuneyoshi told them that the Japanese Army attacking Corregidor had priority on food and other supplies. As to medicines, he told them that all his requisitions were being returned from Manila unfilled or with small quantities.

The senior American officers were even more dismayed by the commandant's position on help from other sources. One day a line of twelve Philippine Red Cross trucks pulled up to the gate of the camp. After some discussion Tsuneyoshi refused to let them enter. Japanese army regulations did not permit it, he said. So the trucks returned to Manila. The commandant did accept one-time donations of food from two neighboring towns but refused all other offers of help whether they came from the Philippine Red Cross, the bishop of Manila, or concerned Filipino citizens. Later Tsuneyoshi would maintain he was fearful that letting such supplies and personnel into the camp would lead to smuggling.

Despite his efforts smuggling took place. American water carriers obtained canned goods and food from Filipinos who hid along the riverbank. Small work groups and truck drivers sent into the town of Capas to perform various tasks occasionally had an opportunity to buy from the Filipinos. Some drugs were slipped to them by representatives of the Philippine Red Cross who, undaunted by the commandant's rebuff, had occupied a house on the road between Capas and the gates of Camp O'Donnell. Once in the camp, items in excess of the requirements of the person who had brought them in were usually sold, and a small but active black market soon flourished.

Money could greatly improve an individual's chances for survival. Despite the inspections, some men got through with substantial sums of money. A few others received money smuggled in from friends in Manila. Generally, officers, being better paid, had more money than the enlisted men. Colonel Hardee was not one of these. He arrived at O'Donnell with sixteen pesos (eight dollars U.S.) in his pocket. He soon learned that a corporal in his unit on Bataan was active in food smuggling. He sought him out and, after borrowing fifty pesos from another officer, bought cans of corned beef, canned fish, pork and beans, and fruit from the corporal from time to time. A friend of Hardee's, sick and unable to eat, bought some eggs for seventy-five cents each. They were worth far more than the inflated price. He was able to eat the eggs and they probably saved his life.

As much as they needed food and medicine, the men at O'Donnell needed some antidote for their mental anguish. They were still suffering from the humiliation, shock, and disbelief of their defeat. For the young soldiers, and even some of the seasoned professionals, all previous conceptions of their country's military power and the weaknesses of Japan's war machine had been abruptly shattered. Men craved some source of hope, some possible end to their plight. Even the forecast of the optimist that U.S. forces would retake the Philippines in six months was little solace. Many of the weakened men, observing those dying around them, figured that they might not last that long. Such men gave up and succumbed to a combination of disease and hopelessness.

For others rumors helped. One of the most encouraging was a report that they had heard about in the Manila newspapers that an exchange was under way and that Japanese interned in the United States were in California ready to load on ships. (Arrangements for an exchange of U.S. and Japanese diplomatic personnel were actually in process.) Men at O'Donnell debated whether the exchange would include them, and some were encouraged greatly during the two weeks that this rumor was prevalent. Meanwhile, deaths at the hospital increased daily.

Men on the graves detail were divided into two groups, the diggers and the carriers. Digging graves was a continuing and difficult task. The Americans dug large holes in which a dozen or more men were laid side by side. The water level in the burial area near the river was high, so many holes flooded when a depth of three or four feet was reached. Each day the procession of men carrying bodies hanging in blankets between poles lengthened. At the grave sites burial was unceremonious. Men on the burial details placed as many naked bodies as possible in the long shallow graves and then promptly covered them over. In all, nearly 1,500 men, about one out of six of the Americans who had arrived at O'Donnell, would meet such an end.

The 14th Army staff was aware of the conditions at O'Donnell. General Kawane, chief planner and overseer of the Death March, visited the camp for two hours soon after the fall of Bataan and other officers inspected periodically. In May an inspection team listened to Captain Tsuneyoshi's complaints about inadequate supplies but was more concerned with the commandant's failure to complete a roster of American prisoners and the condition of the fence around the camp. But with a reported two hundred men (Americans and Filipinos combined) dying each day, inspectors' written reports described Tsuneyoshi as "not intelligent," "a reserve officer," with "no common sense." In late May, 14th Army relieved the commandant and a few days later ordered the camp closed: too many people were dying there.

★ ★ ★ 5 ★ ★ ★

In other parts of the now far-flung Japanese empire, Americans captured earlier in the war were doing much better than those in the Philippines.

On the island of Java the Japanese moved the *Houston* survivors at Serang and Americans of the 131st Field Artillery along with captured Australians and British soldiers and sailors to a Dutch military barracks near Batavia. The Dutch had named the place Bicycle Camp, for reasons never determined by the Americans.

Bicycle was a well-run camp. Australian Brig. A. S. Blackburn served as senior officer of the 2,000 Australians and 800 Americans there. The camp had running water and electricity. Sanitation and hygiene standards were excellent. Food rations of rice and a thin stew were mediocre but could be augmented by trading outside of the camp. Some of the Americans, particularly the officers, had large amounts of money. Some of it went into a pool to provide supplements for all of the Americans in the camp. Other officers used the money to obtain luxuries such as liquor and tobacco for themselves. The officers had an outdoor mess hall with two Chinese messboys from the *Houston* to serve them. After complaints from the enlisted men, the officers moved their dining facilities inside.

The privileges of rank notwithstanding, all shared in recreational activities. The boxing matches between Americans and Australians were popular. Even in stage shows the Americans and Australians competed. Two Marines from the *Houston* were the organizers and producers of an original musical comedy called *Mexican Fandango,* complete with scenery and costumes fashioned from scrap wood and rags. Not to be outdone, the Australians produced a mystery thriller called *The Monkey's Paw.* Individually, when not on work details men whiled away the time with various hobbies. One man was able to find enough parts to put together a Ford Model A engine.

Rumors abounded. But not as at O'Donnell, they were fed by a secret radio. Two American sergeants had brought in a shortwave radio on which they monitored broadcasts from San Francisco. The Americans were particularly cheered by the report that Tokyo had been bombed by American planes in April.

The Americans, Dutch, and British at the prison camp near Makassar on the Celebes had no news except what the Japanese told them, which from an American point of view was all bad. Life was dreary and the guards were rough. One day a guard nicknamed the "Mad Monk," using a piece of heavy rope soaked in water, beat an American naval officer in the presence of a number of other prisoners until the man collapsed. Lt. R. W. Antrim, a survivor of the USS *Pope* and before the war a dirigible pilot, could not stand it and volunteered to take the remainder of the beating in place of his fellow officer. His actions brought cheers from watching prisoners. Antrim's move and the reaction to it caught the Mad Monk and other guards off balance. Stunned and confused, the Japanese called off the beating and ordered all men, including Antrim and the victim, to the barracks. After the war Antrim was awarded the Congressional Medal of Honor for his heroic and selfless act. He would be the only man to receive his nation's highest military decoration for actions as a prisoner of war.

Far to the north in Woosung near Shanghai the Mad Monk had a counterpart who, as was to happen often, gained an American nickname descriptive of either his actions or his appearance. The Japanese was a camp interpretor named Ishihara—"The Beast of the East." Neat in appearance, he spoke excellent English, which he had learned while living and working in Hawaii. At first Ishihara tried to be friendly to the Americans but it was not long before his domineering manner showed through. He considered any disobedience or infraction of orders to be an expression of disrespect for the emperor and himself. Slapping and cuffing were dealt out liberally to miscreants. All but a few accepted his abuses of authority as unavoidable. One who didn't was Marine Sgt. B. O. Ketner. At an evening muster Ishihara slapped Ketner for no reason whatsoever. Ketner responded by knocking Ishihara down. Then Ishihara and a Japanese guard gave Ketner a terrible beating and kicking, after which they commended him for taking his punishment like a man but confined him to the guardhouse for four days. Ketner had little trouble with Ishihara after that.

By spring two men had died accidentally and one man had been shot by a guard for an alleged escape attempt. Except for these misfortunes and the abusive reign of the Beast of the East, life was bearable for the men at Woosung. Rising temperatures brought relief from the discomfort of the icy barracks. The enlisted men planted a camp garden and attended classes taught by the officers. Occasionally they had a chance to play softball. An International Red Cross representative arranged for extra supplies of food and clothing to be brought into the camp. Most of this was drawn from American Red Cross supplies left in Shanghai, purchases in the open market, and donations from Europeans living in the city. The Red Cross representative also obtained some medical equipment, including an old X-ray machine, and surgical supplies.

The Japanese permitted a radio in each barracks, adjusted,

they thought, to receive only the Japanese-controlled Shanghai station. American radio technicians soon modified the sets to receive other stations. On May 8 the 1,500 Americans at Woosung received some good and bad news. The American Navy had won a major victory in the Coral Sea, but the Japanese had conquered Corregidor.

3

CORREGIDOR TO CABANATUAN
May–June 1942
The Philippines

★ ★ ★ 1 ★ ★ ★

After the fall of Bataan, Japanese artillery and bombers had pounded Corregidor and the three other fortified islands at the mouth of Manila Bay without letup. The island defense complex, the last vestige of Allied military power in the Far East, was in easy artillery range of guns positioned near the tip of Bataan, just two miles away. On May 4 Corregidor itself, three and one-half miles long and from the air looking much like a tadpole, was struck by over sixteen thousand shells. Casualties were surprisingly light. This was because of the labyrinth of tunnels which had been bored into solid rock in parts of the island. Originally constructed for headquarters and storage use, the virtually bombproof space became a haven for thousands of men on Corregidor. The largest of the tunnel systems was the Malinta Tunnel, running from one side of 400-foot-high Malinta Hill to the other. Branching off the 30-foot-high main tunnel were twenty-five lateral tunnels each about 400 feet long. An underground hospital was housed in another tunnel system, and Navy and Quartermaster Corps personnel occupied still other subterranean space. Elsewhere, most of the men in the gun positions had the protection of reinforced concrete. But those with the unenviable job of beach defense had only their foxholes and sandbags, and it was among them that most of the casualties occurred.

Protected or not, many of the men on Corregidor had by this time reached the limits of their physical and mental endurance. The almost constant noise and reverberation of the explosions, the trapped feeling, the short rations, and the threat of imminent attack drove down the men's spirits to a low ebb.

The heavy bombardment continued the following day and that night the long-expected assault on Corregidor began. Though a combined force of Marines, Navy and Army men inflicted heavy losses on the landing forces, the Japanese, once ashore and reinforced with tanks, overwhelmed the defenders, compelling General Wainwright on May 6 to send a message to General Homma announcing that he desired to surrender and that he had ordered the U.S. forces to cease fire at noon that day. Americans hauled down the American flag on schedule, but after unsuccessfully trying to persuade General Homma to accept the surrender of the harbor defense force, General Wainwright late that night had to surrender all forces in the Philippines to the colonel commanding Japanese forces on Corregidor. The next day the Japanese took Wainwright and some of his staff to Manila and required him to broadcast a surrender message to Maj. Gen. William F. Sharpe, commander of the Visayan-Mindanao force. (The Visayan island group includes Cebu, Leyte, Negros, Panay, Samar, and other smaller islands in the central Philippines. Mindanao is the southernmost island of the Philippines and second in size to Luzon.) His message also reached officers commanding forces still holding out in northern Luzon. Following the broadcast Wainwright and some of his immediate staff were held at the University Club, now converted to Japanese officers' quarters in downtown Manila.

Back on Corregidor, the Japanese allowed the Americans and Filipinos in the tunnels to remain there. Relieved that the shooting had stopped, the men talked and wondered what was going to happen next.

Their conquerors did not let them wait for long. Beginning on May 7 and in the early hours of May 8, the Japanese started moving groups of men to the 92nd Garage Area. This relatively flat ten-acre space on the south shore just east of Malinta Hill had been used for a motor pool for the 92nd Coast Artillery,

hence its name. The usual Japanese procedure for movement
was for an English-speaking Japanese soldier to go to a lateral
or a gun position and give the order "Outside!" No questions
were asked or explanations given, only the admonition "Outside!" Americans reacted in different ways to these commands.
Not knowing whether they were going to return or not, some
would leave with little more than the clothing they had on
them.   Others with more foresight carried packs and equipment and some rations that they had a chance to grab.   Once
outside they were all forced into a column and marched to
the 92nd Garage Area. Along the way they saw the terrible
destruction that the bombing and heavy artillery fire had inflicted on the island. They saw the bodies of dead Americans
and Filipinos but no Japanese. All the Japanese bodies had
been taken away and, in the Japanese custom, cremated. By
the end of the day most of Corregidor's defenders were concentrated in the 92nd Garage Area. About eight hundred
wounded and sick along with their doctors, medical corpsmen,
and nurses remained in the hospital area. The sixty-seven
nurses, christened the "Angels of Bataan and Corregidor" by
their grateful patients, were later separated from the other
captives and interned in Santo Tomas, a civilian internment
camp in Manila, for the rest of the war.

Elsewhere the Japanese were consolidating their conquest.
Landing craft went to adjacent islands of the harbor defense
group to accept their surrender. At one, Fort Frank, the commander, Col. Napoleon Boudreau, gave the Japanese major
who was coming ashore a roster of his command. Boudreau's
name was at the head of the list. With considerable humor,
the Japanese commander said, "Well, Napoleon, show me
around."

In the 92nd Garage Area the nearly 12,000 men, about 8,700
of whom were Americans, were experiencing the early mental
and physical pains of captivity. As individuals most of the men
felt helpless, depressed, and uncertain. As a jumbled group
of defeated men, they had lost the unity and comradeship that
their military organizations had provided for many of them.
Their captors had created this situation when they had earlier
assigned men to groups of a hundred under a single American
officer irrespective of their former military organization. With
strange officers and with the perception that all real authority

now came from the Japanese, military discipline began to un-
ravel. For a substantial number of Americans it was every
man for himself. The physical trials, though less arduous than
on Bataan, were considerable. The Garage Area was hot all
day, stank from the lack of latrine facilities, and swarmed with
biting blue-black flies. Except in two old shell-riddled aircraft
hangars and a few old sheds there was no shade from the hot
sun beating on the broad expanses of concrete. The Filipinos
had arrived first and had appropriated one of the two hangars.
The other was taken over by some of the first American officers
to arrive. The remaining thousands of men and officers found
what comfort they could in the open on the concrete and on
the beach.

Men did their best to cope. First relief came when the
Japanese issued rice. Up to that time some thought that the
Japanese were going to ignore them completely. The rice issue
along with American rations on hand furnished enough for
two meals a day. Through the efforts of Col. Cyrus Crews,
the Corregidor supply officer, a cistern was uncovered in the
Garage Area, and except for the usual long lines, water was
not a serious problem. The men without shelter began to improvise. Soon the flat beach and lower slopes of the area were
covered with habitations in every conceivable form—makeshift
tents, lean-tos, and shacks with wisps of smoke from cooking
fires rising here and there. Except for the machine-gun posts
on the high ground overlooking the 92nd Garage Area, it might
have been taken for a gigantic version of the hobo jungles
prevalent in the years of the American Great Depression.

To get away from the awful battle with the flies, the stench,
the stifling heat, and the monotony of life on the beach, many
officers were either assigned or volunteered to accompany the
large working parties of American enlisted men which the Japanese frequently demanded. Col. John R. Vance, General Wainwright's finance officer, volunteered for one. The work party
that he took out carried cases of food from the Navy tunnel
to the south dock, where they were loaded on barges to be
shipped to Japanese warehouses. Though their captors let
them have a can or two of rations at the end of the day, it
was still tantalizing to the hungry men to see hundreds of cases
of corned beef, canned corn, bacon, and other foodstuffs disap-
pearing into the holds of the barges. Food was not all that

was leaving Corregidor. Some work details moved machinery, generators, and medical supplies to the docks for transshipment, while still others cleared the roads and helped to restore power and communications around the island.

Sgt. John D. Provoo was a member of one of the early working parties. Provoo had, just prior to being drafted, spent two years in Japan with a friend, a young Japanese Buddhist priest. Provoo seized the earliest opportunity while on the detail to make his knowledge of the Japanese language and culture evident, and a curious guard took him to a Japanese officer. In less than twenty-four hours the Japanese gave him excellent accommodations in one of the laterals and complete freedom of movement around the island. Soon he began acting as a "spokesman" for the Japanese military hierarchy to his fellow Americans. Unsure of what to make of him, his countrymen viewed him with a mixture of fear and contempt.

Aside from the usual cuffings and beatings, which the Americans soon learned to expect as a matter of course, the Japanese on Corregidor committed few of the kinds of atrocities that had been inflicted on Americans marching out of Bataan. An exception was the execution of Capt. Burton C. Thompson. Late one evening Thompson, who was in charge of rations for the American hospital, refused a request by Sergeant Provoo for food for a group of Japanese officers. An argument ensued and Provoo returned and reportedly told the Japanese that Captain Thompson was "anti-Japanese and uncooperative." Subsequently Captain Thompson was shot by a firing squad.

Americans who surrendered in the southern islands of the Philippines fared better initially than their countrymen on Bataan and Corregidor. Most of the Americans who were captured were on the island of Mindanao. Only a small number of Americans, mostly senior officers commanding Filipino units, fell into enemy hands after the surrender of the islands in the Visayan group.

Three days after Corregidor fell, resistance on Mindanao ended and the Japanese began assembling captives in a military installation near the town of Malaybalay, in the northern part of the island. More Americans were brought in for the next three weeks from other parts of Mindanao along with a few from other islands. By the beginning of June about eleven hundred officers and men, predominantly Air Corps personnel, were held here as well as a much larger number of Filipino troops. The Japanese allowed some Americans to travel to the Malaybalay camp in their own vehicles with all the personal gear they could carry. The guards required that all weapons and other military equipment be turned in but conducted no mass shakedowns. Initially, stocks of U.S. military rations were ample and Americans were permitted, in the words of one officer, to "run our own show." The Japanese required them only to provide a few details to repair roads and to maintain their own camp. At first the men listened to news on several radios which the Japanese permitted them to keep. One officer conceded that the Japanese were operating the camp according to the Rules of Land Warfare. But he and others had second thoughts when they later heard that the Japanese in another part of the island had executed Lt. Col. Robert H. Vesey and two other Americans for allowing some of the men under them to escape.

★ ★ ★ 2 ★ ★ ★

On the morning of May 23, after a heavy rain, the Japanese began moving the men from the 92nd Garage Area to Corregidor's docks. Shortly after noon the wet and bedraggled Americans and Filipinos were taken in motor launches to three small tramp steamers. By the end of the day all of the ships were loaded, two with Americans aboard and the third with Filipinos. The men spent an uncomfortable night and the following morning the ship sailed. When the men who could look out saw that the ships were headed in an easterly direction—toward Manila—they were greatly relieved. At least they were not headed for Japan as some had feared.

When the ships arrived at a point about two miles offshore, the first two containing the Americans dropped anchor. The third ship carrying the Filipinos continued shoreward toward the piers. Soon Japanese landing craft came alongside the two ships with the Americans aboard and started carrying them to shore. When the landing craft touched bottom opposite the Manila Polo Club, the hinged bows dropped and the Americans were ordered to wade in. The men complied and soon found themselves in waist-deep water; others were up to their armpits.

As the first sodden Americans stumbled ashore, many still desperately grasped bulky items of equipment—bedding rolls, suitcases. One or two even had small footlockers. The Japanese guards hurriedly formed them into columns of four and started them moving down beautiful palm-bordered Dewey Boulevard. With the ship carrying the Filipinos tying up at a nearby wharf and unloading there, it soon became apparent to the Americans that their movement was to be a deliberate display of Japanese superiority to Filipino civilians. By the time the last men came ashore, a column of nearly eight thousand weary men stretched almost a mile along the hot pavement.

The movement down Manila's most prominent street with all its familiar landmarks was a wearying and discouraging experience. Men near the front of the column soon found their water-soaked gear too much to carry. Blankets, duffel bags, and other heavy gear shed by the unduly optimistic littered the sides of the roadway. In sharp contrast to the disheveled American column, the Japanese guards presented an excellent appearance. Some on horseback, wearing boots and open-necked white shirts, rode up and down the column spurring the slower marchers on.

Just beyond another familiar landmark, the Manila Yacht Club, the column stopped. Here under some palms the Americans were allowed to get water from several large tubs. After their brief but welcome halt, they were ordered back into line again and they resumed the march, passing more familiar buildings as they continued. The U.S. high commissioner's residence had a large Japanese flag flying from its flagpole. Japanese light tanks occupied the parking lots of two buildings nearby. As the column turned east away from the Bay, unknown to the marchers General Wainwright and some of his staff were watching from their quarters in the University Club. At this point a fairly large number of people had gathered on the sidewalks. Many Filipino men and women had tears streaming down their faces. A few made the V sign for victory with their fingers, first making sure the Japanese guards were not watching. All of this was ample proof to the Americans that they still had the respect and sympathy of their Filipino allies. Late that afternoon, after a march of about six miles, the first Americans arrived at their destination—Bilibid Prison.

Bilibid, which would in the next few years become familiar to virtually all of the Americans captured in the Philippines, was built by the Spanish in 1865 as their central prison. Massive stone and cement walls surrounded the prison yard. In the center of the yard was a tall guard tower surrounded by open space. Radiating from the circumference of this space like spokes of a giant wheel were cellblocks, each 180 feet long and 40 feet wide, with barred windows at intervals down the sides. During its use by the Spanish and later under the United States, the prison had housed about three thousand Filipino criminals, with the overflow going to penal colonies located near Davao on the island of Mindanao and Puerto Princesa on the island of Palawan. Just before the outbreak of war in the Philippines all the inmates were transferred from Bilibid to the new prison south of Manila, after which Bilibid became a storehouse for archives. For a brief period after war broke out, U.S. authorities held Japanese civilians there until the Japanese marched into Manila on January 2. The Japanese reciprocated by confining some medical personnel and others captured in and around Manila and now were opening the forbidding steel gates to the first of many large contingents of Americans to enter.

At the direction of the Japanese, arrangements for the men arriving from Corregidor had been made by a group of Americans captured earlier. The senior officer of the group was Col. J. W. Worthington, a Veterinary Corps officer, who escaped from Bataan but was recaptured. As the men cleared the gates, they were divided into groups of 250 and without halting were led away by their American guides to cellblocks and other buildings. To accommodate the large number of men some had to sleep in the space between the cellblocks.

After the poor conditions at the 92nd Garage Area, the Americans found Bilibid, though designed for common criminals, an improvement. There was plenty of Manila city water to drink and the showers were soon running full blast. Crude flush toilets were available. Only the sleeping arrangements left something to be desired. They had only the concrete floor to lie on. The first meal that they got, like most of those that followed, consisted of rice and onion soup made with lard and varied once or twice with a small quantity of meat for soup stock.

Unlike Camp O'Donnell, where access to outside aid was harshly restricted, at Bilibid Americans with money found several ways to obtain additional food and even lifesaving drugs. Colonel Worthington, through a Japanese interpreter, arranged for a merchant to sell sugar, fruit, and tobacco in the prison compound. Some of the sentries provided another source of food, though their prices were not as reasonable as those at the prison market. To do business with the sentries, prospective purchasers would line up for their turn along the wall under a sentry station. The Japanese sentry on top of the wall would then require the purchaser to throw him some money, usually about five pesos ($2.50 in American currency). Next, by means of a rope thrown to a Filipino on the outside, he would pull up a basket the contents of which would be one or more of the following: bananas, mangoes, molasses, coconut bars, papayas, sugar, or candy. The items were hardly ever worth more than two pesos at current market prices. The sentry would let the basket down to the prisoner, pay the Filipino what he pleased, and pocket the difference. An American never knew what to expect for his money. Grab bag that it was, the sentries had plenty of customers.

Still another method of obtaining food was from Filipino boys who at times when no guards were in sight would accept money and take orders through an opening in a seldom-used gate in the wall. Their prices were fair, considering the risk they took if caught—a beating or worse. A large raisin or custard pie from one of them would cost only a peso. They also accepted notes, which they would pass on to people outside the walls. In this way some Americans made their first contact with their families or civilian friends in Manila. A few of these fortunates were able to get material assistance—food, money, or both—in response to their notes. One American, the envy of his fellows at the time, received a beautiful chocolate layer cake and two pies from his friends in Manila.

Far more fortunate than the man with the chocolate cake were those who had the money and were able to buy medicine and vitamins. Even as men were dying from the lack of them at Camp O'Donnell, Worthington and perhaps others got permission from the Japanese to obtain these vital items. In tablet form, the medicine and vitamins were divided on the advice of medical officers into individual medicine kits each containing 150 tablets: 25 sulfathiazole tablets for dysentery, 50 quinine tablets for malaria, 25 aspirin tablets for fever, and 50 Vitamin B_1 tablets for vitamin-deficiency diseases. Each kit cost about fifteen dollars. When the drugs arrived, word was passed which probably reached only a small proportion of the men at Bilibid; and of these some didn't have the money. Despite this the demand for the kits far exceeded the supply, so it was necessary to draw lots to see who would get the kits. Only later would the lucky recipients realize the extent of their good fortune.

★ ★ ★ **3** ★ ★ ★

Bilibid was only a stopover for the Americans from Corregidor. Soon after their arrival the Japanese began to move large groups of them to a new camp that they had established near the town of Cabanatuan, about ninety miles north of Manila.

As these men were leaving, about eight hundred patients along with their medical personnel from closed-down hospitals on Bataan arrived at Bilibid by truck. No sooner had they arrived than men started circulating through the building selling or trading quinine, sulfathiazole, and Vitamin B_1 tablets. In this way a few more men were able to obtain some of the vital drugs and, in some cases, mosquito bars, sheets, raincoats, underwear, socks, and canned rations as well.

While the groups were leaving for Cabanatuan, some of the officers discussed whether or not they should ask the Japanese to segregate all officers in a hotel in Manila where, in the view of some, the provisions of the Geneva Convention could be properly carried out and the officers allowed to live as "gentlemen under restraint." Finally one officer, Lt. Col. Frank Carpenter, composed a letter requesting that officers be moved to better accommodations. Colonel Vance read the letter and considered it to be a pretty good one. Carpenter gave it to a Japanese guard. The Japanese didn't bother to reply to the letter, and in a few days Carpenter and most of the officers had left for the new camp at Cabanatuan. Vance, who along with other full colonels and generals remained at

Bilibid, would later recall this incident as an example of how naive and unprepared many Americans were for captivity.

Like that to O'Donnell, the movement of Americans to Cabanatuan—which was to become the largest American POW camp in the Far East—was poorly executed. The location selected was another Philippine army division training camp situated on the road running northeast from the town of Cabanatuan. This training complex consisted of three separate camps, all in poor state of repair. The Japanese had given each camp a number. Camp 1 was about five miles up the road from Cabanatuan; Camp 2 was four miles farther on; and Camp 3 was six miles beyond Camp 2. Camp 3 had a working water supply. Camp 1 had none at the time, and although water was available at Camp 2 it was more than a thousand yards away from the camp with no connecting pipes.

The first Americans arrived on May 26 and were sent to Camp 3. Successive shipments of about one thousand men per day were sent there also. By the twenty-ninth of May this camp was at capacity. On that day Lt. Col. Shigeji Mori, a classmate at the imperial military academy of Prime Minister Tojo, assumed command of the Cabanatuan camp. He found that in addition to the problem of where to put the incoming Americans, four Corregidor soldiers had escaped from Camp 3 and had just been recaptured. The new commandant ordered the execution of the four men and this was carried out a day later. Mori sent the next group of Americans to Camp 2.

Maj. Stephan M. Mellnik, who had arrived in the Philippines as a first lieutenant two and one-half years before, was in this group. On the hot and uncomfortable train ride from Manila to Cabanatuan he and his companions had speculated that with the war in the Philippines over and time to organize, the Japanese at this new location would be better prepared and things would improve. They were soon disappointed. After spending the night in a downpour in the town of Cabanatuan, they hiked to Camp 2, where they were greeted by Lieutenant Colonel Mori. He told them that the war for them was over; that this camp was their home and that they should cooperate. To their dismay they found that the camp had no water, drainage, or latrines. For the next four days the rice ration was

slim and men depended mainly on rainwater to drink. Finally
the commandant ordered the abandonment of the camp. The
Americans trudged back down the road over which they had
come to Camp 1, where the water system had been restored.
Here Lieutenant Colonel Mori announced to the weary and
disgruntled arrivals, "This is your permanent home."

This "permanent home," as it was to be for thousands of
Americans in the years to come, was a rectangular area situated
in flat rice-growing country. One side faced the road to Cabanatuan on the north, the other three sides abutted open farm-
land. When the first Americans arrived, the camp was not
yet fenced and was guarded only by sentries. The Americans
occupied the larger northern section of the camp, which contained three separate groups of buildings, mostly barracks.
Typical barracks were long, framed, shuttered structures designed to hold about sixty men. But by adding a second tier
of sleeping platforms, the Japanese had doubled the capacity.
Immediately to the south was a road which crossed the camp
and below this was the Japanese area. The southernmost section of the camp was designated as the hospital area. It was
not long before men were occupying the buildings in this area.

At the beginning of June, as the last Corregidor men from
Bilibid moved into Cabanatuan, the Americans at Camp O'Donnell were told by a Japanese officer that they were going to
another camp (Cabanatuan) because "too many were dying
at O'Donnell." The death toll would reach fifteen hundred
Americans by the time O'Donnell was finally closed.

Leaving behind a group of doctors and their patients, the
Japanese moved the Americans to their destination in several
groups. Some rode all the way to Camp 1 in crowded trucks.
Others rode to the town of Cabanatuan in hot boxcars and
then marched the five miles from the railroad station to the
camp. Mellnik and others who had arrived a week before
watched the incoming columns and were appalled at the condition of the new arrivals compared with themselves. The men
looked haggard; they wore ragged clothing; most had no blankets, mosquito nets, or other personal equipment. They were
a sorry sight. But mixed with this sympathy for their fellow
Americans was the Corregidor men's concern that the diseases
that they soon learned were prevalent at O'Donnell would

spread to them. Their worries were well founded. Soon heavy rains turned the camp into a quagmire, overflowing the latrines. When the rains stopped, the flies took over, spreading dysentery organisms everywhere. Rapidly breeding mosquitoes did the same for malaria. It soon became apparent to captor and captive alike that another onslaught of disease and death was under way.

Meanwhile, the Japanese had transferred the senior officers captured on Corregidor and held at Bilibid to a small camp near the town of Tarlac, to the west of Cabanatuan. General King and other senior officers from Camp O'Donnell had already arrived there. Here again the Corregidor officers were shocked when they met their fellow officers from Bataan and saw their gaunt, dispirited condition. All the Americans at Tarlac were cheered when a few days later their commander, General Wainwright, and his immediate staff arrived from Manila.

After the senior officers left, the Japanese converted part of Bilibid Prison into a hospital and transient center and staffed it with American naval medical personnel. Bilibid and Cabanatuan were two among scores of "permanent," long-term camps which were beginning to dot the Prisoner of War Bureau's map of Southeast Asia. Though treatment of captives up to this time had been largely influenced by post-battlefield conditions, directions emanating from Tokyo at this time would have a more far-reaching effect on the lives of the Americans.

4

"NO WORK—NO FOOD"

May–July 1942
Japan—The Philippines

★ ★ ★ 1 ★ ★ ★

In Japan on May 30, Prime Minister Tojo, leader of Japan's war effort but in appearance a bald, short, and unimpressive man, spoke to the commander and staff at Zentsuji, where Americans from Guam were in their fifth month of captivity. In what was to be one of his few visits to POW camps, Tojo publicly expressed a policy which had been decided upon in a Tokyo conference earlier. His government would require that the Allied prisoners be governed by the dictate then being applied to the Japanese people which had come to be expressed in a national slogan, "No work—no food." His directions— which carried the full weight of an imperial decree as well as his own—to the Zentsuji officers were clear:

To this Division is attached a Prisoner of War Camp. Prisoners of War must be placed under strict discipline as far as it does not contravene the Law of Humanity. It is necessary to take care not to be obsessed with a mistaken idea of humanitarianism or swayed by personal feelings towards those Prisoners of War which may grow in the long time of their imprisonment. The present situation of affairs in this country does not permit anyone to lie idle doing nothing but eating freely. With that in view,

in dealing with the Prisoners of War, too, I hope you will see
that they may be usefully employed.

At Imperial Headquarters the Prisoner of War Bureau continued to plan and develop policies for prisoner-of-war administration. Staff officers spent long hours drafting new directives
and revising decades-old regulations. Messages went out sum-
moning all of the chiefs of camps throughout the Japanese empire to a meeting in Tokyo. With all this staff activity the
Bureau did not neglect to take immediate steps to make the
"work" part of the slogan operative.

Within a week of Tojo's visit to Zentsuji, the camp commander sent 150 American sailors and Marines to the city of
Osaka. This was not just another work detail. Some of the
men at Zentsuji had been on those before. For the military
and economic planners it had considerable long-range significance. Japan's military successes across a wide expanse of
Southeast Asia had, in a matter of months, created a tremendous
requirement for manpower. Virtually all the able-bodied men
were in the Army, Navy or Air Force, leaving only a few to
load ships, mine ore, plant crops, repair roads, and perform
myriad other labor-intensive activities. Despite the use of
women and older men, the effects of the labor shortage cut
across all sectors of the Japanese economy. The Osaka detail
was then a small but important experiment to see how Americans would perform on jobs requiring heavy manual labor.
So a short time after their arrival the men from Zentsuji were
hard at work, as part of the port of Osaka stevedore force,
loading and unloading ships from all parts of the greatly expanding Japanese empire.

★ ★ ★ 2 ★ ★ ★

In the Philippines the Japanese military command did not need
Tojo's announcement of the Japanese policy on war prisoners
to set about putting their half-starved, war-weary captives to
work. Beginning around the time of the fall of Corregidor
the Japanese sent out many Americans from Camp O'Donnell,
about one out of every ten men, in details of one hundred to
four hundred men. Most of the work that they were required
to do resulted from the fighting that had just ended. They

had to build bridges, repair roads, and salvage military equipment from the battlefields. For some these details were a blessing, for others a bane. Men never knew beforehand. But whether they were ordered to go out or they volunteered, most believed, or made themselves believe, that things would be better wherever they were going.

Some men found themselves back on the very fields of battle that they had left only weeks before. David Levy, then a young Air Corps private, would later recall his detail back on the Bataan Peninsula as, relatively speaking, a pleasant interlude. He and other Americans, supervised by Japanese service troops, towed away and repaired U.S. Army trucks for use by the Japanese Army. Except for an occasional rap for failure to understand a direction, Levy found his masters fairly easy to get along with, and he and the other men ate better. They got more rice than at O'Donnell and supplemented this by trading tools and other items found in the trucks for food from the Filipinos. Capt. Mark M. Wohlfeld, in charge of a hundred-man Bataan salvage detail, found life there better than the monotony of O'Donnell. Like Levy's, Wohlfeld's problems—none serious—rose out of his and others' inability to understand the Japanese application of their standards of military discipline and propriety. One night he and others in his tent were awakened from a sound sleep and beaten. The interpreter later came in and explained that the Japanese commander of Wohlfeld's detail had learned that the Americans had been visited by Japanese officers from another unit and had enjoyed themselves talking and smoking until late in the night. The beating, the interpreter explained, was for this unauthorized pleasure and for violating a nine o'clock curfew which Wohlfeld and the other men were unaware of. But what surprised the Americans the most was the last offense for which they were told they had been punished: not inviting their Japanese commander to the bull session. Equally surprised were some of a four-hundred-man American detail back on Corregidor. After completing a number of jobs cleaning up the war-torn island, one group of Americans was ordered to convert some storage space into a series of small rooms. This they did and were later astonished to learn that the Japanese had imported seven prostitutes from Manila and were soon using the rooms as Corregidor's official Japanese army brothel.

In sharp contrast to the men in details on Bataan and Corregidor, the men assigned to work on bridges and roads suffered
terribly. After a month on Bataan, where he had been sent
at the end of the Death March, the next work assignment for
Marine Sgt. Earl Dodson and his detail was to repair one of
two bridges spanning the Pampanga River at the town of
Calumpit. The Americans were assigned to work on the highway bridge. The Japanese supervised a Philippine engineering
contractor work force on the railroad span. Dodson and his
companions took their orders from a cruel Japanese sergeant
nicknamed "The Whip Master" and other Japanese soldiers.
The Americans' job was to carry long heavy wooden beams
from the riverbank out onto the bridge to a specific location
where the Japanese engineers bolted them into place and attached steel cables, also carried to the site by Americans. The
work demanded extreme physical exertion with beatings for
slackers. With only rice to eat, and not much of that, the
men began to sicken and die with alarming frequency.
Dodson, distressed by these conditions, started slipping out
of the lightly guarded prison compound at night. With the
help of brave Filipinos—the Japanese dealt very severely with
Filipinos if they were caught helping Americans—he was able
to fill his burlap bag with food and medicine, which he shared
with some of his friends. After ten successful trips out of the
compound Dodson quit when the Japanese announced that if
one man was caught escaping, ten would be shot.

Americans on another bridge suffered as badly or worse.
This detail, working on a bridge at the town of Gapan, fourteen
miles south of Cabanatuan, was so riddled by disease and exhaustion that after two months the Japanese sent the men back
to Cabanatuan. Far south of Manila other Americans worked,
building a road through the jungle in Tayabas Province. Maj.
Charles T. Brown, an Army doctor sent down from Bilibid because of the bad medical situation at Tayabas, was shocked
by the sight of approximately three hundred ill-clad, exhausted,
malaria-ridden Americans working with wheelbarrows, picks,
and shovels. Surprisingly, he found that a fairly adequate supply of American canned goods was on hand but it did little
good. Most of the men were too sick to eat. Two to three
men were dying each day by the time Brown, along with thirty

other seriously ill men, left the work camp to return to the prison hospital at Bilibid.

All the deaths did not result from disease and exhaustion. On another bridge detail south of Laguna de Bay, in southern Luzon, the Japanese carried out their threat to execute ten men if one escaped. After a Filipino guerrilla raid one night in which several Japanese guards were killed, the Japanese took a head count and found one man missing. Next they required the Americans to stand in formation and picked out ten men with the same identifying armbands as the man who was missing. Then, in the sight of the assembled Americans, the Japanese shot the ten men. A month later the edict was carried out again, but this time on a reduced scale. At Calumpit a man escaped while working on the bridge there. Rumor had it that his Filipino wife had arranged for him to escape down the river in a boat. When the Japanese discovered he was missing, they summoned two American captains on the detail. After some negotiation with them, the Japanese agreed to execute five men instead of ten. The unfortunate five were those with numbers on the prisoner roster closest to the escapee. After their names were called, they were trucked away and executed by a firing squad.

Meanwhile, the railroad bridge at Calumpit was finished. To celebrate, Japanese flags flew and military officers stood by proudly. As the first train crossed the bridge a Filipino band from Manila began to play. Americans about one hundred yards upstream working on the highway bridge watched and listened. Years later one of them would swear that interspersed in the medley played by the band were the unmistakable strains of "God Bless America."

As men on the battlefield clearance, road, and bridge details were completing their work, the Japanese military command began to find more permanent work projects for the Americans. Over four hundred men were assigned to the Manila port area as stevedores. A somewhat smaller detail of Americans moved by ship to the port of Puerto Princesa, on the island of Palawan south of the island of Luzon, where they were put to work on a military airfield. Another detail began work improving a former U.S. Army Air Corps base at Clark Field, north of Manila, for use by the Japanese Air Force. In coming months five more airfields requiring the use of large details of Americans would be added to the Japanese list of work projects.

★ ★ ★ 3 ★ ★ ★

In Tokyo at two meetings held by the Prisoner of War Bureau to instruct high-ranking officers in charge of groups of camps and members of their staff, Tojo once again expressed his views on how war prisoners should be treated and used. The first meeting, held on June 25, was attended by the chiefs of prison camps in Korea and Formosa; the second, held twelve days later, was for the four major generals responsible for camps in the Philippines, Thailand, Malaya, and Java. Both meetings lasted two days and followed the same schedule. Each meeting opened with General Uemura reading Tojo's address:

> It gives me great pleasure that you have been appointed Chiefs of Prisoner of War Camps and are starting for your respective posts soon.
> In Japan, we have our own ideology concerning prisoners of war, which should naturally make their treatment more or less different from that in Europe and America. In dealing with them, you should, of course, observe the various Regulations concerned, aim at an adequate application of them, and evince the fair and just attitude of the Empire vividly for abroad as well as at home. At the same time, however, you must place the prisoners under strict discipline and not allow them to lie idle doing nothing but eating freely for even a single day. Their labor and technical skill should be fully utilized for the replenishment of production, and contribution rendered toward the prosecution of the Greater East Asiatic War, for which no effort ought to be spared.

Following the reading of Tojo's address, Prisoner of War Bureau officers lectured on various topics for the remainder of the two conferences and distributed written documents to the conferees. A sampling of the subjects of the over twenty-five individual documents provides some insight on the scope of the meetings: treatment, disposition, labor, punishment, labor (officers), transportation of technicians, information on prisoners, identification cards, sanitation, monetary allowances, personal belongings, information on the International Red

Cross, correspondence, war dead, control of prisoners, daily routine of prisoners, guarding of prisoners.

Policies and instructions in the Japanese Army were typically very specific, and those issued to the newly appointed camp chiefs were no exception. The policy on labor by officers and noncommissioned officers (forbidden by the Geneva Convention and a subject of contention between the Japanese and American officers for months and years to come) read in part:

> Although the imposition of labor upon Prisoner of War officers and non-commissioned officers is prohibited under Article I of the Prisoner of War Labor Regulations (Army Note #139, September 10, 1904), it is the policy of the Central Authorities, in view of the present condition of this country which does not allow anyone to lie idle and eat freely, and also with a view to maintaining the health of Prisoners of War, to have them volunteer to work in accordance with their respective status, intelligence, physical strength, etc.

The directive went on to include a list of suitable work for officers, which ranged from the direction of other POWs to raising domestic animals and chickens.

Significantly, the schedule for the meetings did not mention and the documents and instructions issued did not include a subject that would be of tremendous importance in the life of Japanese prisoners: medical treatment. This reflected the low priority that the Japanese Army gave to this subject in planning and conducting their own military operations. Not surprisingly, the Japanese military would have even less concern about the health and physical well-being of prisoners of war.

The new chiefs left the landmark meetings and journeyed to their far-flung posts to oversee a vast program which in the Orient was without precedent. For the first time Occidentals in large numbers would join the masses of Asia toiling at what was then popularly called coolie labor. The war minister's rules for the new coolie force were tough, exacting, and for Occidentals demeaning. Life for the typical American would become bearable only when camp commanders were to interpret these rules in their most favorable light, or bend them a little. Unfortunately few commanders saw fit to do so.

★ ★ ★ 4 ★ ★ ★

In late July and early August two meetings—this time of ships, not men—occurred which, as those in Tokyo, would ultimately have a major impact on Allied prisoners. Soon after the fall of Corregidor the U.S. government and the American Red Cross, through the intermediation of the Swiss government and the International Red Cross, began negotiation with the Japanese on the exchange of diplomatic personnel and certain civilians who had been in each country at the outbreak of the war and were interned there. The United States also sought to furnish relief packages to Americans captured by the Japanese. In June 1942 the United States chartered a Swedish ship, the *Kanangoora*, loaded it with nearly one million dollars' worth of food, clothing, medicines, and other items, and asked the Japanese government to allow the ship to sail from a U.S. West Coast port to a designated port in the Far East from which the supplies could be distributed. The Japanese from the outset stated that they could not guarantee safe passage of the ship. Discussion got nowhere and the ship was finally unloaded. Failing in this effort, the Americans found that the Japanese were quite interested in the exchange of diplomatic personnel, and arrangements to bring this about went relatively smoothly. The first exchange began when the Japanese ship *Asama Maru*, after taking aboard American diplomatic personnel and civilians at Yokohama, Hong Kong, and Saigon, was joined by an Italian liner, the *Conte Verde*, bringing Americans from Shanghai, China. Both ships proceeded to the port of Lourenço Marques in Portuguese Mozambique, near the southeastern end of the African continent, where on July 23 they met the U.S.-chartered Swedish liner *Gripsholm*, which had arrived earlier.

The *Gripsholm* not only had aboard Japanese diplomatic personnel and civilians but also carried in its hold a substantial cargo of food packages, medical supplies, clothing, cigarettes, toilet articles, and miscellaneous other items. These relief supplies were a combination of contributions by the American, British, and Canadian Red Cross societies. Besides the cargo brought by the *Gripsholm*, the Red Cross Society of the Union of South Africa, a country which bordered on Mozambique, shipped a quantity of bulk foodstuffs to Lourenço Marques for the exchange. The transfer of people (thirteen hundred Americans happily boarded the *Gripsholm*) and cargo was accomplished in four days; and in late July the *Asama Maru* and *Conte Verde,* with their cabins now occupied by Japanese citizens and with relief supplies in their holds, sailed for Singapore and Yokohama.

Shortly after this exchange another was made at the same port. This one involved British and Japanese diplomatic personnel and civilians but also included relief supplies from England, Australia, and India. This time, after loading their countrymen aboard and stowing the relief supplies in their holds, the two Japanese ships, the *Kamakura Maru* and *Tatuta Maru,* proceeded to Shanghai and Yokohama.

The United States and the other countries involved in the two exchanges had no assurance that the relief supplies furnished by the respective countries would go to the citizens of that country. Nor did they know when and how the Japanese would distribute the supplies. Even with this uncertainty and the knowledge that much more was needed, Allied authorities could draw some satisfaction from the knowledge that finally some help was on the way. Unfortunately it would be too late for those interred in the burial ground at Camp O'Donnell and for the growing number of dying Americans at Cabanatuan.

5

ZERO WARD

June–August 1942
The Philippines

★ ★ ★ 1 ★ ★ ★

The end of the first week in June found about nine thousand Americans, mostly Camp O'Donnell survivors, at Camp 1 and nearly six thousand men at the other Cabanatuan camp, Camp 3, nine miles to the northeast. It would be at Camp 1 that the lethal way of disease and death would finally expend itself over the next several months. The men at Camp 3, mostly from the healthier Corregidor garrison and isolated from the pestilence of the other camp, would come through these months relatively unscathed.

During June the wood frame barracks converted to crude hospital wards—about twenty of them—in the southern third of Camp 1 filled to a capacity of about two thousand men. About half of these men, those with dysentery, occupied ten to twelve buildings separated from the hospital buildings. American doctors selected one building in the dysentery section for those men expected to die. It became known as the "Zero Ward." One medical officer would recall that the name was given it because the building was missed when the wards were assigned numbers. But others who were familiar with the ward and its purpose assumed that like "St. Peter's Ward" at Camp O'Donnell, its name referred to the fact that once there a man's chances for emerging alive from the ward were zero. At peak times, one or two additional buildings were

converted to the same grisly purpose as Zero Ward. Maj. Roy
L. Bodine, Jr., a dental officer who had spent his boyhood in
the Philippines and who was a careful chronicler of his days
as a prisoner, would write later: ". . . The men were nearly
all naked, having soiled and thrown away their clothing and
blanket, as there were no means to wash them and no one
to do it. The one doctor assigned to each building could do
nothing for his patients except try to encourage them as he
watched them die; the two medical corps men assigned were
busy trying to distribute evenly the meager amounts of water
and food. Once each day the helpless, bedsore human skele-
tons were moved from their own filth so a crude attempt could
be made to scrape and sweep the mess to one end of the building. A haze of giant green flies covered the area and crawled
over the eyes and in and out of the mouths of the dying
men. . . ." By the end of June 500 men had died—474 enlisted
men, 25 officers, and 1 civilian.* About 300 of these succumbed to dysentery, or dysentery in combination with another
disease, usually malaria.

Little could be done to quell the dysentery scourge. As
they had in the last days at O'Donnell, the torrential rains—
80 inches of rainfall were average for the June-to-December
rainy season—caused the open-pit latrines to overflow. Water
was scarce for washing hands and eating utensils. Sanitary
discipline, in fact all discipline, was seriously lacking. In what
was in Bodine's view "a low point for the science of dentistry"
teams of dentists, armed with improvised shovels made of a
piece of sheet iron on the end of a stick, went around covering
up human waste left by men who could not get to the latrines
or just didn't try to.

With no medicines available, men in the "well" section of
the camp were advised to get some charcoal from the kitchens
and eat a spoonful several times a day. This helped some,
but still the daily trek of men—many so sick that they had to
be carried by their companions—down to the hospital section
grew in numbers. But it never exceeded one hundred, the
daily limit set by the Japanese.

* The Japanese treated the relatively small number of American male civilians captured
with the troops on Bataan the same as the military. Civilians and their families in
Manila and elsewhere were interned in Santo Tomas and other civilian internment
camps for the duration of the war.

As sick men entered the hospital others were leaving in a solemn procession to the cemetery area, sometimes as many as forty corpses a day. In the first few months, for reasons they never explained, the Japanese did not permit the respects normal to human burial. Consequently Americans were compelled to dump their comrades' bodies into a large common grave. No markers could be installed nor were chaplains allowed in the cemetery area. On the many rainy days burial holes often filled with water, and some of the burial detail had to hold down the bodies with poles while others shoveled wet earth over them.

With the deplorable conditions in the hospital area, strong feelings—pro and con—about the American medical staff existed. One officer observed: "Medical treatment was haphazard, generally poor, and frequently a disgrace. Medicines were stolen from patients and sold for profit. Patients were robbed, neglected, allowed to die crying for attendance—receiving only curses. Doctors too lazy to visit the barracks allowed sick men to die without visiting them, then wrote out death certificates without ever seeing the patients. Corpses lay unattended for hours in barracks or underneath in the grass where death had come."

The doctors, working with the most primitive type of equipment and little or no drugs and medicines, had a different view. A medical officer described the ward as a scene of "much fussing, bickering, swearing, stealing; in short, it is something of an inferno. Our doctors who work hard amongst this all day long deserve something better at night. Many of the patients criticize the medical department, saying we keep food and supplies from them. They make the most baseless accusations, forgetting that we are all prisoners and if anything better could be had, we would only be too glad to have them better treated and housed. The officers are about the worst complainers we have. Their ward is about the dirtiest and they spend their days making us of the staff miserable. This situation has shown what a thin veneer of civilization we have."

Disease and death reached their peak in July. Deaths from all causes were 786 by the end of that month. This shocking death rate, if it had continued, would have virtually wiped out the entire camp in ten months. Dysentery and malaria were still the leading causes of death but increasing numbers of men succumbed to diphtheria in a extremely virulent form. About one out of every three men lying in the hospital at the beginning of July died before month's end. Fear of dying haunted those who remained. They mourned little for those who had left or gave little thought to the wives, children, or parents of their deceased comrades. The living's overriding concern was simply "Who will be next?" but in Zero Ward most of the men were not that concerned. They had resigned themselves to death and were beyond caring.

Death hit the young enlisted men the hardest. Of the men who died during July at Camp 1, 85 percent were under thirty. Ten percent of the enlisted men died, compared to about 4 percent of the officers. Given the fact that nearly all of the men, young and old, officers and enlisted, had had their hopes dashed on the Death March and during their stay at Camp O'Donnell and were weakened by disease and malnutrition, some probable causes for the higher death rate among enlisted men might have been: they were being tested for the first time; they had no wife and children who needed them; they possessed little or no money or other means to get extra food and medicine; and finally, they lacked the resourcefulness and determination that usually come with maturity and long experience.

★ ★ ★ 2 ★ ★ ★

Life was not easy for the men in the northern end of Camp 1. Daily they had to contend with Japanese army regulations, inadequate nourishment, related vitamin-deficiency ailments, and a number of discomforts which made each day difficult.

Early in June, Lieutenant Colonel Mori had published a set of regulations for both Camps 1 and 3. The regulations specified that each camp be organized into three groups, each under an American lieutenant colonel. A single officer in each camp reported directly to Colonel Mori. The first such officers appointed were Col. D. J. Rutherford at Camp 1 and Lt. Col. Curtis T. Beecher at Camp 3. The regulations stated that the penalty for attempted escape was "death by shooting." The Americans were required to designate in each barracks ten-man squads. In the event of an escape or an attempted escape by one man, the other members of his squad would be held responsible and subject to the death penalty. Beyond these sobering mandates, the regulations contained sixty other provisions which governed virtually every facet of the Americans' existence, ranging from twice-daily roll calls, use of water, sleeping, and going to the toilet to the requirement that all Americans salute Japanese soldiers and stay at least two meters away from the fence surrounding the camp.

One of the more nettling set of rules—five of them in all—applied to precautions in the barracks to avoid fire: no smoking, fire guards, inspections, disposal of trash, and the formation of a fire bucket brigade if a fire should break out. Such extreme attention to protect what the Americans considered to be little more than shacks was baffling. Even more disturbing was the seemingly false concern for their lives which the rules implied. Few Americans, if any, were aware that the Japanese were applying to the camps the stringent rules (and to some degree a preoccupation with building fires) that grew largely out of a terrible earthquake in Japan which had occurred nineteen years before and had destroyed a third of Tokyo and most of Yokohama and killed 150,000 people. Even had they been aware, it would probably not have made much sense to the Americans to have to live by such rules in a remote camp in the Philippines. But those Americans who then and in the future held that Japanese regulations were a deliberate attempt to demean and humiliate them had more solid grounds for their views in respect to the rule for saluting. The requirement that every American, irrespective of rank, salute a Japanese soldier of any rank left little doubt as to the relative status of Americans under their Japanese masters.

Much as the rules rankled, food was a larger concern. Even after the disastrous experiences of the Death March and O'Donnell, the Japanese camp administration was not staffed, trained, or equipped to provide adequately for feeding large numbers of men in captivity. At Camp 1 a Japanese sergeant working under a lieutenant was responsible for procuring food for over eight thousand men. However, after a poor start the rice ration—the same for both officers and enlisted men—was increased to an amount about equal to or possibly slightly larger than that which had been issued at O'Donnell. The rice, boiled to a pasty soup called *lugao* for breakfast and steamed and supplemented with different types of native greens at the other two meals, was never enough to satisfy the American appetite. More importantly, the diet lacked the vitamins and nutrition necessary to allow the human body to fight off diseases and infections or, were they incurred, to recover from them.

As a result of hunger pangs and an increasing obsession with their degrading state of health, individual Americans sought ways to get more food. Truck drivers, details out of the camp, and Filipinos working in the camp often brought food items and tobacco with them and sold them for exorbitant prices at a daily "thieves' market." An underground communications and supply link (which would continue almost until the end of the war) was a group of carts pulled by native oxen which the Japanese had authorized to haul rice and other supplies daily from the town of Cabanatuan to Camp 1. Aaron Kliatchko, a refugee from Russia, formerly with the U.S. Army and a longtime resident of the Philippines, along with six American soldiers who had experience with farm animals operated the slow-moving supply train. At considerable risk to themselves, they began almost from the opening of Camp 1 to smuggle messages, medicine, and money from sympathetic Filipinos and members of the Manila international community along with their legitimate cargo.

Another source for food opened when the Japanese authorized the Camp 1 leadership to purchase food and tobacco from Filipino merchants approved by the Japanese. At first the limited quantities led to abuses. Supposedly at the direction of the Japanese, the foodstuffs were made available for purchase according to rank. In one such issue lieutenant colonels got a can of corned beef each, majors received one can of milk for each four men, and a barracks of captains (eighty-four men) had three cans of corned beef and six cans of milk to divide. They usually divided them by drawing lots among those who had the money. The enlisted men's barracks got candy and cigarettes. Such abuses naturally bred animosity among the ranking officers, the junior officers, and the enlisted men but this was largely eliminated when supplies increased. The increase in quantities had another beneficial effect. The officially authorized prices were reasonable and drove most of the black market operators out of business. But whatever the source, it was those with money, rank, or cunning who got the extra food which helped so much to make the rice diet endurable and kept the spark of hope burning.

The availability of extra food for the fortunate generated a word which came to be an integral part of the American POW vocabulary. The word was "quan." Derived from a Filipino word, the term was used to designate extra food—quan; the container it was prepared in—a quan can or bucket; and the preparation and consumption ceremony—quanning. Typically, canned fish when added to rice with a little vegetable oil and heated made a good quan. Also used for the purpose but not so common were canned pork and beans, chili con carne, and corned beef. It was during the infrequent occasions of quanning that the Americans' morale was the highest.

The small quantities of supplemental food did little to change the fact that the diet at Camp 1 was nutritionally insufficient for Americans. The vitamin-deficiency diseases which had started for some at Camp O'Donnell now became widespread. Men with "wet" beriberi found their feet swelling, and later the edema would progress up their bodies to their head. Those with "dry" beriberi experienced severe stabbing pains in their feet and legs. To obtain relief they would sit up all night with their feet in pans of water, when it was available. Pellagra and scurvy would afflict a lesser number of men. Deaths from beriberi and the other vitamin-deficiency diseases would not occur in significant numbers until later in the year.

Meanwhile, a seemingly endless number of lesser torments—tropical sores, worms, lice, scabies, bedbugs, and flies—plagued those fortunate enough not to have a serious ailment. Long lines for water for drinking and personal hygiene persisted as Filipino contractors continued digging some new wells for the camp water supply.

Under such dismal conditions some officers sensed a need for diverting men's minds from their seemingly overwhelming situation. One officer, a former Manila auto salesman, organized a series of camp shows. Drawing on a pool of professional and amateur singers, comedians, and musicians, the hour-long shows were an instant hit. Soon each of the three groups had its own show. In addition to variety shows some of the officers lectured on history, language, travel, hobbies, and sports during evening free time and on Sundays. Attendance at the lectures dropped over time but the camp shows were increasingly popular. High-quality entertainment was not a requirement. As

Lt. Col. O. O. "Zero" Wilson, a key promotor of the shows, put it, "The men were down so low that they would listen to anything."

Entertainment, good or bad, was not the only diversion. Some found solace in religion. While the Japanese forbade burial services in the first few months at the Cabanatuan camps, religious services were permitted. At first these services were conducted in empty barracks. Later, special buildings in each group area were equipped as well as possible and used as chapels. But to the Japanese, religious freedom went only so far. They insisted that the chaplains submit their sermons before presentation, and the commandant would often send an interpreter to the services to listen.

As they had been at Camp O'Donnell, rumors continued to be a morale booster. Though a few men scorned constantly emerging reports, many drew hope from each new rumor as it made its rounds and finally died. Most rumors concerned the progress of American forces on the way to reconquer the Philippines. News would come through that Americans had taken New Guinea and were progressing north. Later the men would be told that this was incorrect. Many of the less informed really believed that it would only be a matter of months until they were free. Christmas of '42 was a popular target date. Even more optimistic were the large group of New Mexicans in the camp with their slogan "Thanksgiving turkey in Albuquerque." But by far the most popular were the rumors that a prisoner exchange was in the offing. (The exchange of American and Japanese civilians was actually under way at the time.) The most common version of the rumor popular in the camp was that the Americans in the Philippines would be taken to a neutral country and kept there until the end of the war. Several countries were mentioned but Ecuador was the most frequently suggested.

Among the rumors were true accounts of fighting in Africa and the landing of American Marines on Guadalcanal. The American naval victory at Midway, the major turning point in the Pacific war, was belatedly but accurately reported in the camp. All of this information came from smuggled messages from radio listeners in Manila and from a secret radio which had been assembled and was operated in the camp by Lt. Homer T. Hutchinson, a former mining engineer. The location and operation of this radio was known only to a few American officers. News received nightly from station KGEI, San Francisco, was passed on by these men to the rest of the camp without ever disclosing the source.

In the early days at Camp 1 probably a number of Americans contemplated escape as an alternative to long-term suffering and servitude, but relatively few made serious attempts to get away. The Japanese death penalty for escapees and their supposed accomplices was the primary deterrent. Besides this, most of those physically and mentally capable of planning and carrying out an escape—getting out of the camp was no great problem—lacked confidence that they could make it to the nearest American troops, almost two thousand miles away in Australia. In addition, some worried that Filipinos, upon whom they would have to depend for food and shelter, might turn them in for a reward or to avoid punishment or death inflicted by the Japanese. Despite these obstacles, during the first week of June three Navy ensigns made their decisions and escaped. Unpredictably, the commandant, who a short time before had promptly ordered the execution of the four men at Camp 3 for attempted escape, did not carry out the stated death penalty for members of the escaped men's barracks squads. But later that month when six men were charged by the Japanese with dealing with Filipinos and smuggling food into the camp, he dealt swiftly and cruelly. Prior to their execution the men were paraded through the camp tied to poles. Then they were shot in view of their fellow prisoners. Their death brought the total number of men executed at both camps to ten.

★ ★ ★ 3 ★ ★ ★

The six thousand men at Camp 3 near the Sierra Madre mountains were mostly the healthier men captured at Corregidor. Benson Guyton, a thirty-one-year-old captain, was an early arrival at the camp and had watched in disbelief the execution of his comrades there, but after the initial shock Guyton settled down to camp life and was adjutant of one of the three groups in the camp. In this job he had to receive and consolidate the twice-daily roll call reports from the barracks leaders for nearly two thousand men. Sometimes the Japanese would spot-check the roll calls, counting and re-counting the men until the correct number was attained. While this was going on, as Guyton put it, "the adjutant was on the hot seat."

Other than the vexations of the roll calls, Guyton and others at Camp 3 would later regard the conditions there as relatively good. From the outset, under the leadership of Lieutenant Colonel Beecher, the camp was well organized and clean. Beecher managed to maintain relatively good relationships with the Japanese and set strict standards for sanitation. Adequate latrines were dug and maintained. Men could stay clean. Officers had showers, and the men bathed and washed their clothes in a river that flowed by the camp. (Possibly only by coincidence but perhaps because of the better conditions at Camp 3, Lieutenant Colonel Mori, in charge of both camps, chose to live at Camp 3 until he later moved to Camp 1 in September.) The food ration was supposed to be the same for both camps but the initially healthier men at Camp 3 were apparently able to obtain more benefit from what they ate. Guyton noted that by mid-August, despite the monotonous rice and soup (he himself had been able to buy some extra food), many men were gaining some weight.

By the end of July, 32 of the 6,000 men who had arrived at Camp 3 had died of natural causes, while 1,286 out of about 9,000 had succumbed at Camp 1. While some of this tremendous difference in death rate can be attributed to better conditions at Camp 3, clearly the major factor was the physical deterioration of the Camp 1 men which had begun before their arrival at Cabanatuan.

★ ★ ★ 4 ★ ★ ★

Meanwhile, at the Tarlac camp Lieutenant General Wainwright along with fourteen other generals, ninety-one colonels (or their naval equivalent in rank), three lieutenant colonels, three majors, and a small number of enlisted men were, as the thousands at Cabanatuan were, converting to a diet of rice and a life of humiliation. General Wainwright learned, with anguish, to salute and bow to the Japanese guards, as he and the others tried to get used to the daily roll calls and dull meals of rice with an occasional small portion of meat and fruit added. Since the officers had no assigned duties and reading material was limited, they spent much time rehashing their defeat.

The heated discussions which took place were often laced with recrimination and resentment, but as one officer put it, "no one came to blows." The Japanese wouldn't let some of the prisoners put the war behind them. One day a Japanese colonel who had been in command of the four hundred artillery pieces which had bombarded Corregidor visited the Tarlac camp. A group of Americans was called in for a conference at which the Japanese colonel and some of his officers lectured their captive audience on the operation and were well pleased to hear the Americans comment that the artillery fire had been the deciding factor in the fall of Corregidor.

One of the guards, a corporal named Nishiyama, perhaps because he was impressed with the high rank of his prisoners or because he was genuinely concerned, was one of the more considerate Japanese that many of the Americans at Tarlac would meet. He took a family photo belonging to one of the officers into town and had it enlarged. When he returned it he apologized to the officer, saying that he thought that the merchant had charged him too much. Another time he escorted a colonel to a Filipino dentist for much-needed dental work. On still another occasion he found glue for a violin which one officer had miraculously been able to retain but which needed repair badly. Not as helpful but equally well known was a guard nicknamed "Whisky Pete," who would often return from Tarlac on his day off in a drunken condition and would be punished by a noncommissioned officer. Whisky Pete would frequently seek sympathy from the American officers and on one such occasion summed up his philosophy with the statement "War no good, drunk good."

If whisky was solace for the guard, sunsets were consolation for the prisoners. Col. William Quinn noted at the time, "The coloring and cloud play is so outstandingly beautiful that I really can't describe it." His feelings were shared by many of his companions, who briefly gained a measure of serenity from these natural phenomena.

★ ★ ★ 5 ★ ★ ★

In August at Cabanatuan things turned for the better. The Japanese provided to the American medical authorities a shipment of quinine, which reduced the malaria deaths, and also some antitoxin from Manila which had a like effect on the diphtheria cases. Partly because of these drugs but mostly because the diseases had run their course, deaths for August were 287, a dramatic drop from the 786 of the previous month.

In another favorable development the Japanese finally completed registering the men at both camps, an activity which had been conducted sporadically but, probably under prodding from Tokyo, got high priority in August. Registration required that each man fill out a card with his name, rank, and specialties in military and civilian life. (Selected men whose specialties were already known to the Japanese were interviewed in addition to their filling out the cards.) Colonel Hardee and others put down as little as possible, reasoning that the less their captors knew about them the better. Some men took the opposite view, hoping that by listing experiences in a number of specialty lines they would get an assignment with more food and better living conditions. For a few technicians this approach got favorable results, but for the vast majority the work that they would later perform would have little relationship to their registered "qualifications." But all Americans were pleased that after completion of the registration cards the Japanese announced that they were no longer captives and were now officially prisoners of war and entitled to be paid—an action which for most would not occur for another two months.

About this time, as part of the policy to free Japanese troops for duty in war zones, six hundred Formosan nationals arrived for training as guards. Some of the Formosans were quartered at Camp 1 and others at Camp 2, the camp abandoned for use as a POW compound. On occasion some Americans were able to observe the Formosans in training. The prisoners noted with grim interest the manner in which the Japanese treated men whom they looked upon as social inferiors because of their nationality. The watching prisoners realized that the same Formosans who were enduring a grueling training program of running, marching, and bayonet practice, with the usual slappings and beatings for infractions of rules, would soon be their masters.

In Tokyo officials of the Home Ministry had concluded after reading favorable reports on the 150 Americans working on the docks at Osaka that more prisoners of war were needed to further Japanese industrial output. They wanted to use the first large group of over three thousand for stevedores in the ports of Tokyo, Yokohama, Osaka, Kobe, and Moji. Subsequent groups of prisoners would be put to work in mining and construction.

Meanwhile, the Prisoner of War Bureau had already begun issuing movement instructions which would disperse POWs to new locations throughout the Far East. The first to move would be the generals and colonels at Tarlac.

6

ON THE MOVE
August–December 1942
Formosa—Luzon—Manchuria—
Burma—Mindanao—Japan

★ ★ ★ 1 ★ ★ ★

On a hot afternoon in mid-August, General Wainwright and other senior prisoners of war arrived from Tarlac at Pier 7 in Manila. Tied up at the pier, called the "million-dollar pier" because it was at the time of construction the most expensive and beautiful of its kind, was the Japanese transport *Nagara Maru*, which the Japanese told them they would soon be boarding. While they were waiting and wondering what it would be like on the ship, the Japanese abruptly herded them into some nearby buildings. Then within the view of some of the prisoners, for the next two hours, a long line of Japanese soldiers, like men in an old fire-bucket brigade, passed hundreds of small boxes of ashes of their dead comrades onto the ship for return to the homeland. This accomplished, the Americans boarded the ship for the two-day voyage to Takao, on the southern tip of Formosa. The Americans found the two-tiered sleeping shelves crowded but were pleased that the Japanese provided increased amounts of rice and all the tea they could drink, and allowed them on deck during daylight.

At Takao the officers were transferred to a small, dirty coastal steamer which took them up the east coast of Formosa to a small port, Karenko. From the docks they marched two

miles to a barbed-wire-enclosed prison compound. After the
usual shakedown inspection and a speech by the commandant,
they were assigned to rooms which they would occupy for
nearly a year.

Colonel Vance found the routine at Karenko grim and monotonous. Each day opened with a roll call and a bow to the
emperor of Japan. The emperor was represented by a white
post implanted at the end of the parade ground. (At a later
formation on the eighth of the following month the Japanese
sergeant major would solemnly read the "Imperial Rescript"
to the assembled Americans.) Breakfast was two-thirds of a
cup of rice and a bowl of vegetable soup. Lunch and dinner
were essentially the same. As Vance wryly observed, "This
menu did not vary for the next two thousand meals." The
officers were organized into ten-man squads for most activities—eating, roll calls, bathing, and monthly weighing. Most
disturbing to the seasoned officers, whose average age was more
than fifty-five, were the constant slapping for minor infractions,
the requirement to salute all Japanese, even the youngest Japanese privates, and the menial labor that they had to do. Amidst
this dull routine the Americans were cheered somewhat upon
receipt of their first pay at the end of August. The Japanese
informed them that their monthly pay would range from 395
yen for a general to 20 yen for a lieutenant. But after the
Japanese had made their deduction for food, sundries, and other
items, the officers received only 25 yen, whatever their rank.
At first there was nothing to spend the money for, but later
the men were able to use it to purchase small amounts of cigarettes, soap, toothpaste, and other daily essentials that were
brought in from time to time. In the following months a number of top military commanders and civilian officials (British,
Dutch, and Australian) arrived from Singapore, Java, Hong
Kong, and other areas conquered by the Japanese. They
brought with them news and different outlooks which brought
some new life to barracks discussions.

★ ★ ★ 2 ★ ★ ★

Problems were of a much more serious nature at Camp 1, Cabanatuan. In early September Lieutenant Colonel Mori personally moved there from Camp 3, and for the remainder of

the month escapes would be a major source of concern to Japanese and Americans alike.

In mid-September a hospital patient who had escaped in early August returned to camp and gave himself up. He reportedly had been living with a Filipino family in a neighboring town. After his escape the Japanese locked up the other nine members of his "shooting squad" in the camp guardhouse. They also confined the medical officer of the day and two U.S. Army medical corpsmen whom the Americans had assigned, on the orders of the Japanese, to supplement the Japanese guard force. The camp leaders and the medical staff awaited with deep concern the decision of the camp authorities on the men that they held, since this was the first real test of the harsh camp regulations on escape. Three days later the Japanese informed the American senior officer that the "shooting squad" would be confined at the guardhouse for a month, the officer of the day would be freed, but the two men on guard duty would be shot that afternoon. The American commanders pleaded with the Japanese; and about an hour before the time the execution was to take place, the sentence for the two men was commuted to six months' confinement.

While the men involved were deeply relieved with the outcome, many others in the camp were not. Some officers and men, having seen or experienced the unpredictability of their captors, were far from convinced that a precedent had been set. Consequently, soon after the Japanese verdict officers posted in some of the barracks notices which read, in effect, that in the event that an escape of any man or men led to the death or punishment of any of the men who remained, the names of all parties involved would be recorded. It was the intention to turn over these names after the war to the proper military or civilian court for trial and punishment.

On the evening of the escaped prisoner's return, following a performance of the camp show, the commandant walked onto the improvised stage with the prisoner bound and held by a guard at the end of a rope. Colonel Mori then lectured all present on the futility of escape. The next day the soldier was confined in the guardhouse on two meals a day and sentenced to an indefinite period of hard labor to be done while tied at the end of a rope. In addition, the commandant tightened security of the camp and increased the American guard details, particularly around the hospital area. A week later while Maj. Gen. I. Morimoto, commander of all prison camps in the Philippines, was inspecting the camp, a Marine on a work detail made an unsuccessful escape attempt. This further heightened the tension between the Japanese camp administration and the prisoners of war.

Soon thereafter the three Navy ensigns who had walked out of the camp in early June returned. Though successful in surviving in the jungle for three months, they had been unable to find a way to get out of the Philippines or join guerrilla forces. Lieutenant Colonel Mori again seized an opportunity to deter Americans from thinking about escape. This time he required the three officers to read statements to a large group of assembled American prisoners on the perils that they had encountered—snakes, bad food, polluted water—and the difficulties of surviving outside the camp. In addition, Mori required Col. John P. Horan, a guerrilla leader in northern Luzon who had recently surrendered, to speak about the problems and futility of attempting to hold out in Japanese-occupied territory.

Within twenty-four hours of this lecture, Army lieutenant colonels Lloyd W. Biggs and Howard E. Breitung and a Navy lieutenant, Roydel Gilbert, with all the money, food, and medicine they could gather, attempted to escape. As they were crawling down a drainage ditch which they expected to lead them under the camp fence, an American enlisted man on guard challenged them. A struggle and a loud argument ensued. The noise alerted those in nearby barracks. They tried to quiet the bitter argument between the officers and the guard. But soon the Japanese overheard the still-noisy Americans and came and marched the three officers away to their headquarters. After interrogation the Japanese tied the men to posts near the camp entrance; and as successive Japanese and Formosan guard details finished their reliefs, they beat the Americans with clubs, fists, and sticks. The beatings, witnessed by American prisoners, continued off and on for the next forty-eight hours. On occasion, passing Filipinos were ordered to beat the Americans. During most of this time the rain fell in torrents from one of the worst typhoons in years. The duration and ferocity of the public beatings were probably because the

Japanese wanted to make this the ultimate lesson for the POWs, but also they may have had something to do with the defiant spirit of the tortured Americans. One of the colonels, when asked by guards why he tried to escape, replied that he wanted to re-join the American forces and come back and wipe out the Japanese. Guards finally came and cut the bonds of the three battered men, put them in a truck, and drove out the gate. Soon POWs at the camp heard two volleys of rifle fire. Later it was reported that two of the men had been shot and the third beheaded. The "shooting squads" of the executed men came from two officers' barracks. The Japanese sentenced these men to only thirty days' confinement, took away all of their canned goods, and denied them commissary privileges.

Far across the Pacific, nine American Marines who had been captured in a raid on the island of Makin had been treated humanely. They were held at Kwajalein, awaiting, they thought, transportation to Japan. Actually the Japanese commander of the Marshall island group, Adm. Koso Abe, was undecided on what to do with them. Finally a staff officer from higher headquarters arrived and supposedly informed Abe that established policy did not require captives to be sent to Japan and that he might dispose of the men as he saw fit. Abe ordered them executed, and this order was carried out in what the Japanese officer in charge later referred to as the traditional manner—beheading by sword.

At Camp 1, David Levy heard that a large number of men were being selected for shipment either to Japan or Mindanao, the large island in the southern Philippines. Levy thought that anyplace was better than Cabanatuan so he volunteered. Later his name appeared on a long list of men to be shipped to Japan. Over half the men came from the healthier group at Camp 3; the remainder were from Camp 1. Word around the camp was that the shipment was made up of "technicians," Air Corps mechanics and Army ordnance men, to be put to work in Japanese industry.

This information was inaccurate on both counts. Most of the men had little or no industrial experience, and Japan was not to be the final destination for most of them. In September the chief of staff of the Kwantung army (responsible for Japanese-dominated Manchuria) had wired the vice-minister of war:

> As the technician shortage in Manchuria makes it essential to use 1,500 prisoners of war in the plan for utilizing the Manchurian Machine Tool Company for rapid increase in aircraft production dealt with in No. 3, 129—Army Secret Asia, we intend to open an internment camp and ask you to inform us as soon as possible the time of their being transferred to Manchuria and the number, etc. Considering the necessity to establish a camp before winter, we wish to transfer the prisoners to Manchuria as soon as possible.

October 8 was as soon as possible, and on that date thirty-one officers and about nineteen hundred enlisted men boarded the freighter *Tottori Maru*, which had been converted to carry Japanese troops. The Americans climbed down into two large holds and part of a small one on the ship. Several hundred Japanese troops occupied the fourth and fifth holds. The American holds were filled beyond capacity. Only about three-quarters of the men could stay in the holds at one time; the remaining men had to stay on deck. The holds were divided horizontally by bare, wooden sleeping racks with little headroom. Latrine facilities were primitive "outhouses" hung over the sides of the ship. With a first meal of spoiled rice and fish, the lines for these crude toilets soon grew long and remained so for the whole voyage. Meals were spare—a slim ration of crackers, rice, and soup, with water available from a tank on the deck. The ship proceeded slowly but finally arrived at Takao, Formosa, where the Japanese soldiers debarked except for a small guard force which remained aboard. After that the Americans were moved onto the docks, lined up, and hosed down with cold water and returned to their now smelly holds. The *Tottori Maru* then headed north but returned to Takao twice because of engine trouble. With these delays and the slowness of the ship, it was not until November 8—thirty days from the time they had left Manila—that most of the Americans were put ashore at the port of Pusan, on the southern tip of Korea. The Japanese issued them winter clothing. This large contingent, fourteen officers and 1,188 enlisted men along with about one hundred British soldiers, moved by train north to Mukden, Manchuria. After the Mukden group's departure the *Tottori Maru* sailed for Japan with over three hundred Americans aboard, leaving the rest of the men from the Philippines, most of them very sick, in Pusan.

Levy, among those taking the long train trip to Mukden, had endured the rigors of the voyage north with the hope that in the next camp he would find better accommodations, more food, and humane treatment. He found none of these at Mukden. The men were quartered in long, low wooden barracks with brick stoves that furnished little heat. Fresh from the tropics, surrounded by a bleak, desolate landscape, the men suffered from the subzero weather and the freezing winds which penetrated numerous cracks in the barracks. The food, the second radical change from an American diet for the men, consisted of bread and cornmeal with occasional servings of a native green vegetable similar to kale. Morale slumped, and soon two or three men were dying daily as the rest of the men huddled in the barracks under six thin blankets trying to keep warm.

The Japanese let the sick and exhausted men stay in the barracks but marched the relatively few men who were able four miles to the M.K.K. (the Manchurian Machine Tool Company), where they began training them for various types of work. The men in the barracks were given written tests to determine their mechanical aptitude. Levy, along with many others with little or no experience in factory work, was less than optimistic about his future prospects.

From Pusan the *Tottori Maru* continued to the port of Osaka, Japan, arriving on November 12. The American prisoners then journeyed by train to Kawasaki, a city located between Tokyo and Yokohama. Their camp was situated in the center of the industrial area of the city. Next to the camp was the Showa Denko chemical plant and not far away was the Nippon steelworks. Within a few weeks many of the POWs were put to work in one or the other of these plants.

Of the men remaining at Pusan, those who recovered from the onslaught of dysentery and other diseases would later be transferred to camps in Japan. Over one hundred died and were buried at Pusan.

★ ★ ★ 3 ★ ★ ★

As Americans began to work in some of Japan's industrial plants, Tojo approved a plan which would soon put thousands of war prisoners and native laborers to work on one massive project. The project was to build a new railroad which would run from Thanbyuzayat in Burma south to the town of Ban Pong, where it would join the existing rail system into Thailand. The length of the new railroad was to be 260 miles, much of it through rugged jungle terrain. The Japanese hoped to complete the project in one year.

In September 1942 the prisoners at Bicycle Camp in Java had heard rumors of their movement. In early October a group of 191 Americans along with more than thirteen hundred Australians loaded aboard a Japanese ship for a hot, miserable trip to Singapore. Here they were taken to the huge Changi POW camp, where British and Australian prisoners numbering some fifteen thousand were quartered. To the men from Java, Changi appeared to be a POW heaven but they had little time to enjoy it. After a brief stay the Americans and the Australians traveled on another ship to Rangoon, Burma, changed ships again, and proceeded to Moulmein, where they were confined in a local jail. The jail was uncomfortable and demeaning but at least its windows afforded a view of the pagoda made famous by Rudyard Kipling.

Three days later as the men marched to the railroad station they had an experience which few of them would forget. Fully expecting the indifference and outright antagonism that they had received from the Javanese early in their captivity, the prisoners were surprised by the actions of the people of Moulmein. Lining the streets in the predawn hours, native men and women distributed tobacco, fruit, and food to the marching men despite the protests and threats of the guards. Greatly moved, many men choked up and some wept with emotion. Somebody cared.

After a forty-mile train ride, they unloaded at Thanbyuzayat, the northern base camp for the railroad. Here a group of three thousand Australians under Brig. A. L. Varley had earlier begun work on the right-of-way. After a brief rest the weary newcomers were assembled for a speech by Lt. Col. Y. Nagatomo, commandant of POW Branch Number 3, which summed up his view of the project and what he expected of the men who would work on it. Transcribed later by the Japanese, it read in part:

> You are only a few remaining skeletons after the invasion of East Asia for the past few centuries and are pitiful victims. It is not your fault, but till your Government do not wake up from the dreams and discontinue their resistance all of you will not be released. However I shall not treat you badly for the sake of humanity as you have no fighting power at all. His Majesty the Emperor has been deeply anxious about all the War Prisoners and has ordered us to enable opening of War Prisoners' camps at almost all the places in the southward countries. The Imperial thoughts are unestimable and the Imperial favours are infinite and as such you should weep with gratitude at the greatness of them and should correct or mend the misleading and improper anti-Japanese ideas.
>
> Lifting manners, deportment, salutation and attitude shall be strict and according to the rules of the Nippon Army, because it is only possible to manage you all who are merely rabbles, by the order of military regulations. . . . My biggest requirement from you is escape. If there is a man here who has at least one per cent of a chance of escape we shall make him to face the extreme penalty. If there is one foolish man who is trying to escape, he shall see big jungles towards the East which are absolutely impossible for communication, towards the west he shall see the boundless ocean and above all, in the main points of South and North our Nippon Army is staying and guarding. . . .
>
> At the time of such shortness of materials, your lives are preserved by the Military, and all of you must reward them with your labour. By the hand of the Nippon Army railway works to connect Thailand and Burma have started to the great interest of the world. There are deep jungles where no man comes to clear them by cutting the trees. There are also countless difficulties and sufferings but you shall have the honour to join in this great work which was never done before and you should do your best efforts. . . . In conclusion I say to you "Work cheerfully" and from henceforth you shall be guided by my motto.

No Americans felt "honored" but within a few days they were all hard at work at a camp which was the farthest forward into the jungles at that time. Their work consisted of moving

earth to build the right-of-way. The men worked in groups.
Some dug with picks and shovels. Others carried the dirt to
the place it was needed, Asian style, in a basket hanging from
a pole the ends of which rested on the shoulders of two men.
At first Pvt. Edward Fung, a San Franciscan who before the
war had left home to work as a cowhand in Texas, found the
Japanese requirement that they move 1.2 cubic meters of earth
per day to be reasonable. He and his companions found that
if they met their quota fairly early in the day, they would have
extra time for rest. But it was not long before the Japanese,
noting this, increased the quota. From then on, Fung and
his comrades never tried to make their quota early in the day.

Meanwhile the Japanese had moved another group of 450
Americans from Java to the Changi camp at Singapore, where
they remained until the end of 1942. A third contingent, members of E Battery of the 131st Field Artillery from Java, stopped
briefly in Singapore, then left by ship for Japan. Upon arrival
there most were assigned to camps on the island of Kyushu.

★ ★ ★ **4** ★ ★ ★

In the Philippines another group of about one thousand Americans had been alerted for departure to a camp on the island
of Mindanao. Unlike the large group of relatively healthy men
that had earlier departed for Manchuria and Japan, the men
slated for this transfer included many who were suffering from
various maladies but were still able to walk. Stories began
circulating that the new camp had an abundance of tropical
fruit and vegetables and large herds of native oxen.

The glowing descriptions that were circulating were not
too far off the mark. The prisoners' destination was Davao
Penal Colony, which at the time was a large plantation-type
project where long-term convicts could be taught farming and
trades. Situated thirty-five miles north of the port city of Davao, the penal colony occupied a large rectangular area about
three miles long, traversed by a small narrow-gauge railway.
In this area were a prison compound, warehouses, sawmills, a
rice mill, and a wide range of farm equipment. Surrounding
the penal colony were groves of coconuts, coffee, guava, avoca-
dos, citrus, and bananas. Papaya flourished wild as did peppers,
spices, and cassava. Cultivated crops included large fields of

rice, corn, sweet potatoes, and all types of vegetables. To prepare Davao Penal Colony for its new function as a POW camp
the Japanese moved all but 150 of the convicts to another
prison.

The first Americans to reach Davao Penal Colony were
eleven hundred men who had been held at Malaybalay, in
northern Mindanao. The Japanese did not give them much
work to do. Taking note of this and the abundance of food
around them, some concluded that this was going to be a pretty
good camp.

The morale of the one-thousand-man group from Cabanatuan also rose after they boarded a former American freighter,
the *Erie Maru,* and headed south for Mindanao. Except for
the conditions in the holds—crowded, hot, and smelly—most
of the prisoners found the trip a welcome change from Cabanatuan. They were allowed unlimited access to a small area of
the deck, which was a great relief from conditions below.
The food was the best they had had since they were captured.
There was plenty of steamed rice and occasionally, as a treat,
corned beef seized at the naval base of Cavite and good, thick
vegetable soup. Hardee liked to watch the Japanese cook
steam the rice in large caldrons. To this officer, raised in the
South, the rice appeared to be "as fluffy and nice as a well-
baked hot biscuit."

Besides the food, the Japanese crew and guards treated them
well and on one occasion early in the trip showed rare compas-
sion for one of the POWs. When Comdr. Alan McCracken
suffered a temporary paralysis in his legs (no one ever determined why) his friends carried him up on the deck. Later
the captain of the ship permitted them to place McCracken
outside his door. While Americans brought him food daily,
the stricken officer—sitting in what to the crew must have appeared to be a place of honor—received many presents from
the Japanese. From the ship's doctor he got a can of pineapple
juice and from the chief engineer a bottle of vitamin pills.
Another ship's officer after a trip ashore presented him with
two large grapefruit, and other crewmen gave him assorted
cookies and cigarettes. Probably the most unusual gift and
perhaps the most heartfelt one was a small vase of flowers which
a shy Japanese sailor furtively placed on the deck beside him.

From his vantage point on the deck McCracken watched

each morning as the Japanese crew, facing the sun, recited Emperor Meiji's "Imperial Rescript to Soldiers and Sailors." After their recital they bowed gravely to the rising sun, then faced toward Japan and bowed a second time. Then they would begin their work.

After ten days at sea and two deaths en route, on November 7, 1942, the *Erie Maru* docked at Lasang, Mindanao. Those men that the American Army doctors considered unable to march (McCracken, though he had recovered the use of his legs, was one of these) were permitted to ride in captured American trucks; while the others, starting in the late afternoon, walked the approximately fifteen miles north to the penal colony. Even without their baggage, which was taken in the trucks, it was a rugged march for the Americans. It was not until about 2 A.M. that the weary marchers entered the barracks in the dark and dropped to the floor for what sleep they could manage.

Awake the next morning they discovered that the POW compound consisted of eight barracks about 150 feet long parallel to each other, running north and south. East of the barracks and separated from them was the hospital building. These buildings along with the mess hall and several latrines were surrounded by barbed wire. Soon the Cabanatuan men were mixing with the men who had preceded them. Lt. Col. John H. McGee, a Malaybalay prisoner, was amazed at the appearance of the new men, describing them as "a group of hospital cases." The newcomers were equally surprised to see how well the early arrivals looked and the amount of gear—mosquito nets, bedding rolls, and trunks—they had brought with them. Later, after the initial reaction of the men had subsided, they talked at length about their experiences since the war began. It was during these conversations that the men captured on Mindanao first heard the details of the fall of Bataan, the Death March, and about Camps O'Donnell and Cabanatuan.

Discussions were cut short when the POWs were herded out of the compound to a nearby field for an address by the Japanese camp commander, Maj. Kazuo Maeda. Four months before, Maeda had attended with his superior, General Morimoto, the meeting in Tokyo for the chiefs of POW camps. Through an interpreter the balding and portly Maeda lectured the men in a shrill voice. He put into his own words, with appropriate embellishment, those used by Tojo in his speech. "POWs are here to work, not to sit around idle and eating. They must forget lazy American ways and learn Japanese industry and frugality." Disappointed that they were in such poor physical shape, Maeda closed by saying, "I asked for laborers, not walking corpses."

To get the walking corpses in working condition, Major Maeda ordered increased rations for the next month and initiated a work program for all men under forty-five years of age who were not hospitalized or medically classified as "sick in quarters." Initially, large numbers of the Cabanatuan contingent were in the latter category; but in succeeding weeks their condition improved, and a larger number of their enlisted men began working under Filipino overseers on the various agricultural activities of the penal colony.

★ ★ ★ 5 ★ ★ ★

After the departure of the Americans assigned to Mindanao, the Japanese closed Camp 3 at Cabanatuan and transferred all of the remaining Americans to Camp 1. A new camp commandant, Major Iwanaka, replaced Lieutenant Colonel Mori and soon thereafter a group of men was alerted for shipment. This group, fifteen hundred men including two hundred officers, left Manila on the seventh of November aboard the *Nagato Maru*, crowded into three holds. The other holds and decks above those containing Americans were filled with more than one thousand Japanese troops. Insufficient space was a problem as it had been for other Americans on the *Tottori Maru*, possibly more so since the ship was smaller and there were more Japanese aboard. One officer said they were packed "like pickles in a jar." After seventeen days at sea and the death of ten men, the ship arrived at Moji, Japan, on November 25, 1942. It was during the last several days of the voyage that the weather changed from tropical heat to freezing cold.

As the men, clad only in cotton shirts and trousers, walked onto the docks, Japanese medical technicians, using a glass rod, took rectal samples (probably to determine the presence of cholera germs) from many of them, an indignity to which many later arrivals at this port also would be subjected. Next, after the men were sprayed for lice, the Japanese lined them up and divided them into groups of between four hundred and five hundred men. After hours of this, the men finally were rewarded with the first decent meal they had had since leaving the Philippines. They then climbed into third-class train coaches, a pleasant change from the freight cars used to haul prisoners of war in the Philippines, and traveled to Osaka, where they would become the first American group to implement the "No work—no food" policy on a large scale in Japan.

Just a month before, the War Ministry had published instructions about the basic food allowances for POWs, which would determine with finality the maximum amount of food that prisoners held in Japan, Manchuria, Formosa, and Korea would get if they worked. (Similar but not identical allowances applied to prisoners held in conquered territories, which were mostly in tropical zones.) According to this directive, officers were to receive 420 grams (15 ounces) of "staple food," which was normally rice or barley, per day. Enlisted men would receive 570 grams (1 pound, 4 ounces). Those who performed hard labor—and unfortunately for them a large number of Americans were required to do so—were authorized an additional 220 grams (7.7 ounces). Depending upon availability, the rice or barley ration could be supplemented by vegetables and meat. Assuming that a POW received about 12 ounces of such supplements per day, the total authorized for the hardest work in the temperate zones was about 2 pounds and 11 ounces. In peacetime the ration for an American soldier was approximately 4 pounds 7 ounces. Even if the American got the maximum ration, which was seldom, he was consuming about one-half his former diet. So from the very outset American and other POWs were destined to exist on a substandard diet, both in quantity and nutritional value.

The Japanese would maintain then and later that they fed the Americans a ration comparable to that provided to the Japanese soldier. In some locations POWs did get a ration approaching, but seldom equaling, that of the Japanese soldier. But the average Japanese male was smaller than the average American male and required less caloric intake. Moreover, the Japanese by heredity and upbringing were accustomed to both the type and the quantity of food issued. Americans were not, and they were almost always hungry and nutritionally deprived.

Adequate clothing, not of great importance in the Philippines, was a vital necessity in the colder northern climate. Again, the Japanese virtually guaranteed the prisoner of war's discomfort when in a directive published in December 1942 the War Ministry specified that "the clothing and bed clothes to be loaned to prisoners of war shall be supplied from the stock of clothing of inferior quality held for the non-commissioned officers and enlisted men in each unit." In addition to being hungry few Americans would remember being warm during the winter months in the north.

The Japanese were generally satisfied with the results of the work done by prisoners earlier on the docks in Osaka and the rail yards in Kawasaki. Not only did the prisoners provide additional manpower, but a Japanese official noted at the time that the public, seeing American and English prisoners of war at work, realized "with gratitude the glory of the Imperial Throne," and on a more practical note he observed that Japanese workers in areas where POWs were used got to their jobs earlier and worked harder. Unfortunately for the POW, he had earned a place in the Japanese industrial effort.

For the long lines of shivering Americans getting off the trains in Osaka, the Japanese had varied assignments. One group would become steelworkers, another would become freight handlers, and a third would become construction laborers.

Capt. John S. Coleman, a Texan and a survivor of the Death March and Camp O'Donnell, was with the group of more than four hundred men and officers which marched into Yodogawa Steel Company shortly after a Thanksgiving Day on which they had little to be thankful for. Soon after their arrival, the Japanese issued them coats and pants made of a light gunnysack-type material and put them to work in the mill. It made fifty-gallon drums, sheet iron, and engine blocks out of slab steel. Coleman's first job was loading cinders into a conveyor car. A few days later he was put in charge of a detail of 140 men. These men performed various activities associated with the manufacture of steel products, ranging from the handling of white-hot slabs of steel to cutting sheet iron into strips using steel cutters. Americans worked alongside Japanese men and women and generally got along well with them. After an eight-hour day with only occasional days off, the men returned to their barracks, which because they were situated next to the factory were almost always noisy and smoky.

Cpl. Charles E. Maurer, a Marine captured on Corregidor, was one of 458 Americans assigned to a camp at Umeda, the central railroad yard serving the Osaka industrial complex. As at Yodogawa, Maurer and his ill-clothed companions were put to work almost immediately, unloading and loading freight cars in freezing weather. The men were provided only the basic work rations, 570 grams of rice; and worse, when a man was too sick to work he got only 300 grams. The Japanese sought in this way to prevent men from pretending illness to avoid work. Instead, as it turned out, they lost workers permanently because few of the already weakened Americans could survive on the "sick rations." This ration had no official sanction but was used from time to time in a number of camps during the war.

The third group, consisting of 500 men (178 officers and 322 enlisted men), was sent to a small, newly constructed POW camp near the coastal village of Tanagawa, outside Osaka. The day after their arrival Colonel Murata, commandant of all POW camps in the Osaka district, arrived and made a speech to them cautioning them to "guard your health," and assured them of good treatment at the camp. After a day's rest the Japanese put the men through a period of instruction in close order drill. The Japanese drill sergeant somehow expected them to learn the commands and the Japanese language at the same time. Failure to respond properly to barked orders, and such failures were many, resulted in immediate corrections in the form of slaps and cuffs. Even Capt. K. C. Emerson, a twenty-four-year-old Oklahoman, who was well versed in U.S. Army drill procedures, found the training frustrating. Particularly distasteful to him was the requirement that he goose-step with an eyes right or left when passing a sentry, noncommissioned officer, or officer.

Soon the men were put to work. All of the enlisted men who were physically able were assigned to a construction project which involved carving a drydock for submarines out of a hillside on the bay near the camp and lining it with stones. In addition to the Americans, Korean laborers and Japanese convicts worked on the project. Back at the camp, officers did odd jobs and for their work received reduced rations.

From the outset the hard work performed by the enlisted men and their initial poor physical condition resulted in a high death rate. Emerson was one of those assigned to haul the bodies to a crematory. Once there, after a prayer, the body was burned and the ashes were brought back in a small box. Concerned about the sick rate, the Japanese transferred two American doctors to Tanagawa from another camp. But they had little or no medicine to dispense. The death rate here and at the other Osaka locations would continue to rise.

★ ★ ★ **6** ★ ★ ★

Movements out of Cabanatuan to long-term camps were not confined to distant locations. The Japanese transferred about eight hundred Americans to Pasay, a suburb south of Manila, and quartered them in a former girls' school. Their job was to extend the runways of Nichols Field, a former U.S. military airfield. The tedious, hot work shoveling dirt into small cars on a track, pushing these cars to a dumping point, and unloading the cars and spreading the fill would continue for nearly two years. Several hundred men worked on another Manila airfield, Nielson Field. Smaller groups of men, billeted in and around Manila, drove trucks for the Japanese and did motor maintenance work.

During the time that groups of men were being sent to other locations from Cabanatuan, deaths there, which after the July peak had dropped to just below three hundred in August and September, continued at this level for two more months. In December the number dying turned downward. Also the causes of death changed. Beginning in September the two major killer diseases, dysentery and malaria, had been gradually displaced by diseases which resulted from protracted absence of vitamins in the diet: beriberi (both "wet" and "dry"), pellagra, and to a lesser extent scurvy. Pellagra, resulting from lack of niacin in the diet, caused great sensitivity and pain on the skin surfaces, mental instability, and disorientation, and, like beriberi, in extreme cases an agonizing death. Lt. S. Konishe, one of the rare Japanese medical officers who tried to help the American doctors in their continuing uphill battle with diseases, was very interested in pellagra but his interest did little to quell the disease. Despite the reduction in the number of deaths in December, the death rate in terms of percentages was still high since more than half of the men present earlier had left the camp or died. Medicine was still needed, but in December adequate nutrition had become a more critical factor in the survival of men at Cabanatuan and elsewhere.

On December 8, 1942, the first anniversary of the Pacific war, Japanese troops throughout the Far East, as they had done monthly in some POW camps, stood in formation and once again listened to the reading of Emperor Hirohito's "Imperial Rescript," denouncing Western imperialism and declaring war on the United States and its allies. Though a few top military and political leaders in Tokyo had serious doubts, the dramatic military successes of the past months had imbued Japanese troops with a supreme confidence in ultimate victory.

For Americans the past year had been a disaster. Since their ignominious surrender, they had lost nearly five thousand of their number, with deaths from disease and malnutrition far eclipsing those occurring in battle. The end of December found the survivors in the following locations:

ESTIMATED NUMBER AND LOCATION OF AMERICAN PRISONERS
OF WAR HELD BY THE JAPANESE AT THE END OF 1942

The Philippines	13,250
Japan	2,900
China	1,650
Manchuria	1,200
Malaya	450
Celebes	250
Burma	200
Formosa	150
Wake Island	150
Total	20,200

Although the survivors would not be home for Christmas, as some had hoped, the upcoming Yuletide season would nonetheless turn out to be a dramatic turning point in the lives of the majority of the American prisoners.

7

RELIEF AT LAST

Luzon—Mindanao—Singapore— Manchuria—China—Formosa—Japan

★ ★ ★ 1 ★ ★ ★

Rumors that Red Cross food and clothing had arrived in camp were at first met with disbelief by the men at Cabanatuan. Most of the prisoners had resigned themselves to a lonely Christmas—their first in captivity. But when the American camp leaders confirmed that the supplies were present, their incredulity changed to a feeling of gratitude and hope. Their country had not forgotten them. They did not realize that a large proportion of the Red Cross supplies which they looked forward to receiving were from Canada, Great Britain, and South Africa.

The multinational Red Cross food, medicine, clothing, and other items which reached the Philippines came in two shipments. The first to arrive, sometime in November, was the bulk of the *Gripsholm*'s relief supplies that had reached Yokohama aboard the *Conte Verde* and the *Asama Maru* in August 1942. Items included in the consignment and the country of their origin were as follows:

22,160 eleven-pound food packages	American & Canadian
271 cases of drugs	American & Canadian
210 cases of bulk foodstuffs	South African

2,220 articles of clothing	These and the remain-
640 pairs of shoes	ing articles below
3,680 toilet kits	were all
3,588 toilet articles	American
6,120 cakes of soap	
25,000 packs of cigarettes	
4,896 tins of tobacco	

The second shipment, which reached Manila in December, consisted of about half of the relief supplies which the *Kama-kura Maru* brought back from the British-Japanese exchange (the other half had been unloaded in Hong Kong in October). This shipment consisted of the following, all British:

    13,750 eleven-pound food packages
    8,725 cases of bulk food
    87 bales of clothing

With the wonderful news spurring them on, men turned to preparation for Christmas with enthusiasm. Chaplains scheduled religious services. Choirs practiced. Musicians and entertainers rehearsed. Even the Japanese, caught up in the spirit, promised time off at Christmas and New Year's with meat and extra rations for both holiday meals.

On Christmas Eve a Japanese soldier assigned to monitor a show put on by one of the group's entertainers was particularly enthusiastic when the camp orchestra played "My Blue Heaven." Noting this, some Americans urged him to sing it in Japanese. He did so and received a good hand for his efforts. While the show was in progress, groups of carolers moved through the hospital area, singing to the bedridden men. At midnight men of all faiths attended a Catholic high mass. On Christmas morning, after a breakfast of generous portions of rice with raisins and hot cocoa, Protestant services were held. Then, to the delight of all, the much-relished relief pack-ages—these were from the British Red Cross—were handed out, one to each man. More modest, but deeply appreciated for the personal sentiments that they conveyed, were the small packages containing soap, thread, pencils, and other conve-nience items furnished by Filipino organizations. For dinner the men had all the rice, hash, tomato soup, and beans they could eat with candy and cookies for dessert, and cigars topping off the meal. A big surprise, but only for a fortunate few, was mail postmarked in June. The number of letters was small because of the hurried organization of the diplomatic exchange, and the fact that few families and friends knew when and how to write to men whose whereabouts was unknown to them and who had not been officially announced as POWs.

On New Year's Day another food package was issued to each man; half of them received American packages and the other half Canadian. The contents of an American Red Cross standard package Number 8 for prisoners of war (Canadian and British packages contained similar but not identical items) were as follows:

Evaporated milk, irradiated	one 14½-oz. can
Lunch biscuit (hardtack)	one 8-oz. package
Cheese	one 8-oz. package
Instant cocoa	one 8-oz. tin
Sardines	one 15-oz. tin
Oleomargarine (Vitamin A)	one 1-lb. tin
Corned beef	one 12-oz. tin
Sweet chocolate	two 5½-oz. bars
Sugar, granulated	one 2-oz. package
Powdered orange concentrate (Vitamin C)	two 3½-oz. packages
Soup (dehydrated)	two 2½-oz. packages
Prunes	one 16-oz. package
Instant coffee	one 4-oz. tin
Cigarettes	one 10's
Smoking tobacco	one 2¼-oz. package

Over three pounds of each eleven-pound unit consisted of containers but little was wasted. The POWs used the empty cans for drinking, cooking, and utility containers for months to come.

American cooks used some of the cases of bulk foods— canned meat, flour, fruit—from the British Red Cross to supplement the daily food prepared in the camp kitchens. But the greatest benefit came from the portion of these rations, along with vitamin pills, allotted to the hospital kitchen for those suffering from extreme cases of vitamin deficiency and malnutrition. The effect of a nutritive diet on these men was almost miraculous. Bloated limbs regained their normal size. Skin ulcers and lesions cleared up. Vision improved. Relief from such aggravations brought with it a renewed zest for living.

Medical care also improved greatly with the cases of medicine and equipment received. Once-scarce medicines—sulfathiazole, quinine, and morphine—were now available in quantities sufficient to permit effective dosages. Whereas American doctors previously had to perform surgery under the most primitive conditions, with many deaths from infection, they now had gloves, gowns, and sterilizers. In a matter of weeks the hospital was transformed from a place to die in to a place to live in.

While Red Cross relief supplies would have a beneficial effect elsewhere, probably no single location benefited more than Cabanatuan. At this camp, with the largest concentration of both well and sick American POWs, the full allocation of food, medicine, and clothing was dispensed when it was most needed to salvage men's bodies and spirits. As Colonel Beecher, the American senior officer, and many others would say later, the Red Cross supplies were a lifesaver.

At Bilibid Prison in Manila, the hospital and transient center for POWs on Luzon, William S. Cummings, a Catholic Army chaplain there, had gotten permission to leave the prison from time to time under guard to pick up religious supplies. Just before Christmas he visited the Assumption Convent, where the nuns gave him Christmas tree lights, crib figures, and decorations for the Christmas Eve mass which he celebrated for Catholics and others in the prison compound. On a later trip out of the compound the intrepid priest, working with a Filipino woman, Lulu Reyes, obtained several laundry baskets full of noodles, which a friendly Japanese guard arranged to have taken into the camp, where they made a welcome addition to Christmas supper. Like their companions at Cabanatuan, the men at Bilibid and the stevedores working on the port area detail enjoyed time off, Red Cross packages, and mail. Men working on the airfields, Nichols and Nielson, were under a stricter regime, in which little or no recognition was made of the holidays and those who received Red Cross packages had little time to enjoy them.

Red Cross supplies did not arrive at Davao Penal Colony

in time for Christmas or New Year's Day. But as at Cabanatuan the Japanese were somehow caught up in the Yuletide spirit. The commandant, Major Maeda, declared a two-day holiday. He opened the holiday season by dispensing a package of Japanese cigarettes to each POW. This was followed by a Christmas Eve show in the prison chapel. Unlike the performances at Cabanatuan, this one was a joint affair involving the Japanese staff, American prisoners, and Filipino civilian employees. Lt. Kempai Yuki, a former schoolteacher with a fair command of English serving as master of ceremonies, struggled through the evening with multilingual introductions of the various performers for the benefit of the American, Japanese, and Filipino audience. With a newly constituted American band performing for the first time, POWs put on a variety of song-and-dance acts. The Japanese contribution included ritual dances and singing. In a surprising variation a Japanese interpreter noted for his frequent beatings of POWs performed his own version of an American dance, the Charleston. The highlight of the evening was the traditional harvest dance, gracefully performed in flowing native dresses by wives and daughters of Filipino camp employees. The dance was a particularly welcome break from the dreary, colorless, male-oriented life of the prison camp. After the show the Filipino women gave each man a fried rice stick and later sent each barracks a five-gallon bucket full of candy. Americans gratefully recognized that preparing these delicacies for more than two thousand men had been a formidable task for the small number of women. On Christmas Day the Americans received more cigarettes and generous servings of stew, sweet potatoes, and rice. Even without Red Cross supplies, most of the Americans gained much comfort and satisfaction from the extra food and entertainment.

The Japanese were so pleased with the Christmas show that they asked for another one on New Year's Day. The highlight of that show was a classical piano concert by one of the Filipino wives under the stars in a jungle setting. It all seemed strange to some of the Americans but was nonetheless well received. POW reaction to a Filipino children's singing group was not as enthusiastic. The youngsters' repertoire consisted of lusty renditions of Japanese songs taught them by their new masters.

At Singapore the bulk of the thousands of cases of British

and South African food unloaded after the British and American exchanges found its way to the Changi camp and its large population of British and Australian prisoners. The extent to which men in the group of 450 Americans who had arrived at Changi from Java in October benefited from these Red Cross supplies is unclear. One American recalled that most of the Red Cross food went to the officers' mess. The only way he got any was to sneak a few cans while on a detail carrying food from the food dump to the kitchens. Whatever he got was more than Americans received who were already working on the Burma side of the Burma–Thailand railroad. No Red Cross supplies got to them nor would any reach them for the duration of the war. The reason why some of the substantial quantities of food and medicines unloaded in Singapore were not allocated to the men on the railroad is unknown. Probably it was a combination of the difficulty of transporting supplies to the remote camps and bureaucratic bungling.

★ ★ ★ **2** ★ ★ ★

North in Manchuria eleven hundred Americans, most huddled under blankets in frigid barracks, shivered through Christmas with a meal of buns and corn-and-cabbage soup. Several hundred of the men working at the M.K.K. factory got some extra food on Christmas Day. The rest could muster little holiday spirit with the death rate by the end of December comparable to that in Cabanatuan during its most lethal month. The men at Mukden, like those working on the Burma–Thailand railroad, were provided nothing from the British Red Cross supplies that the Japanese allocated to Korea. With an operating rail line running north from Korea to Mukden, the failure to send any supplies whatsoever can only be attributed to administrative error or neglect. Probably no group of Americans at the time needed the Red Cross supplies more. Had they arrived, the number of deaths would likely have been far less. In sharp contrast the fourteen hundred Americans at Kiangwan, China (in early December the Japanese had moved them to this new location, not far from their first camp at Woosung), were doubly fortunate. A large shipment of Red Cross boxes, estimated at seven boxes per man, arrived in mid-December. Colonel Otera, who had succeeded Colonel Yuse as commandant, released three packages—one immediately, one on Christmas Eve, and a third at New Year's—withholding the remainder for later issue. The POWs benefited further from the generosity of Jimmy S. James, an American civilian who operated a restaurant and nightclub in Shanghai. He along with some other civilians had not yet been placed under detention by the Japanese. Sympathetic to his incarcerated fellow Americans, James persuaded the Japanese to let him send turkeys, sweet potatoes, coffee, and cigars into the camp. Because of James's generous and enterprising spirit the Shanghai POWs were the only Americans in the Far East to eat a traditional Christmas dinner.

At Karenko, Formosa, the top-ranking Allied officers celebrated Christmas without Red Cross supplies. Their allocation, like that at Davao Penal Colony, was delayed. (Three months later they would receive a generous shipment.) Despite this lack the senior officers had a pleasant if not exuberant Christmas. Some exchanged cards fashioned from scrap paper. One small group even toasted the King, the President, and loved ones with some home brew made of potato peels.

★ ★ ★ **3** ★ ★ ★

Americans laboring in Japan had little time to make home brew but all received Red Cross food in varying amounts. Apparently the Prisoner of War Bureau neglected to publish any guidance on the distribution of Red Cross supplies. Consequently POW camp commanders in the several camp jurisdictions in Japan set their own policies, mostly governed by the traditional code of military austerity and frugality. This brought joy to some Americans and discomfiture to others.

At Zentsuji, where some of the first Americans captured still remained, Red Cross supplies had arrived in September soon after being unloaded in Yokohama. Americans, with great expectations, helped stack the precious eleven-pound packages in a storeroom but the hoped-for immediate issue did not occur. Despite appeals by the POW spokesman, the supplies remained in storage until early November. Equally tantalizing to the prisoners were the bags of mail withheld for censoring. One man estimated the Red Cross stock to be sufficient for ten packages per man at the existing camp strength. Finally in early

November the Japanese released the first Red Cross packages. To the Americans' surprise the issue was only one package to be divided among four men. Also to their consternation the Japanese withheld the prized cans of salmon and corned beef and later made the cooks put them in soup. Finally the mail began to trickle out, providing the first contact with home for nearly a year. On Christmas Day the camp commandant assembled the prisoners and grandly announced that each man would receive a Red Cross parcel. Though his audience wondered why he couldn't be more generous, they happily accepted the "gift," expecting more in the future. Since Zentsuji was the War Ministry's premier camp, their expectations were justified and the men there probably got more packages than other camps in Japan.

At Osaka 1, a work camp but also the location for the headquarters of the group of camps in and around the city, Red Cross food parcels had arrived in early fall along with some medical supplies. When no issue was made, some men suspected that the guards were helping themselves to the supplies. But their fears were dissipated when on the day before Christmas each American received an unopened Red Cross box. One of the recipients, Martin Boyle, a Marine captured on Guam, was surprised by the reactions of his companions. He had expected them to be overjoyed and to show it. Instead most men received the packages calmly, walked back to their cramped quarters, and quietly began examining the contents one by one. Spam, sardines, cigarettes, coffee—they savored even the various brand names, which, unseen for months, were a thrill. Trading soon began and after a meal with extra rice and fish, the men spent the rest of that day relaxing.

Amounts of Red Cross food dispensed at other Osaka camps varied. At Tanagawa the Japanese allotted one South African Red Cross box of bulk food to six men. The POWs savored every mouthful of this food from a country that many of them had never heard of. The Americans ate and sang carols on Christmas Day, which was a holiday as was New Year's. Their joy on New Year's was temporarily dampened when, because this day was also a Japanese holiday, the guards lined them up and required them to shout "Banzai" three times, lifting their arms in the direction of the Imperial Palace. This chore completed, the Americans returned to their food and conversation. At the steel mill in Yodogawa conditions were bleak. Christmas passed with little ceremony. Items from cases of South African Red Cross food such as cigarettes, chocolate bars, and canned pudding were given out, but only as rewards for hard work. Since he was a supervisor and did no manual labor, Captain Coleman got just five lumps of sugar. Later, in the true spirit of Christmas some of the men pooled the food that they had received and shared it with others who had received little or none. The Japanese kept most of the cigarettes and chocolate bars, occasionally sharing them with a POW. Farther north at Kawasaki, Hugh Meyers and other freight handlers received mail in late October and South African Red Cross food items at Christmas. The guards did not pilfer here as they had done at Yodogawa. Instead they were all smiles on Christmas Day, hoping that Americans, with all their Red Cross delicacies, would give them a "presento." They got a few.

While some Red Cross food got through to the hungry prisoners, practically none of the medical supplies did. In the Philippines (and later in the Tokyo area) the Americans were allowed to set up their own medical facilities, but in the Osaka area the Japanese used Japanese civilian doctors and hospitals when absolutely necessary to treat severely ill or injured POWs. Some of the Red Cross medical supplies were turned over to these hospitals, where Americans would report seeing them being used for Japanese as well as themselves. Large quantities of medicines and equipment were stored for long periods, some indefinitely, as only another manifestation of the Japanese Army's frugality and conservation ethic.

★ ★ ★ 4 ★ ★ ★

The August exchange of American and Japanese diplomats, with its lifesaving Red Cross supplies, had another by-product. It began a long series of attempts by the U.S. government to secure assurances from the Japanese that American POWs would be treated in accordance with the Geneva Convention.

American civilians returning from the Philippines and China on the *Gripsholm* brought back with them the first information on Japanese treatment of captured Americans. They told American officials in Washington what they had heard about the Japanese brutality on the Death March and about the inhumanity at Camp O'Donnell.   Though information on Americans in the Philippines was general in nature, that concerning the men in the Shanghai camps was more specific.   Working with what they had, State Department officials drafted a protest through the Swiss government which Secretary of State Cordell Hull signed on December 12, 1942.   In his message Hull cited the march out of Bataan, conditions at O'Donnell, and the "illegal sentences" and mistreatment of American escapees at Shanghai.   In addition to insisting that the Japanese treat Americans in accordance with the Geneva Convention, Hull requested the names of all prisoners be reported—only those captured on Guam and Wake and in China had been reported at this time and these lists were incomplete.

The Japanese ignored this, the first of many American protests, but independently of Hull's request they had already begun transmitting the names of men held prisoner in the Philippines.   By Christmas relatives and friends of Americans whose names were on these lists had gained some assurance that they were alive.   Others had to settle for hope that those not on the lists and classified by the United States as missing would somehow return.   But even for the many whose loved ones were on the lists, the feeling was growing that with the Japanese military successes liberation might be a long time in coming.

Thousands of miles across the Pacific, the majority of Americans in Japanese prison camps had come to the same conclusion. These men, who had come through so much hardship and death, were thankful to be alive and few of them expected early freedom.   Drawing some confidence from their survival thus far, they felt that with a little luck they would eventually make it home.

PART II

Working and Waiting

January 1943–
May 1944

8

TROPICAL TOIL

January 1943–March 1944
Mindanao—Burma—Luzon—
Palawan

★ ★ ★ 1 ★ ★ ★

At Davao Penal Colony not long after Christmas the Japanese holiday spirit wore off, and the Americans—officers and men alike—had to resume their daily toil. Frequently in the morning Major Maeda, wearing a khaki pith helmet, a white undershirt, and shorts, would saunter out of his house by the main gate to watch the prisoners form for the day's work and march off.

There were many jobs to be done. One group under an American who had once been a county agricultural agent tended the chicken farm; another, smaller detail looked after the pigs; others worked at the farm warehouse or at the sawmill. About a dozen men became specialists. They learned to drive carabao, the native oxen used for plowing and hauling. Some officers, in deference to their age, were assigned to lighter tasks such as picking coffee, weaving baskets, and making straw hats for the rest of their comrades, most of whom were constantly exposed to the sun. Some prisoners lacked the manual skills and temperament for hat making, prompting a Japanese to comment truthfully, "We find you are very slow at learning to make this hat."

The men who needed the hats most were the five hundred

or more of the healthiest men (over a quarter of the camp's twenty-one hundred POWs) assigned to the rice fields at Mactan, five miles east of the prison compound. Transported to their work daily on flatcars pulled by a small diesel locomotive, these men performed the most important function of the penal colony's agricultural program. Rice cultivation began with plowing. Driving a carabao while clad only in a hat and a G-string, waist-deep in water and mud, was a demanding job. But some of the men became attached to their animals and preferred to do this. After plowing, a planting team of twenty-eight men lined up along a rope across a rice paddy covered to a depth of two and one-half feet by muddy water. On signal each man would plant his handful of seedlings, and again on signal would move backward for the next repetition. It was dull, tedious labor—at the lowest level of the Asiatic work scale. After completing the planting, the men were given one day off to celebrate the occasion in keeping with Japanese traditions.

At the beginning, the food that the POWs got for their work was better than average, with small amounts of fish or carabao meat and larger amounts of vegetables added to their daily portions of rice. The men working in the rice fields got the most generous amount of rice. All others who worked got somewhat less, and the sick and those not assigned work got the least. Late in January 1943 the long-delayed Red Cross supplies arrived—American, British, South African, and Canadian. Each delighted POW got two eleven-pound packages plus toilet articles. Sorely needed medical supplies including quinine, sulfa drugs, anesthetics, and vitamins were put to immediate use. In addition to individual packages the shipment included cases of canned corned beef and meat-and-vegetable stew. The Japanese gave out two cans to each man for about eight weeks until the supply ran out. Unfortunately the Japanese reduced the previously liberal vegetable and meat ration as an offset for the Red Cross food.

Shortly after the distribution of Red Cross supplies came another morale booster. Each man was allowed to send an Imperial Japanese Army postcard containing a maximum of fifty words to the United States. All cards were censored and those who tried to sneak disguised information through as to the camp's location or to describe bad conditions were subject to punishment. Because of the censorship the cards conveyed little more to their anxious recipients in the United States than the fact that whenever the card was prepared (usually the Japanese did not permit dating the cards), the POW could be presumed to be alive. These and cards sent later from Davao and other camps took on the average about a year to reach the addressee.

After the Red Cross supplies were exhausted, the Japanese maintained the reduced vegetable ration imposed because of the Red Cross food. With vegetables and fruit all around the camp often left to rot, the POWs could not understand why more of this food was not provided, or, at the very least, why workers outside the camp were not allowed to carry some of it back with them at the end of the day. Protests by the camp leadership for more food did no good. The official response was that the food was not available. On one occasion an interpreter stated, "We dare not give you too much to eat. You will get strong and hurt us." Equally aggravating were the shakedowns of incoming work details for smuggled food. The Japanese denounced POWs attempting to bring in food, calling them "robbery men," justifying the action on the basis that in the Japanese view, if all the men could not have extra food, it was wrong for a few to get it. What baffled and dismayed the Americans was why *all* did not get the food. The POWs never did get a satisfactory answer to this question but continued to smuggle food in whenever the opportunity presented itself.

One reason that POWs were able to get food into the camp was the relatively light security. Guards were posted at the gates at all times and others accompanied outside work details. As a result of the large number of details and their many locations, the guard force was spread thin. Despite this, the Japanese were not overly concerned since they considered the camp's remote jungle location a major deterrent to escape. But some of the healthier and more aggressive Americans were beginning to think otherwise.

★ ★ ★ **2** ★ ★ ★

Three such men were Capt. Austin C. Shofner and Lts. Jack Hawkins and Michael Dobervich. All were members of a fifteen-man plowing detail. Their work took them to nearly all parts of the camp and afforded excellent opportunities to forage for extra food, which restored their lost strength and vigor. Soon they were permitted to work around the central part of the camp without guards and with such freedom that they began discussing among themselves possibilities for escape. About the same time Capt. Ed Dyess, who had started with the plowing detail, graduated after an illness to bull cart driver, delivering tools and supplies to various details around the camp. He soon became a familiar figure to the guards—an American airman piloting a bull cart—and could move about the camp unchallenged. While on his daily rounds Dyess began to consider organizing some sort of escape. Two men that he had in mind as possible collaborators were his old Air Corps buddies, Lts. Samuel C. Grashio and Leo Boelens. Comdr. Melvin H. McCoy, U.S. Navy, and Maj. Steve Mellnik were in charge of a lightly guarded coffee-picking detail. With no manual labor duties themselves, they had time to study the area and struck up a friendship with a Filipino agricultural advisor, Candido "Pop" Abrina. In long conversations with Abrina the two officers gained much information on the roads, trails, and geography of the area around Davao Penal Colony. It was not long before the two had roughed out a plan, built around McCoy's nautical ability, to escape and obtain a boat and sail it to Australia. Soon they arranged for two Army noncommissioned officers, Paul Marshall and R. B. Spielman, to join their detail as collaborators in their plan for escape.

During late February and into March the three groups contemplating escapes were active. The Shofner-Hawkins-Dobervich group had contacted and joined with Dyess, Grashio, and Boelens. Later Shofner talked with McCoy and the escape group was expanded to include Mellnik, Spielman, and Marshall. The group now totaled ten men with McCoy, the senior officer, assuming overall leadership. Their objective was to reach a coastal town northeast of the camp, Cateel, where they hoped to commandeer a boat and sail it to Australia. Planning took on new life when Pop Abrina gave them a map of the surrounding area and arranged for two Filipino convicts to act as interpreters and guide the escaped group through the difficult swampy terrain to the north. Gratefully, McCoy and

Mellnik promised the two convicts that they would, when free, arrange to have the men pardoned.

Plans and preparations now intensified. They assembled supplies for the escape: a compass, a crudely fashioned sextant, drugs, bolos (jungle knives), and food for five days. They had earlier judged that Major Maeda was not as tough as Lieutenant Colonel Mori at Cabanatuan, since he, Maeda, had not emphasized the ten-man "death squads." On the strength of this, the men concluded that the likelihood of serious measures against the POWs in the camp was slim. To avoid possible disclosure to the Japanese and minimize the implication of others in their escape, they decided to leave the camp on a Sunday. Escaping on the camp's day off would mean that they would probably not be missed until roll call Monday morning. This would give them a twenty-four-hour head start on the Japanese. To provide an assembly point, McCoy got approval from the Japanese for himself and other members of the escape group to work on a shelter for the coffee detail on Sundays. The men on the plowing detail also got permission to check grazing arrangements for their animals on that day. The group set March 28 for their escape and during the week prior to this date cached most of their supplies along the trail leading out of the camp. The date changed to April 4 when Lieutenant Hosume abruptly ordered most of the camp to work on the 28th as punishment for a case of food smuggling. The week beginning March 28 was one of anxious waiting for McCoy and the other nine men. Fear of discovery of their recently hidden supplies increased when during the week a trigger-happy guard shot and killed an American sergeant near the camp fence for an alleged escape attempt. Guards scurried around the camp and the POWs feared their supplies might be found. They were not, and, as scheduled, on Sunday morning, April 4, McCoy and his supposed extra work detail marched out of the compound with no good-byes to their American comrades and smart salutes to the Japanese guards.

Their troubles began when, after a two-hour delay awaiting their convict guides, they set out only to find that the Filipinos were hopelessly lost. McCoy then took over, using a map and compass. In oppressive heat they hacked their way through jungles and later in the day found themselves slogging through a swamp. On the following day they heard shots indicating that the Japanese were close. On the third day, exhausted but driven on by their hunger for freedom, they emerged from the jungle onto railroad tracks which were on their map but which they had avoided up to now because they feared the Japanese might spot them. Hoping that the Japanese had given up pursuit, they decided to move in the open along the railroad. They moved rapidly until they found a small Filipino village where they felt secure enough to take a rest. While they were relaxing, a band of Filipino guerrillas* appeared out of the jungle. After verifying that McCoy and his group were really Americans (their darkened skin made them look like natives), the Filipinos took them to their headquarters. Now out of reach of their pursuers, they met the guerrilla leader, Lt. Col. Claro Lauretta, and planned their next move.

Lauretta, in command of several hundred poorly equipped men, showed them a letter from an American officer, Lieutenant Colonel McLeish, leader of a guerrilla group located at Medina, a town on the north coast of Mindanao about 125 miles away. According to the letter, McLeish had five hundred rifles, plenty of ammunition, and three diesel-powered boats. He was anxious to establish communications with Lauretta's group. After hearing about the powerboats and McLeish's strong position in the north, the Americans dropped their plan to go to Cateel and accepted Lauretta's offer to carry his pledge of cooperation to the American guerrilla commander.

While resting up for the long trip, the Americans' thoughts turned to the men they had left behind. McCoy and Mellnik, emphasizing the light security around the camp, asked Lauretta if he would try to liberate the Americans at Davao Penal Colony. Lauretta said he could not. He did not have the men or firepower to take on the Japanese who would be sent against him if he attacked the camp. In an all-out battle with the Japanese he feared he would lose everything it had taken him nearly a year to organize. He did offer to deliver a message to the camp. Disappointed, the Americans composed one and

---

* By this time a number of Filipinos, mostly former Philippine army soldiers, had banded together in remote unoccupied parts of the Philippines, under Filipino and American officers who had evaded capture. They carried out various missions ranging from active harassment of the Japanese occupation forces to organizing to support the return of U.S. forces.

gave it to Lauretta, then turned to preparations for their expedition to Medina.

With a native tribesman as their guide and a dozen others as bearers, the Americans struck northward over territory that did not show on their maps. Days of climbing mountain trails followed. Giant leeches wormed through openings in their shoes and leggings. After crossing the mountains the natives built rafts and they floated down the Agusan River—a tremendous relief to the Americans, most of whom by then had completely worn out their shoes. Finally, the exhausted Americans reached Medina, a city which because of a strange truce with the Japanese remained under Philippine control. A Filipino lieutenant escorted Mellnik to a house where he was assigned a bedroom with lace curtains and a four-poster bed.

The POWs' newfound luxury didn't end with their sleeping quarters. The next day they were guests at a birthday party for the governor of the province. Dressed in fresh khaki uniforms and with new shoes, they went through a receiving line and looked with admiration at the beautifully gowned women. They tried not to eat too much or too fast from the platters of food on the buffet. The snow-white linens, silver bowls, and a five-piece orchestra reminded them of a world that they had almost forgotten.

With all the cordiality, McLeish was not encouraging about their escaping by boat to Australia. He explained that the coastal waters were thick with Japanese patrol boats. He suggested that the men contact another guerrilla leader, a former mining engineer named Wendell Fertig, who was at the time serving with the rank of colonel. Fertig, according to McLeish, was in radio contact with MacArthur's headquarters in Australia and was receiving supplies by submarine. He also told them that he had heard that an American agent named Parsons was in the area. Hearing this, the Americans changed their plans a second time, deciding to send McCoy and Mellnik ahead to meet with Fertig.

After a harrowing trip through Japanese-occupied territory McCoy and Mellnik met with Navy commander "Chick" Parsons, and with him continued to Colonel Fertig's headquarters at the town of Misamis. Fertig told them that he would inform MacArthur's headquarters of their presence, but weeks went by with no reply. Meanwhile Ed Dyess, impatient with the delay, arrived from Medina. Soon after his arrival, and two and one-half months after their escape, a message finally arrived which read in part: "MCCOY-MELLNIK-DYESS—AUTHORIZED TO BOARD SUBMARINE—WEEK OF JULY 15–25." Exultant, the three men turned next to their friends in Medina. A quick review determined that it would be impossible to get a message to them and have them make the trip to Medina in time to board the submarine (as it turned out the submarine could hold only five passengers). In a letter to Captain Shofner, McCoy explained the situation and urged Shofner to keep the men together until arrangements could be made to get them out on the next submarine. Later Parsons and three ex-POWs were prematurely forced to start for their rendezvous with the submarine when a Japanese landing party, part of a large sweep of the coast, came ashore at Misamis. After some narrow scrapes with the Japanese—first pursued by a destroyer and later, as they moved across country, brushes with enemy patrols—on July 15 they arrived at the town of Kabasalan. After a night's rest they boarded a small launch that took most of the day to reach the rendezvous point. Within thirty minutes of the prearranged time a submarine broke surface, quickly took the men aboard, dove, and headed for Australia.

When McCoy, Mellnik, and Dyess reached Australia aboard the rescue submarine in late July they were immediately ordered to discuss their experiences only with authorized persons. They then flew to MacArthur's headquarters in Brisbane. There General MacArthur decorated them and after hearing their accounts declared his resolve that the Japanese would pay for American prisoners' humiliation and suffering. Next the men returned to the United States, where they were debriefed and their report was reviewed at the highest governmental levels. After rest leaves the three men returned to active duty with their respective branches of the service. The remaining seven escapees did not get out on the next submarine but did eventually return safely to the United States later in the war.

At Davao Penal Colony immediately after the escape the Japanese conducted an intensive manhunt, with frequent bulletins stating that the Japanese pursuers were close on the heels of the Americans and that capture was imminent. But when no POWs or dead bodies were brought back after a week, most of the Americans assumed that McCoy and the others had successfully eluded the Japanese.

The men involved in the escape had been right about Major Maeda. He did not invoke the "death squad" rule but did put the entire camp on a rice-and-salt diet for a week. He also ordered 550 Americans occupying the barracks in which the escapees had lived to be moved to cramped quarters in another compound north of the camp, where they were kept for a period of one month.

Reactions to the escape varied. Lt. Col. John H. McGee and other aggressive-minded POWs grudgingly admired it. McGee had himself had been organizing an escape of an entire work group with the intent of joining the guerrillas. His plan to escape during the week beginning April 4 was thwarted by the McCoy group's departure. Many Americans, convinced of the futility of escape and still remembering the executions at Camp O'Donnell and Cabanatuan, cursed the escapees and the troubles that these men had brought down on those who remained. But even among the most bitter, few wanted to see their fellow Americans captured. As for the Japanese, fellow officers put some of the blame for the escape on Lieutenant Yuki for his more liberal and humane treatment of the POWs. Thereafter the Japanese became more strict and demanding.

POW life was never quite as good as it was before the escape. Large details were turned out for hard labor in the Mactan rice fields. The Japanese eliminated most of the Filipino employees, who had always been helpful to the Americans. More intensive body searches of returning work details were carried out. This made smuggling of fruits and vegetables into the camp extremely difficult. Money was of little use. A small commissary carried native tobacco and on a few occasions stocked edible items like peanuts and peanut brittle but these items were quickly exhausted. Rumors of U.S. military progress in the Pacific were not encouraging. The camp choir, too tired to sing after exhausting work details, was disbanded. Religious services helped some contend with the bleakness of prison life. For the more ingenious and energetic state societies, chess and checkers, recipe collecting, and house designing helped make the time pass a little more pleasantly.

★ ★ ★ 3 ★ ★ ★

Life during most of 1943 was far from pleasant for men working on the Imperial Japanese Army's ambitious project, the Burma–Thailand railroad. Americans in Colonel Nagatomo's Branch 3 had been working southward for three months when, in January, 450 more of their countrymen arrived at the railroad's northern base camp at Thanbyuzayat. The new men had come by ship from Singapore and on the way had narrowly escaped being sunk by Allied bombers. Soon after they arrived they began work as part of Branch 5, a POW administrative organization which included about nineteen hundred Americans, Australians, and Dutch (considerably smaller than Branch 3, which would reach over nine thousand men at peak strength).

Though the Japanese engineers used dynamite to blast rocks and sometimes elephants to uproot trees, they relied on manpower to move earth. Weather conditions at this time were good, so the Japanese, anticipating the onset of the rainy season in May, began to raise the quotas of dirt to be moved by each work party. From the original 1.2 cubic meters the quota rose to 1.5, then to 2.0, and finally to 2.5 cubic meters. The Japanese engineer supervisors demanded that the quota be met no matter how long it took, so workdays became longer. Some Americans found ways to avoid the excessive requirements. In one work party when the guards weren't looking, the American officer supervisor would move the wooden stakes marking the day's quota closer together so the men would have less to dig and move that day. But opportunities like these were scarce, and most of the time hundreds of Americans had to do a job which in their own army would have been done by a few bulldozers.

Besides the heavy work demands, the Americans on the railroad had to contend with a guard force composed mostly of Koreans. These men both disliked and feared their masters the Japanese and often vented their feelings on the workers over whom they stood guard. Worse, unlike in the Philippines and some other locations where Japanese held Allied POWs, interpreters were seldom, if ever, present on work details.

Instructions were issued in a combination of English and Japanese and sign language. The Japanese expected the Koreans to understand also. Naturally, beatings over misunderstood directions occurred often. The prisoners' senior officers complained but Colonel Nagatomo, while he agreed that the language barrier was a great obstacle to good work relations, did nothing about it.

Americans working in Branch 3 had a short respite from their daily labor when their officers persuaded the Japanese to give them a day off to stage a "Race Day" in the style of the Melbourne Cup, a popular annual racing event in Australia. On Race Day men in improvised jockey costumes rode wooden horses; a crude pari-mutuel board showed the bets and the odds; and men lined up at betting booths to place wagers on their buddies, using their hard-earned pittance—ten cents a day. Though this kind of festivity was strange and different to the Americans, the high spirits of the Australians were contagious and everyone enjoyed the brief escape from the brutal reality of their daily life.

Spirits were dampened later by a report of an unsuccessful escape attempt. One man, of a three-man group of Australians heading west to India, became ill and fell into the hands of natives who turned him over to the Japanese. The other two evaded capture for two weeks before Burmese police killed one of them and captured the other. After executing the leader of the escape the Japanese felt reassured that they need guard their prisoners with only a minimum number of men because the great distances, the jungles, and the native population provided an effective barrier and deterrent to potential escapees. If any Americans had thoughts of trying for freedom, they were discouraged by this news; and during the entire time the Americans worked on the railroad none were known to have made an attempt to escape.

When Americans in Branch 5 were moved farther south, the Japanese put them to work building a bridge. It was one of many crude wooden structures on the railway and of a type which would later be seen by millions in a motion picture (*Bridge on the River Kwai*) about the Burma–Thailand railroad. Again, man did the work of machines. As prisoners stood waist-deep in the water, hauling on ropes attached to a heavy steel hammer mounted between two vertical guide poles, a Japanese supervisor would shout cadence to them for each pull until the hammer hit the top and then dropped to drive another wooden pile into the riverbed. Others, not busy as human pile drivers, clambered onto scaffolding to secure the timbers by tiers in a lattice fashion. It was at this time that the first three Americans died, all of malaria.

With the advent of the rainy season in May, life became even more difficult. Both groups moved farther into the jungle. The monsoon rains, as heavy and intense here as any other place in the Far East, increased daily. Soon the work sites were seas of mud, making all tasks more difficult. At night, returning to their huts, the men found them to be leaking, the floors and bedding a sodden mess. Colonel Nagatomo and the senior Japanese engineers in charge of constructing the railway became fearful that the men's increasing fatigue and the poor work conditions would jeopardize meeting the target date for completing the railway. To avoid this they demanded that work quotas previously established be met despite the weather. As more men became ill and incapacitated and were unable to make work calls, the Japanese countered with measures to get more of them out to work. One way they chose was to reduce the already slim rations reaching these camps deep in the jungle. A full rice ration was henceforth allowed only for those on the job. Sick men remaining in camp were to receive only a part of a ration or none at all. But the rations were distributed in bulk to each camp kitchen. Since no one would deliberately short the sick, workers and sick alike got less to eat. Dysentery and beriberi began to make deep inroads among the prisoners. Along with these diseases, tropical ulcers had a high fatality rate. Capt. S. H. Lumpkin, who was greatly admired by the POWs for his attempts, despite terrible pressures, to keep genuinely sick men off the work rosters, and Comdr. W. A. Epstein tried to treat the painful and lethal tropical ulcerations by having the men soak their sores in hot cloths soaked in boiling water. This system was less successful than that used by two Dutch doctors, Hans Hekking and P. Bloesma. They used a sharpened spoon and would dig the rotten flesh out of the ulcers daily as the patient was held down by comrades. Despite the dreadful pain, these doctors had considerable success with this radical method.

It was during the period from July to October that pressures to finish the railroad reached their peak. As guards constantly shouted "Speedo! Speedo!" the men began to weaken and die in rapidly increasingly numbers. Among the 644 Americans, 9 died in June, 29 in August, and 37 in September. One of those who died in that month was the respected Captain Lumpkin. Finally, in mid-October, the prisoners working from Burma southward met those who had been working north from Ban Pong, Thailand, and the two rail lines joined. A month later Colonel Nagatomo in a "letter of condolence" read to all prisoners announced that the first stage of construction was over. He expressed sympathy for the hundreds of Allied prisoners who had lost their lives. This number would include 127 Americans—4 officers and 123 enlisted men—20 percent of those working on the railroad.

On the day following his announcement Nagatomo ordered merry-making, consisting of Japanese music in the morning and an Australian-style race meeting in the afternoon. After that work tapered off, and beginning in December the Japanese started moving the Burma workers south into Thailand. Life there in camps west of Bangkok improved considerably. Rations and living conditions were better and the work details were relatively light. This, combined with the centralization of medical staff in a huge hospital at the town of Nakhon Pathom, resulted in the death rate dropping dramatically. During the remainder of the war only seven Americans died in the Thailand camps.

★ ★ ★ **4** ★ ★ ★

The death rate had also reached normal by March 1943 at Cabanatuan in the Philippines. Only nine of nearly six thousand died there that month. In April and May only one man died of natural causes in each month and no appreciable increase in deaths occurred after that. The ravages of disease were finally over, but the survivors still chafed under the Japanese yoke.

As the year wore on, the Japanese put increasing numbers of POWs to work on a three-hundred-acre farm near the prison compound. At the peak nearly three thousand men dug, hoed, planted, and hauled water to grow squash, beans, corn, and a variety of other vegetables and rice. One officer was told that the Japanese had a five-year plan for expanding the farm which would include a huge rice field. Work on the farm was tedious, demeaning, and hated, but unlike the work at some other locations it was not so harsh and demanding as to cause death. Occasionally, easier work details provided some respite.

One of these put POWs to work as extras in production of a movie, *Down with the Stars and Stripes*. On the first day of shooting, more than one-third of the Americans in the camp acted in a scene depicting a mass surrender of American troops. After the scenes at Cabanatuan were completed, about one hundred men, mostly officers, were taken to Bataan for a week's filming. Poor weather greatly restricted photographic activity so the prisoners spent most of their time on Bataan sitting around, a pastime much preferable to working on the farm. Finally, after participation in four or five scenes, the men returned to their dull routine as POWs.

The unpredictability of their captors was almost as aggravating to the Americans as the tougher work details. The experiences of Gene Forquer, a young captain from Pennsylvania, were not unusual. One day an amiable guard befriended Forquer when he was officer in charge of the detail in the camp stockyard. The Japanese had apparently come from a Christian background and seemed pleased that he and Forquer could hum "Rock of Ages" and other hymns together. Later, to Forquer's surprise, the Japanese handed him his rifle and asked the American to show him how the U.S. Army executed various movements with the weapon. But a week later, returning from a detail which required carrying large bundles of straw, Forquer was feeling weak. When he passed the sentry at the gate he gave the man only a quarter bow instead of the required hand salute. The guard called him over and, holding his rifle by the muzzle with both hands, swung it at the American, striking him across the hip and thigh. Stunned, Forquer finally managed to get off a salute and walked off, glad to end the session with one blow, but baffled by the difference in behavior of his captor.

To the Americans the actions of the commandant were equally inconsistent. On Memorial Day, after announcing earlier that American attendance at the cemetery would be restricted to only thirteen men, the commandant permitted more than one thousand men to attend what turned out to be a

beautiful ceremony. The general in charge of prison camps
in Manila sent a wreath; and Major Iwanaka, the camp commandant, presented his, a large and beautiful one, personally. The
prisoners' wreath, small by comparison, was placed by two
Army chaplains. Then Americans and Japanese together stood
silently as Protestant, Catholic, and Jewish prayers were said
and two choral groups rendered hymns in tribute to the 2,644
men buried in the cemetery. Now neat and well drained,
the cemetery bore little resemblance to the dismal, muddy
burial ground of a year ago.

The following week the Japanese, mourning the death of
their national hero Adm. Isoroku Yamamoto (shot down by
American fighter planes in the South Pacific), decreed that the
prisoners must not sing or smile for two days. Probably not
by coincidence, the commandant also sent a record number
of men to work on the farm, more than twenty-six hundred,
and included many majors and lieutenant colonels who had
never been required to work before. It was not long after
this that Major Iwanaka assembled all the American senior officers in the camp and in a conciliatory speech congratulated
himself and the American staff for the improved conditions
in the camp, particularly the recent reduction in the death
rate. He said that he regretted the beatings, attributing them
to POW laziness, noncooperation, and the language barrier,
but promised that he would do all he could to reduce brutality.
He closed his speech with the personal wish that cooperation
in the camp continue and "when the war is over, you will
rejoin your families in good health."

Despite their almost constant incompatibility with their captors, the men at Cabanatuan were considerably better off than
those at most of the Asian POW camps during 1943. This
was particularly true in the vital area of food. The Japanese
maintained the rice ration at a reasonable level, and for those
Americans with money, supplementary food was available in
the commissary. Items which could be purchased there included coffee, eggs, corned beef, sardines, sugar, chicken, cooking oil, and assorted vegetables and fruits—onions, peanuts,
mangoes, and limes. With their monthly pay officers were
able to take advantage of the commissary, run by an infantry
officer, Lt. Col. Harold K. Johnson, an enterprising and fair-
minded regular Army officer, who twenty-one years later be-

came Army Chief of Staff. The enlisted men, with their pay of about the equivalent of ten cents per day, did not benefit as much. American officers in the grade of major and above did allot money from their pay to a welfare fund which was used to help enlisted men who had little money. But for those who could buy extras the custom of quanning (the all-purpose word most commonly used by the POWs in connection with consumption of food) was popular. A good quan might have consisted of hotcakes made of rice flour, one or two fried duck eggs, sausage, and onions.

Some of the quanning was possible because of money and food smuggled into the camp on an increasing scale during 1943. The principal organizers of the smuggling activities were two American women, Margaret Utinsky and Claire Phillips. Both were wives of American soldiers who had died in Cabanatuan during the summer of 1942. They had by clever ruses avoided confinement in the civilian internment camp, Santo Tomas, in Manila.

Utinsky, who had provided food and medicine to POWs at Camp O'Donnell, was the first to make contact at Cabanatuan. Acting under Utinsky's directions, a young Filipino woman named Naomi talked with Lt. Col. Edward Mack while he accompanied one of the farm details leaving the camp. Naomi soon recruited two other Filipino women (one was the wife of a POW) and together they began selling vegetables and fruit in the marketplace in Cabanatuan. This made it possible to sell peanuts and other native produce to the Americans on the carabao cart detail when it journeyed into the town and also to POWs as they marched to and from the farm. Concealed in the peanut bags were money and notes sent by Utinsky which she had obtained from American sympathizers in Manila. Financial and other aid came from well-to-do Filipinos, members of the Manila international community, and religious groups. Among the most active in the well-organized network of workers were Ramon Amusatague, a wealthy leader of the Spanish colony, Father Lolar of the Malate Convent, and Mr. Parvino, an Italian. Inside the camp in addition to Mack, Chaplains Frank Tiffany, Robert P. Taylor, and John Wilson as well as Lt. Col. Jack W. Schwartz, a doctor, acted as intermediaries in getting the outside money and supplies to designated recipients and, when requested, in getting receipts and answers back to people in Manila. As the volume of material getting into the camp increased, "Miss U," as Utinsky came to be called, through her agent, Naomi, enlisted the aid of a merchant who had several large vegetable stalls in the marketplace. This merchant agreed to mix vegetables and other produce sent by Miss U by truck from Manila with his own. Under the system that evolved, Americans escorted to the marketplace to purchase for the camp commissary would by covert means also include some of the donated items. These nearly always included money, notes, and medicines. In this way the Americans were able not only to get greater quantities of food for the limited amount of money that the Japanese permitted them to spend, but were also able to pick up more pesos to use for purchase on the next trip. In addition to the underground channel, Father Buddenbroch, a priest who was a German citizen, was occasionally permitted by the Japanese to bring packages and medicines into the camp.

Later Claire Phillips, who ran a Manila nightclub catering to Japanese, began serving as an additional underground channel. Using her nightclub office as a meeting point, Phillips, whose code name was "High Pockets," contributed money herself and collected aid from others in Manila. (Some of her contacts were the same supporters contributing through Miss U.) Both operations functioned smoothly and together were of substantial benefit to many recipients at Cabanatuan. Lieutenant Colonel Johnson estimated later that while the underground was in operation and by keeping two sets of books, one for Japanese audit and the other for American use, he spent nearly one and one-half million pesos on food and other items with an apparent income of only one-half million.

If the food at Cabanatuan was somewhat better than at most camps, entertainment at the big camp was probably unequaled elsewhere. The stage shows which had begun the previous December continued to be a great source of diversion. On Wednesday nights there was usually a popular band concert and on Saturdays a stage play or variety show. Cabanatuan had its own version of the *Hit Parade* and the camp orchestra, the Cabanatuan Cats, did imitations of well-known orchestras. The Mighty Art Players, with Lt. Col. O. O. Wilson and Lt. Al Manning as producers, performed many shows based on well-known books or plays: *Gone With the Wind, Uncle Tom's*

Cabin, Frankenstein, and *Casey Jones* were just a few. Movies were shown about twice a month, starting early in the year, with *Room Service* starring the Marx Brothers, Lucille Ball, and Ann Miller. Unfortunately the fare of old American movies had to give way at times to some Japanese films. Some of them depicted the capture of Bataan, Corregidor, and Java and the bombing of Pearl Harbor. They drew much applause from the Japanese and stony silence from the Americans.

Even with the weekly entertainment and relatively adequate nutrition, personal relationships did not always go smoothly among the nerve-frayed Americans after their first year of activity. Lt. Col. Curtis T. Beecher, as American senior officer, though given little authority by the Japanese commandant, attempted through his staff and group commanders to run a tight ship. Some of his methods and actions were not popular with the POWs. His inspections of the troops, sometimes prior to Japanese inspections, and his demands that unsightly articles be concealed irked the men. The junior officers in particular resented the fact that beds, mattresses, footlockers, and other amenities were provided for Beecher's staff officers and even for some of the headquarters' noncommissioned officers. Things came to a head when the farm work details were drawing more and more men and lieutenant colonels and majors and the enlisted men working for them were not required to go on detail. A group of junior officers banded together and drew up a petition. After much wrangling with one of the group commanders, the matter was presented to Lieutenant Colonel Beecher. He ruled that enlisted men working for the senior officers would work, sick men would not, and that if the occasion required, higher-ranking officers would go on details. This action soothed most feelings at the time but Beecher remained unpopular with many of the junior officers. Beecher's role, indeed the role of any officer representing POWs with the Japanese, was an onerous test of leadership. If the officer demonstrated an unflinching resistance to the rules and demands of the Japanese and totally supported the POW positions, the Japanese would inevitably replace him. In contrast, if he deferred completely to the authority of the Japanese and exercised little control over the Americans, disorganization and breakdown of discipline would result. This would end in the Japanese assuming complete and absolute

control over the POWs, as they did in a number of camps.
It was Beecher's job and that of a few others in the larger
camps to try to maintain a middle ground, neither kowtowing
to the Japanese, as he was accused of doing by some, nor letting
the Japanese run the camp completely. Though unpopular,
Beecher was probably reasonably successful in maintaining the
middle position and men at Cabanatuan were better off because
of this.

At Bilibid Prison in Manila, Comdr. Thomas H. Hayes,
U.S.N., faced some of the same problems in his job as the senior
medical officer of the combined hospital and temporary holding
facility for POWs being transferred between camps. Very
much a realist, Hayes from the day he took over had character-
ized the job of POW camp leader as a constant fight against
selfishness on the part of individuals who for their own personal
advantages would sacrifice the good of others. His credo was
to try to get the best of a bad bargain for all.

★ ★ ★ 5 ★ ★ ★

A bad bargain it was for most of the nearly three thousand
men assigned to work on six Japanese military airfields during
1943. The airfield projects, like the Burma–Thailand railroad,
were in direct support of the Japanese war effort. They were
not situations in which the POWs were expected to work primarily to provide food for themselves and the Japanese, as
was the case at Cabanatuan and the Davao Penal Colony.
At most of the airfields the Japanese had a sense of urgency
about the work to be done and they reflected this in their
treatment of the Americans.

The nearly eight hundred men housed in the former Pasay
School and working on the strip at Nichols Field, outside of
Manila, worked the hardest and were treated the worst. Daily
the POWs, clad in straw hats and loincloths, many without
shoes, marched to the airfield. There after being divided into
work groups they dug rocks and dirt with picks and shovels,
loaded them into small railcars, and pushed the cars to a designated area to unload. The Japanese established daily quotas
for each work group for the number of cars to be filled and
dumped. Failure to meet the quota resulted in beatings or
other punishment. The supervisors and guards under the con-

struction boss "Wolf" Ikota were particularly cruel. Beatings were frequent, and for offenses considered more serious the Japanese often resorted to physical torture: tying and hanging men by their arms from a tree or forcing them to ingest water and then kicking them in the stomach. The POWs hated and feared Ikota and another work supervisor named "Cherry Blossom" Matsomura because they frequently resorted to such inhumane punishment. Injuries resulting from punishment or work, except for the most serious or incapacitating, were left untreated. Only when the Japanese considered a man completely unfit for labor did they send him to Bilibid for medical treatment. Commander Hayes would later record that in one day alone at Bilibid, twenty men came from Pasay all in bad shape, some with crushed arms and legs from cave-ins at the digging sites.

With no shows or other recreation life was bleak. On occasion some of the POWs got some extras through the efforts of friendly Filipinos working with High Pockets. At great risk to themselves the Filipinos would pass food and money to prisoners as they marched back from the airfield. The lucky recipients used the money to buy food from a few profit-minded guards.

Elsewhere, American prisoners worked on improving and maintaining two other U.S. airfields. Some worked on a new runway at Nielson Field, a commercial airfield situated about three miles north of Nichols Field. Treatment and general conditions at Nielson were not as bad as at Nichols. Neither were they as bad at Clark Field, seventy miles north of Manila, where the U.S. Army Air Force heavy-bomber field had become the major air base for the Japanese in the Philippines. Here Philippine contractors built new concrete runways while as many as six hundred POWs drove trucks and performed various maintenance tasks on existing airstrips.

Meanwhile, the 350 men sent to Puerto Princesa on the island of Palawan in late 1942 were told when they got there that they were going to build a new airfield (not an enlargement or improvement of an existing facility such as was the case at Clark, Nichols, and Nielson fields) and it was to be completed in three months. Equipped only with axes, picks, and shovels, one roller, one tractor, and a few trucks, the Americans would take over two years to clear a strip of land over a mile long and 600 feet wide out of the jungle and build an airstrip on it.

The Americans at Puerto Princesa attempted more escapes than at any other American camp of comparable size. The first attempt, soon after their arrival on the island, was the most successful. Of the six who escaped during the night one was shot to death by a Filipino who was a Japanese sympathizer. The rest made good their escape. The commandant placed all POWs on one-third rations for three days and tightened security. Not long after this, two more Americans escaped, and by Japanese standards light punishment of the remaining POWs was imposed. The two escapes that followed were largely unsuccessful. In one, four men got out of the camp but two were recaptured and a third killed. The last escape, in late June 1943, resulted in the recapture of both men making the attempt. They were led off under guard and never seen again. Strangely, it was not until after this attempt that the Japanese commandant announced that if one man escaped, the men in his ten-man squad would be executed. This announcement came nearly a year after the Japanese had imposed the stringent provision at Cabanatuan.

Early in 1943 the Japanese sent five hundred men to build an auxiliary military airfield near Lipa, about seventy miles south of Manila. In September still another auxiliary field was begun at Las Piñas, south of Nichols Field. The Americans here worked moving, digging, and loading earth in small cars like those used at Nichols. The Japanese set high quotas, and one Marine would describe his work there later as the hardest that he had ever done in his life. As the pressure increased, the men took turns working in the leading cars, where the worst beating occurred, thus evening out the punishment among them. Still others got their buddies to break their arms so that they could get off work. With work not proceeding rapidly enough for them, the Japanese brought in some Formosan laborers and worked them under lights on a night shift as well as during the day. Despite all the attempts of "speedo," Americans were still working on the airstrip when the threat of American invasion compelled the Japanese to move the POWs elsewhere later in the war.

The work done by the four hundred men of the Manila

port area detail—loading and unloading ships—was hard and demanding. But unlike the laborers on the airstrips, the port area men got some rewards. The Japanese civilian in charge of the detail had worked with a shipping company in the United States and felt favorably toward the Americans and treated them well. In addition to an adequate ration of rice, fish, and vegetables, the men were able to obtain extra food on the docks, through the black market and contacts with the Philippine underground. They were probably the best-fed Americans in the Philippines.

★ ★ ★ 6 ★ ★ ★

Across the Pacific, in September 1943, the exchange ship *Gripsholm* set sail for the second time carrying Japanese nationals and a large cargo of relief supplies for POWs and civilian internees in the Far East. The 140,000 food packages it carried were specially prepared by women volunteers in the Red Cross packaging centers at Philadelphia and New York. Late information (probably obtained from the escapees Mellnik, McCoy, and Dyess) caused important changes to be made in the package. Additional butter, canned meat, coffee, and cigarettes were included. In order to have the larger packages—weighing thirteen pounds instead of the eleven pounds of the standard package—ready in time for the *Gripsholm* sailing, volunteers worked extra shifts and the packaging centers operated night and day. In addition to the food packages the relief shipment included medicines and drugs aimed at combating vitamin deficiencies, malaria, and dysentery. The Army and Navy supplied sets of heavy clothing for personnel in the northern camps. This clothing consisted of overcoats, shoes, blankets, woolen underwear, socks, shirts, sweaters, coveralls, caps, and gloves. The cargo also included next-of-kin parcels addressed to individual prisoners and hundreds of bags of U.S. mail.

In mid-October the *Gripsholm* met the Japanese ship *Teia Maru* at the Portuguese port of Mormugão, India, where personnel were exchanged and the cargo of the *Gripsholm* was loaded onto the Japanese ship. The *Teia Maru's* itinerary for the return trip included stops at Shanghai to drop off supplies for POWs in China, Java, Malaya, Thailand, and Burma;

Manila for prisoners in the Philippines as well as civilians; and Yokohama for prisoners held in Japan, Korea, Manchuria, and Formosa.

The *Teia Maru* docked in Manila in early November. POWs from Bilibid helped unload the relief supplies, much of which were stored at the prison hospital. As thousands of boxes and cases began to pile up, the Japanese were awed by the amounts of food and clothing that their captives were receiving. Soon after the unloading and storing of supplies was completed, fifty Japanese military policemen arrived at Bilibid and for two days they opened and inspected the contents of the various boxes. The net result of the inspection was the confiscation of some American newspapers and the withholding of all Old Gold cigarettes because each pack had "Freedom" printed on the back of it. Even without the Old Golds the POWs at Bilibid were soon enjoying a thirteen-pound American Red Cross box with more coming at Christmas. Later a group of beaten-down men from Pasay arrived. Commander Hayes, finding that each of the arriving men had gotten only a portion of the Red Cross package, issued each of them the rest of the package.

The Red Cross supplies didn't get to Cabanatuan until the end of November because of the worst flood in central Luzon in nearly twenty years. After the withdrawal of the infamous Old Golds, Major Iwanaka, the camp commandant, took three cases of cigarettes, one thousand pairs of shoelaces, some athletic equipment, and several decks of cards for Japanese use. In doing so he commented to an American officer who was standing by, "Surely you don't mind if we take this after we worked so hard to bring this to you." When word of Iwanaka's actions got out, there was much complaining among the prisoners; but to Maj. E. R. Fendall such griping was not only useless but ill founded. He speculated that were the situation reversed, 90 percent of Americans would have taken as much as or more than the Japanese did.

Christmas of 1943 and New Year's were good days at Cabanatuan. There were religious services, a Red Cross food package for each man (two more were issued in partial quantities over the next few months), extra food, and performances of *A Christmas Carol* and *The Best Shows of 1943* by the Cabanatuan players. However, most of the Americans found the whole holiday period less uplifting than the previous one.

Then the packages had meant much more and the general feeling among the POWs was that they would be home by Christmas of 1943, but another year found them still in Cabanatuan. Admittedly they were better fed. But with the camp's secret radio reporting MacArthur still slugging it out with the Japanese far to the south in New Guinea, most saw a distinct possibility and some the inevitability of spending another Christmas as POWs. One man conceded that this was not a true Christmas spirit but found solace in the fact that at least once a year the Americans with their Red Cross packages were better off than their captors.

He was probably right as far as the Japanese were concerned, but the Americans in the Far East were a deprived lot compared to the Americans held in POW camps in Germany. In addition to the three packages that each Cabanatuan POW would eventually receive from the *Gripsholm* shipment, some got one next-of-kin package from families or friends. In contrast, most of the Americans in German camps received one Red Cross food package per week and mail on a fairly regular basis. Years later, learning of this, an amazed former POW of the Japanese would write: "Boy, we could have owned Japan with a full box once a week!"

South at Davao the Americans were also hopeful that MacArthur's progress would speed up. The men there were kept informed of the war's progress by a clandestine radio set. The officer who assembled the set out of spare parts he collected while repairing the Japanese camp radios, Capt. Russell J. Hutchinson, by odd coincidence had the same surname as the man at Cabanatuan, Lt. Homer T. Hutchinson, who assembled and operated the set there. Hutchinson entrusted his tiny radio, small enough to be packed in a corned-beef can, to a close friend, Capt. Charles Brown, who hid it in a hole under his barracks. Several nights a week Hutchinson would go to Brown's barracks, set up the radio, and listen to the news. Later he would pass it on to the American senior officer, Lieutenant Colonel Olson. Through the other American senior staff, Olson saw to it that the news got around, usually in the form of rumors.

No rumor was the disappointing announcement by the Japanese that Red Cross supplies were on the way but would not arrive for Christmas. Instead, in mid-December, several hundred Japanese schoolchildren were trucked in for a look at the POWs and to stage a field day, which the Americans were invited to watch. The children delighted the Japanese camp personnel with a program which included mass calisthenics, flag exercises, and singing. Some of the performances were accompanied by the POW camp orchestra, which had practiced for several weeks to master the strange Japanese musical scores. All of the Americans appreciated the day off but a few watched with particular interest as the effectiveness of Japanese regimentation and discipline on children in their formative years was displayed for them.

The POWs enjoyed the Christmas Eve variety show and could feel some satisfaction in knowing that nearly a year had passed without a single American death. On Christmas Day the larger servings of soup, the forty cigarettes, and some old magazines fell far short of what they had hoped for when they had heard that another shipment of the prized Red Cross supplies was on its way.

Eight Americans decided to add some extra cheer to their holidays. Somehow they obtained some native alcohol and were apprehended by the guards in an intoxicated condition. The Japanese, for unknown reasons, judged the offense, obtaining and consuming alcohol, to be a very serious one. In an attempt to find the source of the alcohol the Japanese forced the men to stand in pans of water and touched them with live electric wires. Fortunately none of the men died or sustained serious injuries from this treatment, nor did they reveal the source.

By New Year's Eve, with their wrath over the alcohol apparently cooled, several of the Japanese officers invited the American senior officers, Lieutenant Colonel Olson and several of his staff, to dinner. Lieutenant Yuki, the officer who had always been fair to the Americans, provided beer, sake, and corned beef hash. When the beer was exhausted he sent for interpreter Shunusuke Wada's beer ration and the group consumed it. Later Wada let Olson and other Americans who had attended the dinner know that he deeply resented their part in the appropriation of his beer. The incident would have had only minor significance were it not for the fact that later

Wada would be placed in a position to influence the life or death of the Americans at the dinner and hundreds of their comrades.

In early January 1944 the Japanese told the Americans that the Australian and Canadian Red Cross had sent them New Year's greetings. Some of the Americans thought at the time that it was strange that none had been sent by their own country. But their government was involved in more serious matters. In Washington, White House and State Department officials were putting in final form the statements on Japanese atrocities that would send shock waves through the United States and its allied countries.

Not long after his return to the United States, Ed Dyess had written a detailed account of his experiences in the fall of Bataan, the Death March, and at the POW camps at O'Donnell, Cabanatuan, and Davao. Under wartime security he had submitted an account to the War Department for clearance. This created a dilemma for the War Department, the State Department, and ultimately the office of the President. Would the release of the information, by weight of world opinion, cause the Japanese to improve their treatment of POWs? Or would it have the opposite effect, possibly causing the Japanese to refuse to accept or otherwise obstruct the delivery of the Red Cross supplies then en route on the *Gripsholm*? In early September, President Roosevelt ordered Dyess's account to be kept under wraps until the *Gripsholm* supplies were delivered.

Problems arose almost immediately after the President's order to suppress the story. Responding to accounts of Japanese atrocities (apparently based on Australian sources) published in the *Washington Times Herald* in early October, the War Department sent a message to all theater commanders reiterating the President's decision on withholding atrocity information. In his reply General MacArthur pointed out the difficulties of doing this, noting that the Australian government was planning to investigate and publicize atrocities and that the British might also do this. After being informed by the Army that he was not to interfere with the Australian inquiry, MacArthur in characteristic fashion took matters into his own hands. He issued a stern warning to the Japanese field marshal Hisaichi Terauchi, whose command included the Philippines, that he, MacArthur, would hold the enemy leaders responsible for any failure to accord the prisoners proper treatment. He went on to say that the surrender of the United States in the Philippines had been made in the belief that the military prisoners would be treated in accordance with the rules and customs of war. Since then he had received unimpeachable evidence of the degradation and brutality to which these prisoners had been subjected in violation of the most sacred code of martial honor.

Apparently the Australian stories and MacArthur's message had some effect on the Japanese. In late December 1943 the chief of the Prisoner of War Bureau issued an instruction to all chiefs of POW camps: "Care should be taken to avoid issuing twisted reports of our fair attitude which might give the enemy food for evil propaganda and bring harm to our interned brothers." (The interned "brothers" included Japanese civilian nationals held by the United States.)

Meanwhile, the U.S. government, having learned that the Red Cross relief supplies had reached Japan, and expecting, because of the handling of the previous shipment, that supplies should reach most of the POWs by the end of January 1944, decided to release the information at the end of that month. The first release was the Dyess story in hundreds of newspapers across the country. This was followed in a few days by statements by the White House and the State Department, and more press releases based on the accounts of Mellnik, McCoy, and Dyess. Secretary of State Hull dispatched a formal detailed protest through Geneva to the Japanese, stating that repeated protests had been lodged with the Japanese to no avail but that the United States would continue to assemble information on Japanese ill treatment of war prisoners and intended to punish those responsible.

The American reaction to the atrocity accounts was widespread indignation and a demand for renewed efforts to intensify military efforts to defeat the Japanese. But with subsequent massive events on the western and eastern fronts in Europe, the invasion of France, and major victories by the Russians, the emotional reactions subsided; and except for their relatives and friends, the POWs were, as they had been before, left to work and wait. A month later the Japanese replied through Geneva to Hull's protest. They denied most of the allegations and stated that some others were being investigated.

In early March 1944 the Japanese, showing increased sensitivity to the U.S. announcements on atrocities, again resorted to bureaucratic edicts to correct the situation. This time the vice-minister of war instructed all army and POW camp commanders:

> In the light of recent intensified enemy propaganda warfare, if the present condition continues to exist, it will needlessly add to the hostile feelings of the enemy and it will also be impossible for us to expect the world opinion to be what we wish it to be. Such will cause an obstacle to our prosecution of moral warfare. Not only that, it is absolutely necessary to improve the health condition of POW's from the standpoint of using them satisfactorily to increase our fighting strength.

This admonition was followed by instructions to be sure that the prisoners were given their full allowance of food and clothing and that efforts be made to improve medical care.

The international attention and orders from Tokyo did nothing to improve the life of the POW. At Cabanatuan, after filling out six postcards each over the past year without receiving any answers, the POWs were delighted to learn that about 25,000 letters had arrived. Their elation turned to disappointment when they found that only one interpreter was censoring the mail, with an output of about one hundred letters per day. Once again it was a waiting game. A day after the mail arrived, the POWs learned via the secret radio of the U.S. announcements on the atrocities. This news caused much less of a stir than the Japanese announcement shortly thereafter that the rice ration was to be cut. This, the first of a series of reductions in food for POWs at Cabanatuan, stemmed from a serious and growing food shortage throughout the Philippines and the rapid inflation in commodity prices. The relatively good life at Cabanatuan was on the wane.

9

IN COLDER CLIMES
May 1943–March 1944
Manchuria—Formosa—China

★ ★ ★ 1 ★ ★ ★

In early May of 1943, as their fellow Americans were sweating under the tropical sun, the POWs at Mukden, Manchuria, had welcomed the first signs of spring and the warmth that it provided their cold, drained bodies. This same change in temperature prompted the Japanese to order the burial of 150 POWs, most of whom had died during the winter months and who had been placed in vacant barracks because the ground was frozen too hard to dig graves. The Japanese let the Americans hold their own burial services for their comrades. After each of the dead had been placed in an individual wooden coffin, Lt. James K. Levie, whose parents had been American missionaries in Korea, read a short religious service. Then the POWs carried the wooden coffins out of the camp to a cemetery, where a long trench had been dug. In a major concession, the Japanese allowed those POWs not on work assignments to go to the cemetery. Here the boxes were covered over with earth. With the prisoners and the Japanese staff and guards at attention, a soldier from New Mexico blew taps on a bugle that appeared out of nowhere.

By this time most of the Americans were physically improved and had completed or were completing training in the various types of work involved at the Manchurian Machine

Tool Company. Designed by four American engineers, the plant had been completed in 1940 as part of Japan's massive expansion of industrial facilities in Manchuria. Mr. Yoshio Kai, an American-born Japanese who had returned to Japan with his family in the twenties, had been the interpreter for the American engineers, and he stayed on after their departure. When the arrival of the war prisoners was imminent, the plant manager made Kai responsible for coordinating the work of the prisoners. Kai sympathized with the Americans and was the person who had arranged for extra food to be given to the few hundred men who were able to get to the factory on their first Christmas. Thereafter he did what he could to make life at the factory (he had no influence in the prison compound) as bearable as possible. The Americans soon swung into a weekly routine of six days' work at the factory, with Sundays off. The day usually started with a bowl of hot mush made of corn or kaoliang (a barleylike grain) and a wheat bun about the size of a baseball. Then the men would march under guard to the plant. There each man would put on white coveralls which he kept hanging on a wooden peg with his POW number on it. Next the POWs would report to various work stations, where they would carry out assigned tasks on milling machines, lathes and shapers, as well as in the smelting operation. They worked under Japanese civilian foremen in groups of six to twenty. Usually they worked in the same area but were separated from Chinese employees, who engaged in the same (or related) plant operations as the POWs.

Lunch was the highlight of the day. The Americans ate in a large industrial-type lunchroom separate from their Japanese supervisors and the Chinese workers. POW cooks prepared food in kitchens adjacent to the lunchroom. The meal was usually vegetable soup made of boiled soybeans, sometimes with cornmeal and vegetables (potatoes, carrots, or onions), and a wheat bun. Kai, with approval from the factory management and the agreement of the military commandant, did some trading with the local merchants for more vegetables and occasionally small amounts of meat, though the quantities of the latter dwindled to practically nothing after the first six months. Fortunately the supply of soybeans, which was the primary source of protein for the POWs, continued to be adequate. After lunch the men returned to work; and at the end of the

day the POWs removed their industrial coveralls, placed them
on pegs, and marched back to their prison compound.

Smuggling was not uncommon. Some Americans concealed
Chinese newspapers that they got from their Chinese co-work-
ers and brought them back to the barracks. With an ingenuity
born of the intense desire for news, they were able to get some
idea of war events from the careful study of photographs and
related ideographs in the newspapers. Other men fashioned
metal utensils such as cigarette holders and eating implements
on their machines when the foremen weren't looking and
brought them back to their quarters. Americans also bought
and bartered cigarettes from the Chinese and occasionally were
able to conceal small amounts of food when working at loading
docks and other parts of the factory. As at other POW camps,
the Japanese conducted shakedown inspections and punished
those caught with contraband. But overall, the American factory workers found their job not overly demanding and certainly a welcome break from the tedium of prison life.

For three men the improved food and weather conditions
brought renewed energy and kindled an intense desire for freedom, even though they must have known that they had only
a slim chance of reaching Allied forces from their remote location. In late June 1943, two Marines, J. P. Chastine and Victor
Paliotti, and a Navy man, F. E. Mariongolli, escaped from the
camp. The path they took and how they planned to reach
U.S. or other friendly forces are not known. But sometime
in the first few days after their escape, they were spotted by
Chinese (Mongolian) civil policemen, and according to Japanese
records, in the encounter the POWs killed one of them. The
police took the Americans into custody and turned them over
to the Japanese military authorities. Back at the POW camp,
some of their comrades next saw the three arrive bound in
the back of a truck and showing signs of severe physical abuse.
The Japanese military made them reenact their escape and
then took them to Mukden. They were tried by a Japanese
military court and found guilty of theft (the record is silent
on what they stole) and murder. The sentence of death by
firing squad was carried out on July 30. This escape, the only
one to be attempted at Mukden, resulted in relatively mild
punishment for the Americans in the camp. In retribution
for those who might have had some part in the escape, the

commandant, an aging colonel named Matsuda, ordered the Americans on night watch at the time of the escape confined in the guardhouse on a reduced ration for ten days, and the men in the escapees' barracks were required to sit at attention for long periods during the course of one week.

Though the punishment was light by comparison to that in the Philippines, POW life was not without harassment at Mukden. Discipline was strict and some of the Japanese used their authority in a cruel and abusive manner. One who was particularly disliked by the Americans was Cpl. Eichi Noda, who worked in the camp administrator's office and sometimes functioned as an interpreter in the POW barracks. Like Kai at the factory, Noda had been born and educated to the high school level in the San Francisco Bay area, and he later returned to Japan. At first the POWs were impressed with Noda's American ways and speech and his friendly manner. But it was not long before Noda began using his language skills to turn informer on the Americans, with the result that harsh punishment was meted out to offending POWs. On a number of occasions, though not part of the POW guard force, Noda took the opportunity to beat Americans. For his cruelty and enmity toward Americans, Noda was called "The Sadist" or "The Rat."

In July 1943 the POWs moved out of the labor camp huts that they had been occupying since the previous November into a new building complex. This was one of the rare occasions when the Japanese constructed a large permanent compound specifically to accommodate POWs. The new complex consisted of three two-story brick barracks buildings similar in construction to Japanese army barracks. Besides the living quarters, there were separate buildings for a mess hall, storeroom, boiler room, general workshop, and a bathhouse. For sanitation-conscious Americans the bathhouse and flush toilets were among the most welcome improvements. Enlisted men were allowed to bathe every other day and officers daily. Medical treatment was provided in a hospital building with the capacity to handle 150 patients. The medical equipment, though crude by American standards, equaled that of a Japanese army branch hospital. As in other large camps with medical facilities, the American doctors handled most of the medical treatment. Improvement though it was, the new compound was still a prison. An eight-foot wall enclosed the buildings on four sides with guard towers at the corners, and around the perimeter were electrically charged wires. The Japanese looked forward to keeping their American workers on the job for many years to come.

While most Americans at Mukden did not share their captors' outlook, they were nevertheless reconciled to spending their second Christmas as POWs. It turned out to be a big improvement over the last one. The Manchurian Machine Tool Company had a Christmas party with extra food and sweets for all POWs working at the factory. But the best news came in February 1944, when word was passed that Red Cross supplies were at the railhead.

This shipment, the Mukden POWs' first and only one, came from the second *Gripsholm* exchange. In contrast to the procedures at the other large camps and most of the smaller ones, no individual packages were issued intact to the men at Mukden. Maj. Stanley H. Hankins, the American senior officer, decided on a different approach. With Japanese approval, Hankins issued one or two identical items at a time from the boxes to each POW. The men griped about the system at first, but soon got used to it and began making wagers on what item would be issued next. With this system, which discouraged bartering, the Red Cross supplies—the equivalent of two and one-half 13-pound packages per man—lasted for months. Another morale booster arriving with the food was a supply of shoes and a small amount of other clothing and equipment. The shoes, replacing for many men hand-fashioned wooden clogs, were particularly welcome protection against the rigors of the cold northern winter. Again, a careful and meticulous procedure was worked out by Hankins to assure that the distribution of shoes was made in an equitable manner to all POWs. Unlike food and clothing, the medical supplies were taken over by the Japanese and stored for future use.

★ ★ ★ 2 ★ ★ ★

For the American generals and colonels at Karenko, on the east coast of Formosa, together with the high-ranking British, Dutch, and Australian military officers and civilians, 1943 had been a year of ups and downs, but, in general, conditions improved somewhat over time. During the early months the guards had harassed the officers continually for minor offenses. Some of the POWs attributed this to the failure of their fellow prisoners to make favorable comments on their treatment to a group of visiting Japanese reporters. Others said it was retaliation for the American ill treatment of Japanese in the United States, which was being reported in English-language newspapers furnished occasionally to the POWs. The commandant attempted to get some of the top-ranking officers to write letters of protest about the conditions in American internment camps. They refused, and shortly thereafter a guard, probably more out of a fit of temper than any concern over international relations, gave General Wainwright a black eye. Then in March, with most of the officers at their lowest weight in years—one general weighed what he had weighed when he was fifteen years old—Red Cross supplies arrived at Karenko. The shipment (from the British-Japanese exchange during the previous fall) was a generous one. For about four hundred officers and men it contained over seventeen hundred food parcels, substantial quantities of canned meats, British marching shoes, and over 16,000 pounds of a much-craved commodity: sugar. However, because the shipment had originated in England, it was not accompanied by mail from the United States. The Japanese issued food boxes and other supplies during April and May, and by the end of May men were regaining much of their lost weight and many ill men in the hospital were recovering.

In early June everyone except Generals Wainwright, King, and Moore, and about thirty other Allied officers and civilians of high rank, was moved to a new location at Shirakawa, near the town of Kagi on the opposite side of the island from Karenko. The new camp was an old Taiwan army installation consisting of one-story huts nestled in a small inland valley. In weather warmer than Karenko's, most of the officers worked on a nearby farm plot clearing and planting sweet potatoes and peanuts. In the following weeks the camp commandant, with the unpredictability that many of the Americans had come to expect from their captors, increased the daily issue of rice and made more items available in the POW camp commissary. About the same time harassment by the guards subsided. By the end of June, Quinn, with a cache of over a dozen cans of corned beef, two cans of milk, and ten pounds of sugar, thought that if the Japanese didn't cut the rations, he could get along fairly well for some time in the future. Vance and other bridge players began enjoying regular games under the newly relaxed rules on card playing. Shirakawa was an improvement over Karenko.

It was also better at Muksaq, a tiny village in the northern part of the island, where Wainwright and the top generals and civilians had moved after an intermediate stay near Tamazato to the south. Each top officer at Muksaq had his own chair, table, and a reasonably comfortable cot in buildings situated on a hill overlooking a pleasant valley. Though the men had adequate living quarters and orderlies to take care of their cooking and washing, they still shared some of the same psychological burdens as other POWs: a sense of isolation from the outside world and a deep yearning for letters from family and friends.

The men at Shirakawa shared these feelings but also suffered from other personal difficulties. By the end of 1943 they had been confined together, nearly always at very close quarters, in three locations. While this provided an opportunity for comradeship, the close and continuous contact also led to frayed nerves, hypercriticalness, and resentments. Such attitudes ranged from the petty to the serious: avoidance of the man who inflicted the same old stories or endless lectures on anyone who would listen; muttered charges by some colonels that the generals didn't labor in the fields; and the feeling by some that certain members of the American camp hierarchy were doing more for themselves than for those they were supposed to represent. These personal conflicts, common in one form or another in nearly all POW camps, were probably more pronounced in the senior officers' camp because these men had relatively light work demands and more time to think about their real or imagined grievances. But when Christmas arrived, as in more normal times most ill feelings disappeared; and with what one colonel considered the best meal since he had become a POW, and with entertainment and games, the year closed on a convivial note.

In early 1944 the long-awaited news from home arrived. In February a truck arrived at the camp with bags of mail. At Shirakawa censorship was not as great a source of delay as it was in the large Philippine camps. Quinn was one of the first to get letters. During late February and early March he got a total of twenty-two letters and cards. Others would receive mail over the next few weeks. Though their Red Cross packages (from the second *Gripsholm* exchange) were once again slow in arriving, the mail was more than enough to boost the men's morale higher than it had been for months.

★ ★ ★ 3 ★ ★ ★

The first months of 1943 found Marine enlisted men and American civilian construction workers at the Kiangwan POW camp near Shanghai hard at work on a long-term project which would demand most of their energies until mid-1944. Before work began, the assistant camp commandant, with Ishihara as interpreter, told assembled POWs that they were to build an Imperial Japanese Army recreation area. Its major feature was to be a long man-made hill. Soon between eight hundred and one thousand men were daily shoveling earth into carts, pushing the carts to the side of the hill, and dumping them. Ishihara assumed personal control of the project and drove the men to meet increasing quotas of earth to be moved. As the 500-foot-long mound of earth grew—it would eventually reach a height of over 30 feet—the Americans, ever fond of nicknames, christened the project "Mount Fuji" after Japan's most sacred mountain. But soon some of the experienced Marines concluded (correctly) that "Mount Fuji" was not a decorative feature at all, but an essential part of a military rifle range. The huge earth mound, they surmised, would furnish the usual backstop for bullets fired at a line of targets. To the very end the Japanese never acknowledged that the project had any other purpose than a park.

Hard labor on "Mount Fuji" notwithstanding, the Americans at Kiangwan had a better life than a large majority of their comrades elsewhere. Most of the men at Kiangwan had defended Wake Island together, and friendships forged there in prewar days provided a feeling of mutual support and continuity to their lives. The food rations supplied by the Japanese were augmented by a more generous allocation of Red Cross supplies than at any of the other camps in which Americans were held. Those with money could get some extra food through black market dealings with Chinese workers in and around the camp. When not at work the more energetic men played softball, volleyball, and basketball, weather permitting. Interbarracks rivalry was intense. A library of about four thousand books housed in a separate barracks was very popular. The men's health, comparatively speaking, was good. The tropical scourges dysentery, beriberi, and malaria were practically nonexistent and an excellent American medical staff kept other diseases in check. Their efforts were enhanced by the support of Doctor Shindo, the Japanese medical officer for the camp. In addition to his medical role, Shindo provided a steadying influence on other Japanese camp staff and, on occasion, interceded on behalf of the POWs. Also helpful to morale were two radios secretly operated by Americans, one by Lt. John F. Kinney, a Wake Island Marine pilot, and the other by Marine Sergeant F. B. Mohr, and later taken over by two Marine sergeants, B. F. Carrrachi and M. J. Sousek. Rumors based on U.S. news broadcasts kept the men at Kiangwan fairly current on the war's progress.

The ninety-six civilian construction workers who had been kept at work on the defenses of Wake Island for a year and a half were less fortunate. Throughout most of the time they had no knowledge of the war nor did the U.S. government know that they were still on the island. By early fall of 1943 the U.S. Navy controlled the seas around Wake Island, and on the sixth of October, American warships shelled the island heavily. On the following day Rear Adm. S. Sakaibara, commander of the island's defenses, ordered the execution of all the POWs. He would later claim that he had received orders to do so from higher authority. The order was carried out that same day. On a beach in the northern part of the island, in quasi-ceremonial fashion, the Japanese forced the prisoners to sit in a single rank along the beach with their backs to the sea. Then, after blindfolding each man and tying his hands behind him, the platoon commander reported that all was ready. Upon the order of the company commander, who had just arrived on the island that day, the firing squad began its work. After the massacre was completed, the Japanese buried the Americans on the beach where they had been executed.

Though not meeting the terrible fate of those they had left at Wake, some of the men at Kiangwan were punished brutally in the only major clash with the Japanese authorities at that camp. Found guilty of black market activity, two officers and several enlisted men were subjected to the water cure, an interrogation technique in which a person is tied up and water is poured in his mouth until he chokes or loses consciousness or gives the proper responses. All the men subjected to this brutal treatment survived but never forgot their experiences. Meanwhile, nearly five hundred men who had been transferred to Japan the previous summer had joined the growing number of Americans working in the Japanese homeland.

10

UNDER THE RISING SUN

Early 1943–May 1944
Japan

★ ★ ★ 1 ★ ★ ★

Early 1943 found most of the American POWs in Japan concentrated on the main island, Honshu. The largest group was in the Osaka/Kobe area, with other Americans in prison camps on Honshu and on the island of Kyushu to the south.

The first winter exacted a heavy toll on the nearly fourteen hundred men who arrived from the Philippines on the *Nagato Maru* in November 1942. They had been assigned to three camps—Umeda, Yodogawa, and Tanagawa—in the Osaka area. For the starved and disease-ridden men, the hard work, lack of food, and bitter-cold weather at the three camps were life-sapping. Conditions at the Umeda camp were about the worst. Rations, insufficient from the time of arrival, were further reduced in March 1943 when the Japanese Army turned over the food-supply responsibility to Nippon Tsuun Kaisha, a railroad forwarding company. Pushed hard by Japanese overseers, the POWs, fingers and toes numbed with cold, loaded and unloaded freight cars without machinery for ten hours a day. As elsewhere, the Japanese wanted the maximum number of men on the job. An enlisted Japanese medical attendant consistently sent ill men out to work despite requests by two American medical officers to keep them in the barracks.

Malnourished and with bodily resistance at the lowest ebb, more and more men succumbed to dysentery, beriberi, and pneumonia, until by late spring about 115 of the 458 who had arrived had died, about one out of four.

Working conditions in the steel mill at Yodogawa, like those in the rail yards, taxed the weakened Americans to the limits of their endurance. While some men sweated handling hot sheets of steel, others shivered and coughed on other jobs in the drafty buildings with their cold concrete floors and soot-filled air. Pneumonia became a frequent cause of death. While not usually lethal, severe foot problems aggravated many. In early months the Japanese had taken some of the men with the worst foot cases resulting from the cold and poor circulation or beriberi or a combination of the two and sent them to the hospital in Osaka. Noting that few men returned from the hospital, the ailing Americans refused to go there, fearing amputations or death. Even with their feet swollen and their skin and flesh peeling away, the men preferred to doctor themselves with the meager dressings available. Besides the physical discomforts, hunger was ever present. On one occasion Captain Coleman saw a man kill and eat a rat. Requests for more food by the American senior officer, Maj. W. B. Reardon from Albuquerque, New Mexico, had no effect. With no opportunities to steal food in the factory, some of the starving POWs found ways to buy it from guards and civilian workers. Some of the Japanese workers seemed sympathetic toward the Americans. In an act of kindness which he never forgot, a Japanese woman gave William Spizziro a bowl of rice. This small gesture helped get him through a tough period. Many others could not physically endure the conditions, and by the end of May eighty-seven men had died, of the four hundred assigned to the steel mill.

At Tanagawa, where POWs dug and hauled earth to create dry docks for submarines, sixty-nine died of the original five hundred. In addition to death from disease and malnutrition, two men died as a result of surgery by inept medical students at the hospital in Osaka.

Medicine and bandages were always in short supply. When Red Cross shipments were distributed in limited quantities in Osaka camps, the medical supplies were withheld. In March 1943, Chief Boatswain's Mate Philip E. Sanders, U.S.N., saw forty cases of such supplies arrive at the headquarters camp for the Osaka group. Even though American medical personnel capable of using the medicines and equipment were present in the branch camps, Colonel Murata, commander of the Osaka group camps, would permit only a trickle of the vital supplies through. His action and similar actions by other Japanese POW camp commanders probably stemmed from blind adherence to the Japanese army and navy regulations requiring them to maintain a one-year reserve of medical equipment and supplies. Once again, traditional Japanese frugality and strict adherence to orders worked to the detriment and death of American prisoners.

With the arrival of spring, as had happened at Mukden, Manchuria, the death wave subsided in the Osaka camps and the survivors took on a little more hope. Conditions at the Yodogawa Steel Company camp improved dramatically, if briefly, during the summer of 1943. In early July Sgt. Maj. Hirokazu Tanaka took over as camp commander. One of his first acts was to inspect the POW kitchen, after which he expressed displeasure at the paucity of food. The action he then took amazed the American senior officer, Major Reardon, who recorded in his journal: "The C.O. started a strike. He told the factory that unless there was more food, there would be no more work. He said, 'One-half ration, one-half day's work.'" The factory came through with more food, but a month later Colonel Murata replaced Tanaka with a new camp commander. Reardon attributed the sudden and premature relief as the result of pressure from the steel mill administration, which was displeased with the commander's attitude toward POWs. Reardon would later recall Tanaka as the fairest Japanese he encountered in prison life.

On the day after Tanaka's relief, an American soldier at the Tanagawa camp escaped from the POW compound but was recaptured. Attempted escape in the Japanese home islands, with virtually no reasonable chance of gaining freedom, was a rarity then and would continue to be so for the remainder of the war. Because of this, Colonel Murata considered the incident a reflection on his professional honor. To cover the "disgrace" to him personally, Murata ordered Doctor Nosu on his staff to give the American a "severe punishment" by drug injections. The POW died in a truck en route to Ichioka Hospital in Osaka from overdose of drugs. Murata's cover-up of the escape was effective. He remained as chief of the Osaka group camps, which reached nearly twenty in number, for over two more years.

South of Osaka, Zentsuji, the Prisoner of War Bureau's "model camp" and headquarters for a growing number of camps in the southern part of Honshu, was assigned an additional mission. In Japan, as they had in the camps in the Philippines and elsewhere, the authorities faced the nagging problem of how to apply Tojo's "No work—no food" policy to officers, who they knew were not required to work under the Geneva Convention but under the strict Japanese code must not remain idle. While at Davao Penal Colony, and later at Cabanatuan, field commanders made officers work on a number of occasions, the Prisoner of War Bureau decided that in Japan officers would be used as supervisors only on POW industrial details. Beginning early in 1943 the Bureau transferred those not needed for this purpose to Zentsuji. The earliest and largest of these transfers were from Tanagawa and Umeda. These men were joined later in the year by officers from other Osaka group camps. The relatively well treated prisoners already at Zentsuji were appalled at the condition of the first groups when they marched in—dirty and lice-ridden, many emaciated. After a three-week quarantine during which they were deloused, bathed, and issued new clothing, the newcomers were quartered with their more fortunate comrades from Guam and other parts of the Far East. In addition to American POWs, the Japanese had over time brought in a number of prisoners from other Allied nations, making the overall camp population quite international in its composition. Captain Coleman, arriving from Yodogawa, found himself assigned to a room with twenty-eight officers. In the room were two Dutch captains taken prisoner in Java, three British captains captured in Singapore, one Canadian officer who had been captured by a submarine after his commercial ship was sunk in the Indian Ocean, two Australians, two American officers from Guam, and an officer who had been on the USS *Houston* when it was sunk in the Java Sea. With the last arrivals the total number of POWs in the camp was in excess of seven hundred, mostly officers. It would remain an "officers' camp" until the end of the war.

Though the quality of life in Zentsuji dropped off somewhat after the arrival of the Philippine POWs, it was still better than at other camps in Japan. The barracks were cold and the food was minimal, but the work details for officers were usually light and when off duty the officers remained in the barracks compound, where they played cards, walked, discussed the war, or participated in educational and recreational activities which were rarely possible in other camps in Japan. Conversation about world affairs centered around the information contained in copies of the two English-language newspapers published in Japan, which the camp commandant provided to the POWs from time to time. Though they were obviously propaganda, the newspapers accurately reported locations of major military actions, so that discerning POWs could determine with varying degrees of accuracy the progress of the war. For some, speculation on such matters was not enough. K. C. Emerson, who started studying Spanish and Russian but tired of it after a few weeks, was impressed by the mental versatility of his fellow officers. Mike Ushakoff taught Russian to Steve Farris and Fred Yeager, who became very proficient in the language. Nathan Lowe had been a language teacher before the war and compiled a dictionary in several languages. Burt Backstrom taught commercial baking and Al Washer taught geology. These and other classes were started when someone expressed an interest in learning about a particular subject and the teacher volunteered to teach the course. The Japanese had transferred former ambassador to Japan Joseph Grew's library to the camp, where it was later augmented by a shipment of books from the Red Cross. The library with over two thousand volumes contributed greatly to the mental well-being of the prisoners, as did the Sunday night's entertainment—singers, minstrel shows, or dramatic performances.

The state of health at Zentsuji was above average for POW camps. Capt. H. J. Van Peenan, U.S. Navy Medical Corps, who was the senior American doctor in the small medical facility in the camp, did much to make it so. Lieutenant Saito, the Japanese medical officer, was very unsympathetic to the POWs and kept most of the Red Cross medicines and supplies in storage. Through courage and perseverance Van Peenan managed to get enough supplies to perform twenty-four major surgical operations while he was camp surgeon, and his efforts along with the other doctors' kept the death rate at a low level.

★ ★ ★ 2 ★ ★ ★

The Japanese did make a concession to the medical needs of POWs. In 1943 they established a hospital for seriously ill persons at Shinagawa, near Tokyo. The hospital was actually a building converted for this purpose with a barracks which would hold about three hundred men. The hospital itself had an operating room, an X-ray machine, a dental room, and a pathology laboratory. Though the Japanese may have intended it to serve a larger area in Japan, most of the patients—a diverse assemblage of Americans, British, Canadians, Dutch, and Java-nese—came from the Tokyo area and camps in central Japan. An American and British medical staff worked with extreme difficulty under the supervision of a Japanese army doctor and a medical master sergeant. The American physicians fought a continual battle of wits with the two men, who never let them forget that they were prisoners first and doctors second. Though the quality of treatment and conditions at Shinagawa were far from what the POW doctors would have liked them to be, they were probably better than those existing at most branch camps and in Japanese army and civilian hospitals.

Elsewhere in the Tokyo/Yokohama industrial area, Ameri-cans who had arrived in Japan during 1942 were confined in camps at Omori and Kawasaki. Omori was the headquarters camp for the Tokyo group and the commander of the camp had his offices there. The relatively small number of Americans at Omori during 1943 (most of the prisoners there at the time were British) would recall the extremely rigid discipline and harsh punishment meted out by the commandant and his assis-tant, Sergeant Watanabe. Watanabe had a particular dislike for officers. Problem prisoners from other Tokyo camps, in-cluding some Allied doctors whom the Japanese found "uncoop-erative," were sent to Omori for "training."

The regime was also strict at Kawasaki, south of Tokyo, where about three hundred Americans worked at a nearby steel foundry or chemical plant or handled freight at the Kawa-saki railhead. In addition to being harsh to the Americans, "Little Hitler," as the commandant was called by the POWs, allowed more pilfering by his subordinates than occurred at most camps. Japanese staff at Kawasaki took over half of the Red Cross packages that arrived at the camp in late 1943.

Farther south near Yokohama was a POW camp, Ofuna, whose function was markedly different from the work camps'. Here the Imperial Japanese Navy interrogated selected Allied POWs, mostly U.S. Navy fliers downed in the southwest Pacific, along with some Air Corps pilots, submariners, and naval personnel of other ranks. The Japanese did not consider Ofuna a permanent camp so men there were not reported as POWs. Lt. Stefen A. Nyarady arrived at Ofuna on Christmas Eve 1943 after his plane was shot down over Rabaul, New Britain. Immediately after his arrival the Japanese questioned him about his ship and his actions. If he didn't respond properly, the interrogators hit him with a baseball bat. The Japanese gave POWs at Ofuna one cup of rice and some thin soup three times a day and, not as at the work camps, kept most of them in separate cells on a long cellblock. Nyarady endured nine months of "interrogation and intimidation," as he termed it, before he was transferred to Omori. He and others who had accompanied him to the new camp had expected it to be a great improvement. It was not. Nyarady became a frequent victim of Watanabe's wrath against officers.

Ill treated as he was, Nyarady was more fortunate than hundreds of other American fliers downed in the Pacific beginning in 1943 and continuing until the end of the war. He was among a relative few who got to Japan. Many probably met the fate of an unnamed American pilot who was downed near Salamaua, New Guinea, in early 1943 and whose death was described in the diary of a Japanese soldier who wrote: "He is apparently resigned. The precaution is taken of surrounding him with guards with fixed bayonets, but he remains calm. He even stretches out his neck and is very brave. When I put myself in the prisoner's place and think that in one more minute it will be good-bye to this world, although the daily bombings have filled me with hate, ordinary human feelings make me pity him. The Tai [unit] commander has drawn his favorite sword. It is the famous Osamune sword which he showed us at the observation post. It glitters in the light and sends a cold shiver down my spine. He taps the prisoner's neck lightly with the back of the blade and then raises it above his head with both arms and brings it down with a sweep." Some died less quickly of starvation and beatings while others, selected for interrogation in Japan, died along with their captors aboard torpedoed ships en route.

After the fall of the Philippines, the Japanese took few Army and Marine ground troops prisoner except for a short period of battlefield interrogation. Virtually none were shipped to Japan. During most of the war, the U.S. Army took prisoners for the same purpose when they could and, on occasion, sent some to the United States. In the final days of the war the Japanese soldiers' attitude toward becoming a POW changed, and thousands surrendered and entered U.S. Army prison stockades.

★ ★ ★ 3 ★ ★ ★

As military reverses began to place greater demands on Japan's far-flung armed forces, the Prisoner of War Bureau continued to transfer Americans and other Allied POWs to Japan to replenish their labor pool. Three hundred and fifty men were transferred from Shanghai during 1943. Most of these men were assigned to camps in the Osaka group. A larger number of Americans left the Philippines during the summer and early fall of 1943.

The first shipment, 500 men (10 officers and 490 enlisted men), boarded ship in Manila harbor late in July. They and others leaving the Philippines after them probably had mixed emotions about the move. In 1942 conditions at Cabanatuan were terrible and anyplace would be an improvement. But by 1943 most surviving Americans (those at the tougher airfield construction camps would be an exception) had settled in and were accustomed to the life and routines in the Philippine camps. Change in and of itself was not necessarily attractive to them, and despite General MacArthur's seemingly slow progress, the Philippines were, after all, first in line for liberation. But the POW had little choice. A few men were able to substitute for each other or dodge a shipment by exaggerated illness, but the rest, as they had since capture, accepted the transfer as unavoidable and hoped for the best.

The Americans arrived at Moji, Japan, on August 9, 1943,

Japanese officer and guards conducting General King's surrender representatives to meet with the Japanese commander, April 9, 1942. Colonel E. C. Williams wearing the military sun helmet, with Major M. H. Hurt on his left.
SIGNAL CORPS

Discussing surrender terms, April 9, 1942. Facing Japanese Colonel Nakayama: Colonel E. C. Williams, General E. P. King, Major Wade Cothran, and Major A. C. Tisdelle.
SIGNAL CORPS

Defeated Americans on the "Death March," April 1942.
NATIONAL ARCHIVES

Unknown Americans at Camp O'Donnell, circa April 1942.
SIGNAL CORPS

Americans surrendering outside tunnel entrance on Corregidor, May 7, 1942. SIGNAL CORPS

POW garden plot at Cabanatuan, 1942–1943. Man in center is Major J. S. Neary, who died in Japan in February 1945 after the sinking of the Oryoku Maru. SIGNAL CORPS

Cabanatuan, 1943. Two of the carabao carts that hauled food (and smuggled money and notes) to the camp.
SIGNAL CORPS

POWs on their way to freedom after the Ranger raid on Cabanatuan, February 1945. NATIONAL ARCHIVES

The Oryoku Maru *on fire and sinking, December 15, 1944.*
U.S. NAVY

Freed Cabanatuan POWs celebrate after reaching safety, February 1945. SIGNAL CORPS

POWs at Bilibid prison await movement after arrival of troops of the 37th Infantry Division, February 1945. SIGNAL CORPS

Officers at Rokuroshi, Japan, divide air-dropped supplies, September 1945. SIGNAL CORPS

Camp Omori, near Tokyo, as it appeared from an American aircraft, September 1945. NATIONAL ARCHIVES

American and British POWs at Omori greet rescuers arriving by sea, September 1945. NATIONAL ARCHIVES

after a very uncomfortable voyage but, surprisingly, with no deaths en route. From Moji they traveled by train to Fukuoka Camp 17. This camp on the island of Kyushu, the southernmost of the Japanese islands, was near the town of Omuta, forty miles south of the town of Fukuoka. In 1943 the Fukuoka group consisted of some POW camps on Kyushu and others on the southern end of the island of Honshu. Americans from Japan and Wake Island had been at two of the camps on Kyushu, Camp 1 near Nagasaki and Camp 3 near Yawata, since 1942.

In an unusual display of emotion, villagers stoned the Americans as they marched through the camp gates. The POWs later deduced that the Japanese were fearful that employment of Americans by the Mitsui Coal Mining Company would cause layoffs of local workers. Regardless of the effect on the Japanese job market, the Americans (joined later by British, Dutch, and Australian POWs) labored eleven to twelve hours per day with thirty minutes off at lunchtime. The work was divided by nationalities: Americans and Australians dug the coal; Dutchmen shoveled it into stalls near the camp; and British prisoners sweated in the zinc foundry. Work in the mine shafts, loading the trucks below ground and hauling the coal to the surface, was hard and hazardous. An underground stream ran through the mine and prisoners were always faced with the possibility of cave-ins and blast injuries. Fortunately, among the prisoners was an experienced American coal miner who instructed them on safety hazards and preventive measures. Despite these dangers, and though there were many injuries, no Americans died as a result of mine accidents. This record would not have been established had it not been for the surgical skills of Capt. Thomas H. Hewlett, an American Army doctor, and other Allied physicians who worked on the broken limbs and torn bodies of the POWs with dental novocaine as an anesthetic and sharpened table knives as scalpels.

When not working, POWs at Fukuoka 17 found little to make life more bearable. The camp commandant, Lt. K. Uri, an arrogant disciplinarian, ran a very strict camp, with a Japanese military guard force which constantly enforced the Japanese disciplinary code with frequent beatings and other physical punishment. The interpreter for the Mitsui mining company, an American-born Japanese who went by the name of "Riverside"—the California city he was raised in—was at times an informer and grew to be strongly disliked by most of the Americans.

The senior American officer was Maj. John R. Mamerow, but for most of the American POWs and others in the camp, the influence of Navy Lt. E. N. Little was the most strongly felt. Early, the Japanese appointed Little as mess officer, and in discharging this responsibility he antagonized many POWs. Aware of the often overwhelming desire of the POWs to get more food, sometimes at the expense of others, Little set up very strict measures in the mess hall. To prevent men from going through twice, he would personally stand in the mess line and see that each man's POW number was punched on a board. He also established an American guard force to see that men didn't steal from the kitchen. In some cases of jumping the line the punishment was denial of a meal or a beating by the American guard detail, which the POWs christened the Goon Squad. In December of 1943 a Marine corporal was turned in—many thought by Lieutenant Little—to Lieutenant Uri for stealing. He was held in the guardhouse without food for over a month, at the end of which period he died of starvation. Captain Hewlett examined the body and estimated that the weight of the deceased had gone down from about 170 pounds to around 60 pounds at the time of his death. Little remained in his position as mess officer until the end of the war, during which time he was said to have turned in two other Americans for stealing food, one of whom was bayoneted and the other beaten to death by the Japanese. Little was one of the few ex-POWs tried after the war for actions against fellow prisoners. Ultimately he was cleared of the charges against him.

In October 1943 eight hundred more Americans from the Philippines arrived in Japan aboard the *Corral Maru*. They, like most of those arriving before and after them, were soon working in the steel, mining, and transportation activities which were vital to the Japanese war effort. Over four hundred of the new arrivals went to two camps in the Osaka group. Most went to Hirohata, sixty miles west of Osaka, where they fired the furnaces, broke the slag, and laid railroad tracks for the Seitetsu Steel Company, while others unloaded and loaded ships at the docks near the plant. A smaller detail joined British

POWs at Sakura-jima, near Osaka, where they became shipfitters and laborers in the Osaka Ironworks, a factory which produced steel for Japanese destroyers and fuel tankers. About 350 Americans took a long train ride to Niigata, a seaport and industrial city on the west coast of Honshu. POWs working out of this camp, one of the Tokyo group, labored in the Niigata Ironworks, coaled ships, and stevedored at the docks. As it had been for their predecessors, the first winter in Japan was a hard one for the men arriving on the *Corral Maru,* but with an additional year to adjust to POW life, the death rate was not as high as it was for the 1942 arrivals.

★ ★ ★ **4** ★ ★ ★

Red Cross supplies from the second *Gripsholm* exchange helped make Christmas of 1943 a little brighter for some of the Americans in Japan, but once again the quantities and timing of distribution varied widely from camp to camp. At Zentsuji individual boxes were issued to each man and many POWs received letters and "next-of-kin boxes" from family or friends. Along with very useful personal items these packages occasionally contained some odd selections such as a strop razor without the strop, or a football. At Umeda the packages came late for Christmas but were later issued on an individual basis to the men working in the freight yards. The distribution to the Americans at Hirohata and Fukuoka 17 was probably typical of the camps serving Japanese industry. At Hirohata thirty-two Red Cross individual packages were distributed to over four hundred men, while at Fukuoka 17 the Red Cross supplies were not issued until early 1944 and then as rewards to coal-mine workers for good attendance and production. In some camps the Japanese forced men to sign for boxes that were never issued.

While the packages sent by the various Red Cross societies of Allied countries were the most visible form of aid to POWs in Japan, other agencies attempted to better the lot of Allied prisoners by visiting the camps where they were held. These included representatives of the International Red Cross, members of the Swiss legation—Switzerland was the "protecting power" for the United States under the Geneva Convention—as well as officers of the Swedish legation and the Vatican dele-

gate to Japan.   During 1943 the Japanese authorized eighteen
visits to various prison camps.

Arranging for and conducting such visits was a frustrating
job.   Problems encountered by the Red Cross representative,
Dr. Paul Paravicini (who had made the first visit to Zentsuji
by a Westerner, in 1943), and later his assistant, Max Pestalozzi,
were typical.   The Japanese required that the prospective visi-
tor apply for permission to go to specific camps and locations
but refused to give more than general locations of the prison
camps.   Consequently, many visits were to some of the same
camps in the Osaka, Fukuoka, and Tokyo groups, leaving out
a number of camps within these groups and other camps not
part of the larger groups.   Often the neutral representative
did not know until the very last moment whether the visiting
permit was to be granted or not, and who would be permitted
to go.   The duration of a camp visit was usually two hours—
one hour for conversation with the camp commandant (usually
a lecture by that official), thirty minutes for visiting the living
quarters, and thirty minutes for an interview in the presence
of Japanese officers with a POW senior officer.   No communication with other prisoners was authorized.   Camp commandants
frequently refused to reply to questions put to them and explained as their reason that they had not received authority
to give such information.

Despite these difficulties, the Swiss legation and the International Red Cross continued to ask the Japanese Foreign Ministry
for increased opportunities to visit camps in Japan, Formosa,
and China and for more open access to POWs.   These attempts
met with little success.   Meanwhile, the Japanese continued
to deny all requests to visit camps in the Philippines and other
conquered territories, a position which would remain un-
changed for the duration of the war.

From the POWs' standpoint, the visits had little effect.
Because of the restricted nature of the inspections, the POWs
at the camp—except for the camp leadership—often were unaware that a neutral observer had been at the camp.   When
the Japanese did announce a visit, the only benefit to the POWs
might be a slight increase in a meal that day.

But if the visits did little for the American POWs themselves,
they did provide some benefits for their relatives and friends
in the United States.   The American Red Cross had early in

the war begun the publication of the *Prisoner of War Bulletin,* which was sent to next-of-kin and which included available information on American POWs and civilian internees in Europe and the Pacific. The *Bulletin* provided accounts of efforts to send relief supplies to POWs in the Far East (both *Gripsholm* trips were covered). Procedures for writing to POWs were outlined, and excerpts from letters received from POWs were reprinted in the publication. Also included were reports of visits by International Red Cross representatives to the camps. Among these were 1943 visits to the Osaka and Fukuoka group camps as well as to Shinagawa and Omori. While these reports described camp conditions in the best possible light (critical reports would have caused immediate cessation of camp visits), they did meet an urgent need among POW families and friends for some information on where the camps were and what they were like.

The *Prisoner of War Bulletin* reported briefly on the papal delegate Monsignor Paul Marella's visits to POW camps in the Tokyo area early in 1943. According to Marella the prisoners (American, British, and Dutch) were "moderately well treated." Marella observed that the men wanted books, and he sent some to them later along with some games. In June of 1943 Tokyo radio described Marella's visits to camps in the Osaka group and paraphrased the delegate's remarks in glowing terms:

> There might be many people in the world who are not acquainted with the real state of things in Japan, but God knows everything. Japan's fair treatment of the war prisoners will soon be recognized throughout the world. He expressed special admiration of the care given by Japanese authorities concerning the food for the captives and particularly at the supply of cod liver oil. He further said that he would report to the Vatican on Japan's good treatment of the war prisoners and that such appropriate an action being taken by Japan would surely become the foundation for final victory of Japan.

Whether Marella's comments were misrepresented or not, his views expressed after the war differed from those of most Western observers. The papal delegate sharply contrasted the Occidental and Japanese attitudes toward POWs. They despised this class of person. Japanese officers told him that what they were doing for POWs was absolutely one-sided, because the enemy would never have any Japanese POWs. He felt that apart from atrocities and abuse, the condition of the POWs in respect to quarters and clothing was that of the common people of Japan. The discipline was that of the Japanese Army, which was extremely hard. The Japanese standard of living had always been lower than that in the United States and European countries, and during the war it dropped even more. The people had almost nothing to eat and could buy little clothing. Housing and working conditions were far below the standards in the West. Marella concluded that such deprivations, while unsupportable and cruel for Allied POWs, had little effect on the Japanese people because they were used to them.

★ ★ ★ 5 ★ ★ ★

A deprivation unique to the POWs, and one which they found difficult to accept, was their limited ability to communicate with families and friends. In this respect some Americans in Japan fared better than those elsewhere. At Zentsuji and a few of the Osaka and Fukuoka group camps, men were on occasion allowed to write letters rather than fill out the word-restricted postcards commonly permitted. (Kiangwan, China, and Mukden, Manchuria, were two other camps where exceptions were made.) Early in the war Americans writing to POWs in the Far East could write letters of any length, but in late 1943 the Japanese informed Allied governments that personal messages must not exceed twenty-five words and must be typed. Though these requirements were probably imposed to cut the time necessary to censor, the speed of this operation continued to be dependent upon the attitudes and abilities of individual censors and their camp commandants.

The bulk of the U.S. mail to and from POWs in the Far East was transported on the two *Gripsholm* exchanges. Later in the war, U.S. Army Air Corps transport planes flew U.S. mail to Tehran, Iran. The Russian government transported the mail by railroad across the Soviet Union through Siberia and from there it was taken by ship to Japan. The route through the U.S.S.R. did not function regularly but did provide some additional mail service until discontinued when Russia declared war on Japan.

Beginning in the spring of 1943 all mail for Allied POWs was directed to the Tokyo prisoner-of-war post office located at the Shinagawa prison camp. American and British officers and enlisted men assigned by the Japanese to man the post office had a most difficult job. They had to sort thousands of letters, many with incomplete identification of the addressee (a dozen Henry Walkers could be POWs in almost as many locations). This, coupled with incomplete, inaccurate, and outdated POW lists, resulted in many letters being placed in the dead letter files, where some remained indefinitely.

In 1943 an American-born Japanese named Uno conceived the idea of a daily scheduled radio broadcast by POWs to their families back home. He hoped to build large listening audiences in America, Australia, and Great Britain and then add Japanese propaganda into the program format. He obtained approval from imperial army headquarters for the project and chose a private-school building in northern Tokyo to house the POW staff. Using questionnaires that thousands of POWs had been required to fill out after capture, Uno selected fifteen Allied POWs and had them shipped to Tokyo in December 1943. Among these was an Australian major who had been a radio commentator, a British lieutenant who had been an actor, an American civilian who had been a nightclub master of ceremonies, and a number of other POWs who had some skills related to the broadcast or journalistic fields. Uno gathered the group together soon after their arrival and told them of their mission. When a New Zealander named Williams declared that he would be guilty of treason and asked that he be returned to his former camp, he was promptly dragged from the room, beaten, and taken away. Though Williams's ultimate fate is not known, the incident left the remaining POWs in a cooperative mood.

Soon they were participating in a daily program, *Humanity Calls*. The program was broadcast from the studios of Radio Tokyo in the downtown area and followed a standard format. After a few bars of music, the announcer would say, for example, "This is *Humanity Calls*, bringing you messages from your missing men in Japanese prison camps. We know that when you hear these messages, you will help us by relaying them to those for whom they are intended. The first one today is from Lieutenant B—— in the Shanghai camp." A message would then be read. After a dozen or so messages, one of the POWs would play a piano, guitar, or accordion selection. Next there would be a sequence usually written by one of the POWs in which two men would talk about their experiences in camp—gardening, mending their clothes, arrival of Red Cross supplies—or a discussion of postwar plans. Then more messages would be read, this time followed by Japanese propaganda. Sometimes the Americans were required to read prepared scripts which extolled the culture of the Japanese in an attempt to counter the view of Americans and Europeans that Japanese were brutes and barbarians. Less often, fortunately for the POWs, they had to make directed comments adverse to the Allied cause. The Japanese apparently felt that the program was successful because some months later another half-hour segment, *The Postman Calls*, was added. The programs continued until the end of the war, during which time thousands of POW messages were read. In the United States the program got mixed reviews. The *Prisoner of War Bulletin* published a letter by an American shortwave radio operator asking whether there was any objection to his relaying messages that he received from Japan to the prisoner's family. The *Bulletin* replied that the U.S. government authorities had informed them that no trust could be placed on the reliability of the reports from Axis nations broadcasting information about American prisoners. Furthermore, the *Bulletin* stated that the War Department monitored all shortwave broadcasts from enemy territories and usually advised the next-of-kin as to whether the broadcasts were reliable. The article closed with the admonition that no mention should be made of enemy broadcasts in letters to POWs because such letters would be rejected by the U.S. censor. Despite the official opinion, a number of shortwave radio operators along the West Coast of the United States received and relayed thousands of these messages, most of which later proved to be genuine.

The POW programs were only a small part of Radio Tokyo's world broadcasts, the dominant theme of which was a continued assertion that despite reverses, Japan would remain preeminent in the Far East. Actually, on the far-flung Pacific battlegrounds the Japanese Imperial Army and Navy were finding it increasingly difficult to stop the advancing forces of General MacArthur and Admiral Nimitz.

In March, Col. Tadashi Odashima, assistant director of the Prisoner of War Bureau, arrived in Manila after a trip which had included stops in China, Malaya, and Java. Odashima conferred with Gen. Shiyoku Kou, chief of POW camps in the Philippines. Kou told Odashima that the situation in the Philippines was very tense and that the POWs should be moved from there. Upon his return to Tokyo, Odashima briefed the chief of the Prisoner of War Bureau; and in the weeks that followed, plans were developed to evacuate prisoners of war from the Philippines. The Japanese actions were well timed. In the spring of 1944, with MacArthur's long campaign in New Guinea in its final stages, U.S. strategic plans for the Pacific called for American forces under Adm. Chester W. Nimitz to seize the Mariana Islands in June and for General MacArthur to invade Mindanao in November.

PART III

Dashed Hopes for Freedom

June 1944–
January 1945

11

VOYAGES NORTH AND DISASTER

June–December 1944
The Philippines—Japan

★ ★ ★ 1 ★ ★ ★

On June 6, 1944 (Philippine time), as thousands of Allied troops clambered out of landing craft onto the beaches of Normandy, 1,239 POWs on Mindanao found themselves tied to one another and blindfolded, aboard trucks headed for Davao harbor. Their captors were taking no chances on another escape like the one that had occurred less than three months before, when six men on a work detail overpowered their guards and reached freedom with the guerrillas.* Sore and weary, the POWs along with Japanese passengers loaded aboard the *Yashu Maru*, where the Japanese issued them individual Red Cross packages, the remainder of the second *Gripsholm* shipment which along with mail had arrived earlier in the year. Munching on their precious Red Cross food, some of the men talked about the possibility that the sick would be exchanged. Most men discounted this old rumor and hoped that the voyage north would be as good as the one that many of them had taken to Mindanao in 1942.

This was not to be. One night several days after departure, while the ship was at the port of Zamboanga, Lt. Col. McGee,

---

* The men were Capt. Mark M. Wohlfeld and Lts. A. T. Bukovinsky, M. H. Campbell, J. D. Haburne, J. E. McClure, and H. C. Watson.

acting on a carefully thought-out plan, dove into the sea, avoided being hit by a hail of bullets, and made it ashore. In Zamboanga, a city familiar to him from prewar duty there, McGee narrowly evaded capture and finally made contact with guerrillas and freedom. His good fortune cost the Americans on the *Yashu Maru* some of theirs. The Japanese, furious, ordered the POWs below severely limited access to the deck, and nailed boards and positioned life rafts along the deck railing as barriers. On the following night, undaunted, Lt. Donald H. Wills climbed over the barriers within a few feet of a careless guard and, in an incredible show of endurance, swam nearly four miles to shore. As McGee did, Wills ultimately joined guerrilla forces and survived the war. For this escape the Japanese reduced the rations and a day later took the men ashore at a port on the island of Cebu, where they transferred to another ship identified only as *824.* On the continued trip north, with Red Cross supplies nearly gone (some unfortunates had been forced to leave theirs on the first ship), men snapped at and stole from each other. In the stifling heat belowdecks, as one POW put it, "Morale reached a new low." On June 26 the weary men got off the ship in Manila, the first of many groups to move north before the threat of oncoming Allied forces.

While the Americans were en route north, an American intelligence agent reached the Davao Penal Colony. He had come by submarine from Australia on a secret reconnaissance planned by Lieutenant Colonel Mellnik, the former Davao prisoner now on General MacArthur's staff. Finding no POWs at the camp, he radioed his headquarters that all Americans had been transferred, unaware that 750 Americans remained not far away at a Japanese fighter-bomber airstrip near Lasang and at another auxiliary strip close by.

North at Manila about five hundred of the newly arrived Mindanao POWs along with about five hundred Americans from Cabanatuan and Bilibid boarded a freighter, the *Canadian Inventor,* on July 2. (The other seven hundred men from Davao, most of them officers, had gone to Cabanatuan.) The *Canadian Inventor* sailed on July 3 but turned back for unknown reasons the following day. The ship, with POWs aboard, remained in the Manila harbor until July 16, when it set forth again. The next day fifteen hundred POWs boarded another ship, the *Nissyo Maru,* and sailed north.

For those remaining—by now most POWs were aware that the Japanese intended to get them out of the Philippines—life became increasingly difficult. At Cabanatuan the Japanese reduced the POW meal to a small scoop of rice mixed with greens, a portion of thin soup, and some corn. Those who didn't work (all officers and men were required to do so at this time) got only the rice and soup. Hunger pangs reached new highs and men constantly looked around the camp while they were on work details for something to eat. They ate cornstalks and leaves, squash and pumpkin stalks, flowers, fried grubworms, cooked dogs, cats, rats, frogs, lizards, and roots of various kinds—anything that could be swallowed. When foodstuffs were available through the commissary, which was seldom, the prices were exorbitant. Mungo beans cost fourteen pesos (seven dollars per canteen cup), duck eggs were two pesos (one dollar each), and cane syrup was eight pesos (four dollars for a small can).

Things got worse when the Japanese put an end to the underground operations that Miss U (Margaret Utinsky) and High Pockets (Claire Phillips) and the American sympathizers in Manila had conducted with certain officers and men at Cabanatuan. In May the Japanese military police had suddenly seized Fred G. Threatt and five drivers of the carabao supply train that had been transmitting messages, money, and medicines between the town and the camp along with routine supplies. In the weeks after the seizure of Threatt, twenty-five officers and men were apprehended and interrogated, often brutally beaten, by the Japanese to determine the extent of the individuals' involvement. Later all but six were released. These included, in addition to Threatt, Lt. Col. Edward Mack, Colonel Oliver (chaplain), Capt. Rex Aton, Capt. Robert P. Taylor (chaplain), and P. D. Rogers, a civilian. The Japanese considered these men to be the ringleaders of the operation and held some of them in solitary confinement for up to four months before their release. They treated those outside the camp and in Manila even more harshly. The Filipino women acting as go-betweens in the marketplace at Cabanatuan were put to death. Father Buddenbroch died in Fort Santiago Prison in

Manila. Ramon Amusatague and other men and women in Manila's European community were executed. The Japanese finally apprehended Utinsky and Phillips and held them in Fort Santiago Prison. Though the women were subjected to severe maltreatment, both survived the war.

Of the ships departing Manila beginning in July the first to arrive in Japan, in early August, was the *Nissyo Maru*. The Japanese sent the men aboard this ship to five locations. The largest group, about three hundred, went to work in the steel mills at Fukuoka 3, near Tobata on the island of Kyushu; two hundred journeyed to a coal mining camp, Fukuoka 10, near Moji; and a third contingent of two hundred went to Oeyama, an Osaka group camp, where they worked in a nickel mine and processing plant. Smaller groups of men went to Kameoka and Funatsu, also in the Osaka group, both lead mining camps.

The next group of Americans to arrive in Japan were those aboard the *Canadian Inventor*. The ship, which had left Manila on July 2, arrived in Moji, Japan, on September 1—the longest running time of any ship transporting POWs to Japan. Storms, falling out of convoy, anchoring twelve days at Formosa, and dodging in and out of islands in the China Sea to avoid submarine attacks accounted for the extremely long transit time. En route the POWs nicknamed the ship the *"Matimati Maru"* (*mati* in Japanese means "wait"). From Moji the largest group traveled north by train to Yokkaichi, a camp southwest of Nagoya and part of the POW camp group bearing the name of that city. They began work in a copper smelting plant, along with British and Dutch POWs who were already there. Another contingent of 256 men made a shorter trip to a camp at Omine Machi, near the southern tip on Honshu, where they joined British POWs who had been mining coal for nearly two and a half years. A third group of about two hundred joined Americans working the coal mines at Fukuoka Camp 17 at Omuta, on the southern island of Kyushu. With their arrival this camp became the largest single concentration of Americans in Japan.

★ ★ ★ 2 ★ ★ ★

By late August 750 American officers and men near Lasang had spent five months at two airstrips working in the boiling sun as daily flights of Japanese bombers and fighters took off to the south. After a night bombing of the larger of the two strips, the Japanese told them that they would be leaving; and on August 20 the Americans marched to the docks and loaded into the holds of an unknown ship, which sailed soon thereafter. At Zamboanga they transferred to another ship, the *Shinyo Maru.* During the transfer to the second ship word was passed among the POWs that the Japanese intended to kill them if the ship was attacked by airplanes or submarines. On September 5 in a convoy of five ships with two destroyer escorts they proceeded northward.

On September 7 at 4:37 P.M., Lt. Comdr. E. H. Nowell, skipper of the U.S. submarine *Paddle,* sighted the convoy as it was passing close to the western coast of Mindanao at Sindañgan Point. In a flat calm sea, Nowell carefully chose his targets and at 4:51 P.M. fired four torpedoes at a tanker and two at a freighter—the *Shinyo Maru.* When one of the destroyer escorts wheeled and sped in his direction, Nowell dove to maximum depth. There the submarine was subjected to numerous depth charges but sustained no damages. Nowell recorded in his log the sinking of the freighter and damage and possible sinking of the tanker.

In the darkness below, the POWs heard a commotion on the deck and weapons firing. Moments later the ship shook violently. Some felt two concussions, seconds apart. Deck plates buckled. Beams and hatch covers fell into the hold. The explosive force threw Capt. Morris L. Shoss across the hold he was in. Recovering his senses, Shoss saw dead and unconscious men lying around him but could not locate the friends he was sitting with moments before. Spotting a rope dangling from a hole with light showing through, he clambered over several bodies and pulled himself up on the deck. Adjusting his eyes to the bright sunlight, Shoss crawled to the high side of the ship (it was now listing heavily to port, the side away from the shoreline) and jumped into a calm sea, narrowly missing landing on a life raft full of Japanese guards. When Navy electrician C. V. Claybourne crawled topside and saw guards shooting POWs as they came out of the holds, he quickly dove into the water and swam toward the beach, about a mile and a half away. Capt. W. B. Cain saw bullets splashing around him after he jumped off the stern of the ship. He

made his way over to some Japanese soldiers and sailors swimming together and after doing so ceased to be a target. By
this time about two hundred POWs were swimming or hanging
onto anything that would float off the port side of the ship.
Many made no effort to leave the location. Apparently they
expected that the freighter behind the *Shinyo Maru*, which
was picking up Japanese survivors, would also pick them up.

The Japanese had no such intentions. Lieutenant Hashi-
moto, a guard commander, stood in a lifeboat directing fire
at POWs swimming in the water. The freighter and other
arriving ships rescued Japanese but took aboard no Americans.
Shortly, the *Shinyo Maru* sank, taking with it about five hundred Americans—dead, wounded, or trapped belowdecks.
Aware that their only chance for survival was to reach shore,
many POWs by now had covered some of the distance to the
beach. Here, too, safety eluded them. At dusk Japanese on
the big oil tanker, which had run aground after multiple torpedo hits, opened up on the Americans with deck-mounted
machine guns, killing many of them. Shoss and Sgt. O. A.
Schoenborne and others, observing this, decided to stay out
in the open water and make their approach to land at night.
During the night and early morning singly and in small groups
eighty-two POWs made it to shore. On the day following the
sinking, Filipinos, drawn to the scene by the explosions and
firing of weapons, were shocked to see hundreds of American
bodies (and a few Japanese) drifting in the surf and on the
beach. They also encountered live Americans nearby. These
they escorted to guerrilla groups in the vicinity. Some POWs
struck out through the jungles and they were aided by Filipino
villagers farther inland. Eventually all the survivors were assembled in one place where they heard, with a mixture of
disbelief and elation, that they would all be taken to safety
by a submarine. Later in September a U.S. Navy cargo submarine, the *Narwhal*, carried the Americans to Biak, and from
there they were flown to Australia and later to the United
States.

★ ★ ★ **3** ★ ★ ★

As the lucky survivors of the *Shinyo Maru* journeyed to freedom, their comrades remaining on Luzon had reason to be

jubilant, too.   Beginning at 9 A.M. on September 21 and through
the day the POWs at Cabanatuan watched successive waves
of U.S. Navy fighter-bombers with fighter escorts—over two
hundred planes—fly over en route to Manila.   At Bilibid Prison
in Manila, Captain Nogi, the commandant there, observed with
great pride the exceptionally large number of what he believed
to be Japanese airplanes over Manila Bay.   Moments later, to
Nogi's consternation and the surprise and delight of POWs
standing nearby, the "Japanese" planes began diving again and
again on the over forty Japanese ships riding at anchor in the
harbor.   Soon columns of smoke began to rise over the Bay
and from Nichols and Nielson fields as well.   The Japanese
promptly chased the POWs inside, but as the raids continued
the POWs could see and hear enough to know that U.S. air-
power was over Luzon in force.   At Cabanatuan the POWs
were thrilled when Navy fighters shot down a Japanese plane
within view of the camp.   Major E. R. Fendall reflected the
views of POWs throughout Luzon when he noted in his diary
that September 21 was "the happiest day of my life."

Planes from Adm. Marc Mitscher's Task Force 38 came back
the next day and pounded all available targets on Luzon again.
Air groups from the U.S. carriers *Hornet* and *Wasp* went after
shipping, fliers from the *Intrepid* and *Bunker Hill* attacked
Clark Field, and pilots from the *Lexington* struck Nichols Field.
The carrier pilots hit hard again at shipping in Manila harbor.
By the end of the day virtually every ship in the Bay was either
destroyed or damaged.   Convoys in nearby waters were also
bombed.   In one attack American planes sank a Japanese
ship carrying over eleven hundred British and Dutch POWs.
The ship went down in three minutes.   The fewer than two
hundred survivors swam to safety on the shores of Luzon,
where Japanese rounded them up and sent them to Bilibid
and Cabanatuan.

At the end of the two-day raid American morale was at
an all-time high.   The old advocates of "Thanksgiving turkey
in Albuquerque" were now sure that their prediction would
come true this year.   For many of the optimists liberation by
Christmas was a cinch.   Most POWs were convinced that the
Japanese had neither the ships nor the motivation to attempt
further transfers of men to Japan.

In the days after the devastating air strike some of the POWs' optimism began to wear off. American bombers did not reappear, and the Japanese continued to truck in more men from Cabanatuan as well as Nichols and Las Piñas airfields and other camps on Luzon. By late September Bilibid was jammed with prisoners. The early arrivals took up all available space under roof. Those arriving later had to sleep outside. POWs began to sense that their captors intended to continue sending men to Japan. Any doubts disappeared when the Japanese at Bilibid issued woolen trousers and shirts, ordered the senior American officer to prepare two large drafts for movement, and announced that the target date for the first shipment would be October 1.

Most surviving American prisoners of war are still baffled today as to the reason why the Japanese continued to ship prisoners to Japan after September. Actually the Japanese persistence is consistent with the attitudes and behavior that they had displayed throughout the war. First, the military code called for obedience. Earlier in the year Gen. Shiyoku Kou, chief of prisoner-of-war camps in the Philippines, had received orders to evacuate all POWs. This order was still in effect. The imperial Japanese staff did not change the order for political reasons. The thousands of Americans held in the Philippines were symbols of Japanese power in East Asia. To be forced to liberate large numbers of these men to victorious American forces would be an unacceptable loss of national prestige. The Japanese also were concerned that the testimony of thousands of liberated POWs about their maltreatment would embarrass Japan. The stories told by the relatively few escaped POWs had already cast doubts about the veracity of the Japanese government's continued assertions that POWs were being treated fairly. Finally, there was the value of the American (and other Allied) prisoners. In the eyes of Japanese military and industrial administrators, the POW workers had proven to be an asset in keeping up national production. The Japanese had also learned as the war progressed of the high value the United States and other Allied countries placed on their soldiers, sailors, and airmen held by the enemy. Some Japanese may have thought that such leverage would be useful later in the war. These attitudes, though puzzling to the Western mind and a source of despair to Americans in the Philippines at the time, caused the Japanese to persist. The October

1 shipment of POWs got out on schedule.

On that day about one thousand Americans and a hundred or more British and Dutch survivors of the ship sunk ten days before boarded the Haro Maru, a small weather-beaten collier. The POWs crammed themselves into two holds. One was partially filled with coal, and horse manure lay on the bottom of the other. The men stayed belowdecks for several days in sweltering heat with little water and food, and only four buckets in each hold to carry out human waste. Requests for more water by the senior officer Lieutenant Colonel Gaskill were, as usual, futile. On October 3 the ship finally got under way as part of a convoy of eighteen ships, and some air began to flow down to the suffering POWs.

With this small relief the men turned to other concerns. One was the possibility that American bombers would attack the convoy. The other was a new threat (they were not aware of the fate of the Shinyo Maru): that their ship would be torpedoed. This apprehension was based on news heard through the grapevine (the secret radio) that American subs were taking a heavy toll.

The grapevine was accurate. Packs of American submarines patrolled in force in the South China Sea all along the western coast of the Philippines. North, more American submarines looked for victims in convoys between Japan and the Philippines using the Formosa Strait. This group of submarines was aptly called "Convoy College." Tankers carrying Indonesian oil to Japan were high-priority targets. Fewer and fewer Japanese ships—tankers and freighters alike—were getting through the undersea gauntlet. Those that did had to take a variety of defensive measures: traveling only in daylight, hugging the coastline, and seeking refuge at night in protected ports or small coastal inlets off normal shipping lanes.

On the third day out, American medical officers treating some sick men on the deck of the Haro Maru were abruptly ordered below. Before descending into the holds the men saw a large fuel tanker on the port side and a cargo ship to the rear hit by torpedoes. Down in the holds Americans heard a mixture of the explosion of Japanese depth charges and what they perceived to be torpedoes hitting ships. Surprisingly, there was no panic among the men. Some prayed, some talked, and others waited, resigned to whatever might happen. The

Americans' luck held. Their ship was spared. Some POWs contended that the American submarine skipper didn't want to waste a torpedo on a rusty little freighter like the *Haro Maru*.

Ten days later, after losing nearly twenty men to heat, dysentery, and exhaustion, they pulled into what the men below hoped would be a Japanese port. As it turned out they were in Hong Kong. They had made only small progress toward the Japanese main islands. As if that disappointment weren't enough, two days later American bombers attacked shipping in the harbor. Hits were scored on ships nearby, but once again the *Haro Maru* came through.

★ ★ ★ **4** ★ ★ ★

Meanwhile in Manila, with still no more air activity, the Japanese decided to send out the second detail of Americans at Bilibid—about eighteen hundred POWs. As on the *Haro Maru*, this group contained few officers. Even under pressure the Japanese gave priority to getting workers to Japan.

Among the men in the long column marching to Pier 7 on the afternoon of October 11 was Robert Overbeck, an American engineer, one of hundreds of American civilians who had joined the U.S. armed forces in various capacities when the Japanese invaded the Philippines. While boarding, Overbeck noted that the ship was a relatively new freighter. The Japanese forced the long line of men down into the second hold from the front of the ship. Once below, the men moved along a passageway down the center of the hold. On each side were three levels of wooden shelves with about three feet between each shelf. As more POWs moved into the hold the men already there found little room to stand up or move. Loading continued, with three hundred Japanese—some passengers, crewmen, and guards—occupying space in other parts of the ship. Just after dark the *Arisan Maru* left the harbor with the men below wondering how they could possibly survive the trip to Japan under such crowded conditions.

Soon after they departed, the Americans found out from some of the men who had been allowed to go above that the ship was headed south—the opposite direction from Japan. On the following day the *Arisan Maru* joined a convoy of thirteen ships with a destroyer escort and continued southward. On the same day a more pleasant surprise occurred when the Japanese moved about eight hundred of the men out of the jam-packed second hold to the forward hold, and life became a little more bearable. After two days the convoy broke up and individual ships found shelter in coves among islands about two hundred miles south of Manila. POWs on the *Arisan Maru* spent about six days in one of these coves on two meals of rice and one canteen cup of water per day. Suffering in the hot and smelly holds, the men wondered why the Japanese were keeping them in this remote place.

The Americans were not aware that they had narrowly missed being bombed by their own forces. The *Arisan Maru* and other ships in the convoy had gotten out of Manila harbor just before the return of the U.S. Navy's powerful Task Force 38. In a series of actions in support of the impending invasion of Leyte, a large island in the center of the Philippine archipelago, Navy bombers hit the Aparri airfield on the north coast of Luzon.* On October 15 the carriers returned to Philippine waters and bombed Manila and other targets on Luzon for three days before retiring. Satisfied that American fleet action was over for the time being, the *Arisan Maru* left its refuge and returned to Manila, arriving there on October 20.

On that same morning, 350 miles to the south, Gen. Douglas MacArthur had waded ashore on the island of Leyte at the head of a force of over 130,000 troops. To face this onslaught, the Japanese high command had, early in October, flown Gen. Tomoyuki Yamashita to the Philippines. Yamashita had in the opening days of the war commanded the Japanese forces that decisively defeated the British and Australians in Malaya. His assignment was part of the Japanese decision to reinforce the Philippines and hold these strategically important islands at all costs.

Unaware of these momentous events, M. Sgt. Calvin Graef, a native of New Mexico, and some of his companions hungrily watched as Japanese hurriedly loaded rice, sugar, and bananas aboard the ship. On October 21 the *Arisan Maru* left Manila harbor and joined the convoy. This time they headed north.

* Less than two months before, the plan to invade the Philippines by landing first on the island of Mindanao had been changed in order to accelerate retaking the key island, Luzon.

Conditions in the holds continued to be bad. In addition to the heat and crowding about one third of the men suffered from dysentery and malaria. Though twelve American medical officers and about twenty-five medical corpsmen were aboard they could do little for the sick POWs because they lacked supplies and adequate room for isolating ill men. Though some of the POWs had seen Red Cross supplies loaded aboard in Manila, none were provided to the medical officers. Graef, who served on a cooking and water detail, noted that whereas the Americans were given two meals of rice a day and a canteen of water, the Japanese had three meals a day: breakfast consisting of rice, vegetable soup, fish, and tea; lunch consisting of rice, soup, tea, and vegetables; and dinner consisting of rice, fried fish, beans, and vegetable sauce. During the day the Japanese also got candy, fruit, biscuits, and cigarettes. The Japanese issued life preservers to most of the POWs in both holds on the second day out of Manila. This issue only fueled the POWs' existing fear of being bombed or torpedoed and also created more congestion in the holds. By this time the morale of the men was deteriorating rapidly. Many POWs did not care whether the ship sank or not; if it did, at least, they felt, their suffering would be over.

On the twenty-fourth of October, Graef and the others on the cooking and water detail were on deck preparing the second meal of the day. About 4:45 P.M. the Japanese began running toward the rear of the ship. Graef, glancing over the starboard side, saw the wake of a torpedo speeding toward the ship, barely missing the rear of the ship. Then he saw his captors running forward, indicating that a second torpedo might be in sight. If so, it also missed. At this point the Americans were hustled into their holds. Minutes later, a torpedo struck the *Arisan Maru* midships on the starboard side. The ship was then about 225 miles east of Hong Kong.*

Soon after the torpedo hit, the ship buckled in the middle. The forward part of the ship, where the Americans were, stayed level. The stern dropped partially below the waterline. The Japanese, after cutting the rope ladder to the forward hold and closing the hatches on the second, boarded lifeboats and

---

* The joint Army-Navy assessment committee credits the USS *Snook* with the sinking of the *Arisan Maru*. However, this assessment is by no means certain since the USS *Shark* was also in the area. The *Shark* was sunk without survivors about this time.

made for the two destroyers that had moved in close to the sinking vessel.

The prisoners below had felt the jolt and explosion as the torpedoes struck to the rear of their holds. The stunned men soon realized what had occurred but there was little panic. Because of the location of the point of impact, few, if any, casualties resulted from the explosion of the torpedo. Several officers ordered those with life jackets to put them on and to remain in place. The men waited to see what the Japanese would do. Minutes passed and nothing was heard from above. Then some of the men in the second hold decided to go above. They easily forced open the blocked passageway to the deck. When Sgt. Avery E. Wilber got on deck he saw the Japanese destroyers taking aboard the Japanese passengers, guards, and crew from the *Arisan Maru*'s lifeboats. By this time some POWs on deck had thrown rope ladders down in the forward hold and men from that hold were climbing out. A number of Americans began jumping overboard. Wilber joined them. When Cpl. Glen S. Oliver emerged from his hold he stayed on deck and watched a continuous stream of men swimming toward one of the destroyers and waiting in the water around the destroyer. None was being taken aboard.

Sergeant Graef was one of the swimmers. The sea was rough and a strong wind was blowing. When he neared the destroyer, he saw Japanese with poles pushing POWs away. Weak and buffeted by the waves, many Americans drowned. After being poked himself, Graef swam away from the destroyer. Another American swimmer, WO Martin Binder, along with ten others, was hanging onto a raft made out of some wreckage. His group saw what the Japanese were doing and made no attempt to approach the destroyer. They concluded that the Japanese ship, fearing that the submarine might strike again, did not want to stay in the vicinity but might return later to pick up survivors. On this slim hope Binder and his companions decided to wait it out.

Back on the *Arisan Maru,* many of the POWs had decided to stay on the ship. Sgt. Phillip Brodski, a medical corpsman, and Corporal Oliver were among these. Some of the men made their way to the galleys, where they gorged on rice and sugar, drinking catsup and smoking cigarettes. Oliver stayed aboard until the ship began to break in two before going into the water. Brodski and a companion along with some others had decided to go down with the ship, and around dark the *Arisan Maru* sank. The instinct to survive overcame Brodski's fatalism. He floated to the surface and grabbed onto some wreckage.

As night fell, Overbeck, who had been one of those who had attempted to get on the destroyer earlier, floated next to one of the ship's lifeboats. As if this good fortune was not enough, after climbing into the boat he saw a box nearby and, retrieving it, found it contained a sail. Not long after this, he pulled Avery Wilber aboard. During the night they could hear men calling to each other, trying to get together in groups. Just before dawn, they picked up Pvt. Anton Cichy; and soon after daybreak, Graef and Cpl. Donald E. Meyer climbed into the boat. The five men now in the boat saw no other Americans in the vicinity. Presumably during the night a strong wind had blown the lifeboat some distance from the location of the sinking. Taking stock, they found some emergency rations aboard and one keg partially full of water. Heartened by this and finding that Overbeck knew a little basic navigation, they began to rig the sail for a try for the China coast. They had just started this when a Japanese destroyer approached. Frantically they dropped the sail and remained still in the bottom of the boat. The destroyer circled and left. While others rigged the sail, Overbeck took some crude bearings and with a good wind steered a westward course.

Warrant Officer Binder spent the first night on the raft with nine others. On the following day five men left to hang onto other floating wreckage, leaving Binder, a Navy commander named Egbert A. Roth, and three Army men (whose names Binder never learned) on the raft. Two days later Binder dozed off and when he awoke, Roth and two of the men were gone. The following day the remaining man, mad with thirst, swam away. At the end of the fourth day a passing Japanese transport spotted Binder and took him aboard, thinking he might be a crew member of the sunken American submarine. They treated him roughly until he convinced them that he was a prisoner. On the following day the ship docked in Takao, Formosa.

Both Oliver and Brodski, who had stayed with the ship to the very last, survived the night each clinging to wreckage.

On the following day a destroyer (probably the same that had circled the five POWs in the lifeboat) almost ran down Oliver. The same ship ignored Brodski's waving and yelling to be picked up. Soon after the two men spotted each other and began swimming together. Later in the day they came upon four rafts tied to each other. With the rafts they managed to survive until the afternoon of October 28, when a Japanese destroyer spotted them. This one stopped and took them aboard. A day later the ship landed in Takao, where they were turned over to the Army and subjected to intensive questioning, along with Binder and a fourth survivor named Hughes, whom the Japanese brought to the same location. After the questioning was over the Japanese placed them aboard the *Haro Maru*, which had finally reached Takao from Hong Kong five days before. A week later the Americans on the *Haro Maru* were sent to camps in Formosa. During their long trip nearly forty men had died (including Hughes, the last recaptured survivor of the *Arisan Maru*).

Elsewhere, on October 26, with a final stroke of incredible good fortune, Overbeck and the other four men in the lifeboat were taken aboard a Chinese fishing boat. On land they were conducted to friendly Chinese in an area occupied by Japanese troops. The Chinese made contact with a U.S. Army Air Corps weather station which was only a day's journey away. Shortly, an American from the station arrived and escorted the five men back to the station. Then, after a series of moves by foot, sedan chair, and bicycle with feasts and entertainment along the way, the five Americans arrived at an airstrip in early November. From there they were flown to U.S. Air Corps headquarters in Kunming and later to the United States.

★ ★ ★ 5 ★ ★ ★

In the closing months of 1944 American submarines dealt crippling blows to the Japanese Navy and merchant marine. During the same time the United States began what would be a long and devastating program of strategic bombardment of the Japanese home islands. As it had previously, overwhelming U.S. military power brought freedom closer for some POWs but also brought increased suffering and death to others.

In late October the U.S. Third and Seventh fleets, in one

of the greatest naval battles of all times, defeated the Japanese Navy in the waters around Leyte. This effectively ended Japanese military sea power in the Pacific. Equally devastating was the toll taken by American submarine packs hunting the ocean areas around the Philippines and north to the Japanese home islands. Sixty-six ships totaling over 320,000 tons were sent to the bottom in October. This, coupled with sinkings resulting from air attacks, caused Lieutenant General Muto, General Yamashita's chief of staff in Manila, to recall that at the time "some eighty-five percent of our transports met with difficulty." This was an understated way of saying that out of every ten ships sent to or from the Philippines only one or two stayed afloat. As a result the rice ration of the Japanese soldier, 850 grams at the beginning of the war and later reduced to 600 grams, was finally cut to 450 grams in October. One large shipment of rice did get through to Manila in early November. Much of this was sent to the Japanese troops in Leyte and other southern islands. The net effect on the food supply in Manila was zero.

If the situation for the Japanese was poor, it was even worse for the POWs in the Philippines. At Bilibid, where opportunities to scrounge extra food were limited, the men had to get by on two meals of rice *lugao* a day. Prices for black market food, with beans at fifty dollars a kilogram, were out of reach for most. On a daily intake of less than one thousand calories a day, men became progressively weaker. One diarist noted that just climbing a short set of stairs was difficult for him at that time.

Food was short everywhere. In late October the Japanese sent a ship, the *Hakusan Maru,* to pick up eighteen hundred tons of American Red Cross food and medical supplies which the Russians had been holding in Nakhodka, a port near Vladivostok, for nearly a year. The U.S. State Department contended at the time that the successful negotiations to release the supplies were due to the fact that no official releases of atrocity stories had been made during the six months prior to the Japanese agreement to transport supplies. Given the situation at the time, a more likely reason was that the Japanese wanted to minimize the amount of food diverted from their nation's dwindling food supply to feed POWs.

In November, en route to Japan, the *Hakusan Maru* unloaded some supplies at a Korean port for POW camps in Korea and Manchuria. Most of these supplies seem to have been stored or used by the Japanese because little or none reached Americans at Mukden. The ship continued to Kobe, Japan, where the bulk of the shipment was unloaded and stored to await transfer to camps in Japan and other locations in the Japanese empire. Because of the Japanese Army's conservation ethic and some pilfering, distribution to the camps was limited.

If some hungry Americans were denied the joy of Red Cross packages, those in the Tokyo area did get a big lift in morale on November 24. On that day they saw for the first time American planes in the sky above them. These were not the Navy's low-flying dive bombers and fighters but huge aircraft flying in formation at extremely high altitudes—B-29 Superfortresses, the new American heavy bombers flying from Saipan in the Mariana Islands.

The first B-29 raids on Japan had occurred five months before. Planes from bases in Chengtu, China, flew over one thousand miles to hit targets on Kyushu. Some POWs at or near three of the targets—Yawata, Nagasaki, and Omuta—probably heard bomb explosions but were denied seeing the B-29's because the raids were carried out at night.

In early December the bomber command in China, now using daylight bombing tactics, selected the Manchurian Aircraft Manufacturing Company at Mukden as a target. Ninety-one bombers arrived at Mukden in late morning on December 7 with ceiling and visibility unlimited. Successive formations dropped 262 tons of bombs in the target area, first destroying an arsenal and later the aircraft plant. The Mukden POW compound was in the center of the target area and the POWs had ringside seats during the raid. Unfortunately the seats cost some of them their lives. On the third flight over the compound a bomb fell just inside the wall where men were lying in the open on the parade ground. (They had not been given permission to dig foxholes.) The explosions killed nineteen Americans outright and wounded thirty-five more.

North of Mukden at a remote camp near Chen Chia Tung, Allied senior officers held there experienced only air alerts. In October and November the Japanese had moved all of the high-ranking military and civilian POWs from Formosa to Manchuria, with Wainwright, some other generals, and top civilians eventually located in a separate camp at Sian, northeast of Chen Chia Tung.

Following the November raid on Tokyo, B-29 bombing attacks from the bases in the Marianas on the island of Honshu increased in size and intensity. In the months that followed, these attacks would have growing influence on the lives of the Japanese people and POWs in camps around the principal industrial cities of Tokyo, Nagoya, Osaka, and Kobe.

★ ★ ★ 6 ★ ★ ★

In the Philippines, POWs continued to be caught up in the Japanese struggle to hold these islands. With the conquest of Leyte no longer in doubt, but much heavy fighting remaining before the last Japanese resistance was overcome, MacArthur's next objective was the island of Mindoro. It was to be used to launch air attacks on the island of Luzon. The attack convoy heading for Mindoro, escorted by U.S. Navy warships, entered the Sulu Sea on December 14 and headed north. The Japanese, aware of the large convoy, were unsure of its destination.

One of the possibilities was the island of Palawan, lying along the western side of the Sulu Sea, with its big military airfield built by American POWs. In early September the Japanese had sent in a new commander and a new guard detail from Luzon. The same ship bringing the Japanese took 159 POWs back to Manila, leaving 150 Americans to maintain the airfield. The new air base commander, Captain Kojima, ordered a cut in rations. Camp discipline under the guard commander, Lieutenant Yoshiwara, was tightened. Then on October 28, in support of the Leyte invasion, twenty-nine American B-24 Liberator bombers struck the Palawan airfield, destroying or damaging more than fifty aircraft on the ground and putting the strip out of action for some time. The Japanese, upset by this blow, reduced the POWs' ration and put them to work filling bomb craters. These actions did little to dampen the POWs' raised morale as a result of the big bombing attack.

Smaller raids by American planes followed. At first the Japanese herded the POWs under their barracks when an air attack threatened or occurred. But American officers complained that better shelter was needed and recommended a zigzag open trench near the barracks. The Japanese commander responded by directing the construction of three main trenches about 4.5 feet deep with overhead cover and long enough to hold about fifty men. Each shelter had entrances at both ends. In addition to these shelters there were three or four smaller shelters, holding up to five men. All the shelters were surrounded by barbed wire. Beyond the wire on the southeast side was a steep cliff covered with underbrush which descended 60 feet to the beach below.

On the morning of December 14 the men were sent to work as usual. Later that morning Captain Kojima received a message from headquarters that an American convoy was southeast of Palawan and headed in the direction of that island. Acting on instructions from the commander of the Second Air Division, Gen. Seichi Terada, that POWs not be allowed to fall into enemy hands, Kojima ordered the POWs at the airfield returned to the camp. Here they were given their noon meal. About an hour later outside the POW compound Yoshiwara formed some seventy men. Captain Kojima arrived and announced to the assembled men that he expected the U.S. forces to land, and while he was sorry, prisoners would have to be disposed of.

In the POW compound the men had finished lunch and, still puzzled at their recall from work, heard two air raid alarms sound. After the second one they were herded into the shelters. As the Americans crawled into their dugouts the guards shouted warnings that hundreds of American airplanes were coming.

By this time other Japanese guards armed with rifles and light machine guns had surrounded the barbed wire except for the side adjacent to the cliff. Then selected men went to the shelter entrances and poured gasoline into them. Other guards with long polelike torches touched off the gasoline, which ignited with a muffled roar.

Marine sergeant Douglas W. Bogue, in one of the small shelters close to the cliff, hearing the noise and the yelling of the Japanese soldiers, peered out of his shelter. He saw black smoke pouring from the large shelter nearest the POW barracks. Men on fire were running as a group of Japanese soldiers from the barracks moved forward, shooting and bayoneting them to death. Rifle and machine-gun fire from outside of the POW enclosure was directed at the entrance of the large shelter to keep the men inside. Bogue, yelling to the other two men in his shelter to do the same, made a dash for the fence. Reaching it, he gestured for his comrades to follow. Looking back, he saw that they had both been felled by bullets. Frantic, Bogue tore his way under the fence and dropped from ledge to ledge to the beach below. After fighting and getting away from some Japanese sailors that he encountered, he hid among some rocks.

In another shelter, Navy radioman F. J. Barta heard the noise and confusion. As Bogue had, he went through the fence, leaving behind a pandemonium of gunfire, smoke, shouting, and screaming as desperate prisoners were killed or wounded in vain attempts to escape. Only about thirty POWs, mostly those occupying shelters near the cliff, managed to claw their way under the fence and scramble down to the beach.

Up in the POW compound the Japanese guard detachment, having killed all the Americans remaining there, turned to hunting down those who had gotten away.

When Pvt. Eugene Nielsen got to the beach he covered himself with coconut leaves and lay undetected for three hours. Later he got up and found about fifteen other Americans hiding in a cove. Eight of these left the cove and tried to swim to the opposite side of the bay, a distance of about four miles. All of the men making the attempt were shot by Japanese in a launch patrolling off the shore. A little later when a Japanese search party approached the cove, Nielsen dove into the water and, though wounded, made it to the opposite shore.

Bogue stayed in his hiding place and was missed by Japanese search parties on the beach. After nightfall he cautiously emerged and found Barta and three other men. Later that night the five men were able to enter the water undetected by torch-bearing search parties and gained the opposite shore.

Pfc. Glen W. McDole hid out with a wounded friend on the beach until his companion died on December 18. McDole then swam the bay and made his way to the Iwahig Penal Colony, where he met Bogue and Barta and the three others who had escaped with them. On the following day Nielsen, with the assistance of friendly Filipinos, linked up with five more survivors. Together they were taken to Brooke's Point on the southern end of the island. There a guerrilla leader contacted American forces and a U.S. Navy Catalina flying boat picked the men up and flew them to the American forces on the island of Morotai. Bogue and his companions arrived at Brooke's Point after the Nielsen group and were flown to Leyte later. Altogether 11 men out of 150 survived the Palawan massacre.

The convoy supposedly headed for Palawan had landed its troops on Mindoro against no opposition on December 15. It would be nearly three months before American forces reached the Palawan airfield and discovered evidence of the mass execution.

Meanwhile, with the invasion of Luzon a foregone conclusion, the Japanese in Manila had begun the transfer of the last shipment of American POWs from the Philippines.

12

LAST OF THE DEATH SHIPS

December 1944–January 1945
The Philippines—Formosa—Japan

★ ★ ★ 1 ★ ★ ★

American carriers launched no air strikes on Manila in early December. During this time the Japanese at Bilibid Prison ordered American medical officers to examine and list all POWs who were able to travel. Then on December 12, at the 6:30 P.M. roll call, the dreaded announcement came: all men on the list would leave by ship the next morning. This was the Japanese answer to Comdr. W. P. Portz, the senior U.S. Navy officer at Bilibid, who had that day made a written and verbal protest to the Japanese concerning the potential movement of POWs by water in a combat zone in violation of international law and the rules of land warfare. During the night the men who were part of the outgoing draft packed their meager belongings and said farewell to those too ill to leave. Some left notes for next-of-kin with friends. Virtually all contemplated their impending voyage with foreboding. The next morning, December 13, the men awoke at 4 A.M., ate breakfast, and assembled outside. After hours of seemingly endless checking of rosters and counting off, 1,619 POWs, four abreast, moved through the prison gates toward the dock area.

The ragtag column, stretching one-quarter of a mile, contained 1,035 officers—about one-third of those taken prisoner after the fall of Bataan and Corregidor—and some 500 enlisted men, 47 civilians, and 37 British soldiers. Among the marchers were most of the combat unit commanders, junior officers, and noncommissioned officers engaged in the fighting nearly three years before. For many of these the two-and-one-half-mile march under bright sun brought bittersweet memories of better times. The route passed the once beautiful grounds of the Walled City and afforded a view of the Army-Navy Club and the Manila Hotel, both centers of prewar social life in Manila. Some Filipinos on the route of march gave concealed V-for-victory signs to the pitiful remnants of America's military presence in the Far East in 1941.

Arriving at Pier 7, the prisoners saw a medium-sized ship alongside. It was the *Oryoku Maru*, a seven-thousand-ton passenger vessel built in 1937. Some of the men noted that the ship was armed. It carried two 3-inch antiaircraft guns, one mounted near the ship's bow and another at the stern. Smaller antiaircraft guns were spotted in between. All bore grim evidence of the risks ahead.

Others besides the POWs were being rushed out of the Philippines. The Americans had to wait in the sun while a long procession of over a thousand Japanese merchant seamen and civilians filed slowly aboard, filling all of the passenger space on the vessel. The merchant seamen were stranded survivors of some of the ships whose hulks jutted out of the waters of Manila Bay. The civilians were older men and women and children, many of the latter dressed in vivid, brightly colored kimonos.

The prisoners started to embark in midafternoon. Shunusuke Wada, the Japanese interpreter at Davao, supervised the loading. His superior, Lt. Junsaburo Toshino, who was in charge of the shipment, was somewhere aboard the *Oryoku Maru*. This was the first of many times that the aloof, bespectacled lieutenant delegated his military responsibilities to Wada.

The Japanese divided the Americans into three groups, each to be loaded in turn. It took over an hour to load the first group of about seven hundred men into the rear hold. The second group, numbering approximately six hundred, mostly officers, moved in a long shuffling column to the hatch leading down to the forward hold. The prisoners slowly made their way through the hatch down wooden steps, a distance of about 20 feet. They found themselves in a 60-by-100-foot open enclosure. A wooden shelf about 4 feet above the floor extended around three of its sides. There were no ventilators or portholes. The only source of light and air was the 20-foot-square hatch opening.

The Japanese guards, impatient with the progress of the prisoners, began to push them down the stairs, sometimes beating them with shovels or rifle butts. When the floor and the shelves were packed with sitting POWs, each with his knees drawn up to his chest, even the Japanese guards began to wonder where more men could be placed. Still, as ordered, they continued to force more men down the steps. Lt. Col. E. Carl Engelhart, a former language student with the Japanese Army in the Thirties, pleaded with the guard at the top of the ladder to get permission to stop loading the hold. The guard said that Lieutenant Toshino was not available, but he would ask Mr. Wada. He came back and told Engelhart that Mr. Wada said, "*Ippai.*" This was a colloquialism meaning "chock-full." The guards proceeded to obediently stuff the hold *ippai.*

By this time both holds were stifling hot. In the forward hold the hatch cover was off, but no air moved through the opening. Men crowded against the forward bulkhead and the side plates of the ship, particularly under the shelves, found it very difficult to breathe. One of these was Lt. Melvin H. Rosen, a young artillery officer who found himself in the very bow itself. By reaching out he could touch both sides of the ship.

By six that afternoon the last of the third group of POWs, some three hundred men, mostly medical personnel, entered the midships hold. Shortly afterward, buckets of rice, fish, and seaweed were passed down to the Americans in all three holds for distribution. Despite crowded conditions, most of the Americans were able to get some food. Water, more vital to the POWs than food at this time, was provided in such small quantities that it ran out while being ladled out near the hatch openings.

Meanwhile, the ship had gotten under way but to the surprise of the POWs stopped at the harbor breakwater. Men at the top of the hatch ladder reported that the reason for this was that the Japanese were assembling a small convoy of freighters and naval escort ships.

As evening wore on, conditions became increasingly bad. Men were afflicted with dysentery and diarrhea. No provisions had been made for latrine facilities. After repeated requests the guards passed down some five-gallon buckets. Within a couple of hours these overflowed, covering the bottom of the holds near the latrine locations with human waste. The stench was overpowering. When the men had first entered the ship, the temperature was more than 100 degrees. By midnight it was well above this. Men began to suffocate. Those crammed under the shelves away from the hatch suffered the most. As the prisoners became more dehydrated, weak, and thirsty, some became hysterical and irrational. Others sank into a coma. POWs screaming and moaning for water and air were calmed by the leadership of some of their comrades. Some men would recall later the soothing voice of Lt. Col. Frederick E. Saint, which helped bring some order to the chaotic situation in the forward hold. Not far away, Lieutenant Rosen and his companions in the confines of the ship's bow found some protection from the milling and shoving in the larger space to their rear. Relatively motionless and mentally detached, these men conserved energy and air and managed to endure the hours of darkness.

Finally, at about 3 A.M. on December 14, the *Oryoku Maru* weighed anchor and headed out toward the China Sea. The movement of the vessel brought some fresh air into the holds and helped to remedy the intolerable conditions. At dawn men in the forward hold discovered ten of their comrades dead. More died in the aft hold, raising the night's casualties to thirty, mostly from suffocation.

As the POWs were counting their dead, twelve fighter planes led by Comdr. R. E. Riera, U.S.N., took off at daylight from the deck of the carrier *Hornet*, which with other carriers of powerful Task Force 38 was cruising off the east coast of Luzon. The task force's mission was to seek out and destroy enemy aircraft, airfields, and shipping in the Manila area and western Luzon waters. Riera's planes first investigated two airfields for hidden planes. Three pilots dropped bombs and fired rockets, and the rest strafed the most likely-looking target areas. Riera then flew to Manila Bay and proceeded south along the east coast of Bataan, searching for other reported airfields. Finding none, he led his planes around the tip of the peninsula and flew north up the west coast. It was then that they spotted a large transport and escorts steaming north. The Navy fliers doubled back and headed for the ships.

As the *Oryoku Maru* passed Corregidor and turned north, Lieutenant Colonel Engelhart, under the open forward hatch, watched the crew of the 3-inch antiaircraft gun slip off its covers and prepare it for action. They carefully checked the stack of shells and then stood at attention when a Japanese lieutenant arrived at the gun position. The lieutenant examined the gun, spinning the traversing and elevating wheels, checking the sights, the fuse cutter, and the breechblock mechanism. Then he barked orders and the gun crew leaped to their places. He ran the gun crew through a loading and firing drill about a dozen times and then walked away, leaving the gun crew relaxed, smoking, and eyeing the POWs down in the hold.

Riera's pilots found the transport and escorts in the open sea just to the west of the entrance to Subic Bay. They attacked immediately with bombs, rockets, and machine guns. No bombs hit but smoke was observed from the stern of the transport. Riera had to break off the attack to complete reconnaissance of additional airfields assigned for the day.

The convoy had only a brief respite. Around 10 A.M., twelve more Navy fighters rendezvoused and proceeded to Subic Bay in response to the report that a large transport and escorts were entering the bay. They sighted the transport off Sampaloc Point with escort ships three or four miles behind. Half the planes attacked the transport, the others dove on the escorts. Machine-gun fire raked the decks of all vessels. The planes left but returned later for a second attack. This time the transport was observed just inside the western end of Subic Bay. As the Navy planes approached, the escorts turned seaward. Rocket hits were made on the transport and both transport and escorts were again strafed. This time the *Hornet*'s fliers encountered heavy antiaircraft fire of both medium and heavy calibers. Lieutenant Zaecklin was forced to make a water landing when his plane was hit. Zaecklin was later picked up by an American destroyer. At about four in the afternoon another group of the *Hornet*'s planes pressed their attack on the *Oryoku Maru* but did not seriously damage the ship. To the prisoners belowdecks on the *Oryoku Maru,* the day had seemed endless.

A few POWs near the hatch opening were able to watch the duel between the heavily armed Navy fliers and the Japanese antiaircraft crews. As crewmen were cut down by the murderous machine-gun fire from the U.S. Navy attackers, new men took their place. After the second attack the forward gun was put out of action for the rest of the day. The other guns and those of the escorts continued to fire at the attackers. Finally, the escort ships turned and escaped to open sea.

Japanese casualties were not confined to the gun crews. Machine-gun bullets and rockets penetrated the three thinly protected upper decks and superstructure, killing and wounding more than three hundred civilians and merchant seamen. The wounded—many of them women and children—were laid out in the ship's saloon. The dead were placed in two large rooms nearby.

Late in the afternoon, Mr. Wada shouted for five American doctors to come up to treat the wounded. Lt. Col. Jack W. Schwartz, U.S. Medical Corps, and four other medical officers responded. When they got on deck, they requested water for the men in the hold and described the horrible conditions that existed there. Wada ignored their requests and led the doctors to the saloon, where they worked on the wounded until dusk. Their reward—fresh air and a glass of water—was more than adequate under the conditions. Back in the hold, Schwartz told his fellow POWs of the terrible carnage above and the massive wounds that he had seen and treated.

The POWs in the hold, shielded by the upper decks, were spared the full impact of the Navy's firepower, but they were by no means fully protected. Either machine-gun bullets or bomb fragments opened holes in the side of the ship at the waterline near where Maj. Dwight E. Gard, a former banker, was crouched. The flying metal wounded about twenty men but killed none. But for the POWs, cringing in semidarkness as bullets and rockets hammered the decks above them, there was the constant fear that the next attack would sink the ship. At dusk the battle-wise POWs concluded that the planes had returned to their carriers. The attacks were indeed over, but the prisoners' agonies had just begun.

That night, in Gard's words, was "a real hell on earth." Men were raving and crawling naked in the darkness. Some were temporarily insane, making speeches and threats to their neighbors. Others were stealing canteens, hoping that they contained some water. Few did. Men trying to maintain order found the situation beyond their control. Gard and another officer wrestled with some of the distraught, crawling men near them to keep them from piling up and shutting off the air. They managed to quiet a few of them. Other men, fearful that the Japanese would carry out earlier threats to shoot them if they didn't keep quiet, beat their comrades into insensibility when they refused to stop screaming. Conditions for the thirteen hundred men in the forward and rear holds were in a state of degradation and havoc that defies description.

Things were somewhat better in the center hold, where Major Bodine and other POWs had more room. Bodine, sleepless, heard voices from the forward hold all through the night. Men shouted "Quiet!" "At ease!" amidst a clamor of unintelligible outcries. Bodine thought some sort of riot must be going on, probably over water, and thanked the Lord that he was not in the forward hold.

By early evening the *Oryoku Maru* had moved from its position under the cliff near the entrance of Subic Bay to a position about 300 yards off the seawall at the former U.S. Navy base at Olongapo. Shortly after midnight, Japanese women, children, and the wounded were moved from the ship to shore. Later the remaining passengers and crew left the ship. By 8 A.M. on December 15, only the gun crews, the guards, and the prisoners of war remained on the *Oryoko Maru*.

That morning the *Hornet*'s planes returned for the kill. The first plane took off at 7:30 A.M. on a clear Sunday morning and swept west across the waist of Luzon, reconnoitering airfields for signs of activity. Finding none, the planes proceeded to Subic Bay and soon spotted the transport last seen near Sampaloc Point the previous day.

The fliers attacked first with rockets. Lieutenant Commander Bayer's rockets hit midships and Ensign Rollins's hit the stern. The following planes carried five-hundred-pound bombs. Ensign Bethel's bomb hit about midway between the stack and the fantail. Lieutenant Sisley dropped his bomb on the fantail and Ensign Williams's bomb was a near-miss. About this time another group of planes from the *Hornet* arrived. The pilots scored two near-misses with five-hundred-pound bombs, six rocket hits, and they strafed the decks continually. The bomb that hit on top of the aft hold was the most lethal single blow the POWs received. It probably killed over 150 men. Soon after this bomb hit, fire began spreading toward the front of the ship.

Bodine, in the center hold, felt the concussion of the big bombs striking the rear of the ship. The impact was so great that it shook the hatch planking loose, dropping it on men in the hold below. Sensing that the ship was sinking, Bodine and his companions were relieved to hear a sentry shout, "All go home, speedo!" They immediately scrambled up the ladders to the deck. For some it was the first daylight they had seen in over forty hours.

Captain James E. Alsobrook was among the first to leave the forward hold. Emerging, he noticed the coolness of the air and how good it felt. Then he heard the crack of rifle fire to the rear of the ship. Looking back, he saw a Japanese guard and four Formosans firing at prisoners swimming on the starboard side of the ship, the side away from the shore. Alsobrook, reasoning that the guards thought the men on that side were trying to escape, decided to go to the port side. On his way around the deck Alsobrook passed the door to the ship's galley and saw a friend, Lt. W. A. Brewster, inside eating. Alsobrook continued on and looked back to see if Brewster had followed him. It was then that he saw Lieutenant Toshino standing at the galley door with a drawn pistol. A few seconds later Toshino shot Brewster, killing him instantly. Alsobrook jumped overboard and swam toward shore.

When Bodine arrived on deck he saw many Americans and some Japanese making their way to shore, swimming or using improvised rafts or wreckage for support. Hearing shouts that the ship was sinking fast, he stripped off most of his clothing, jumped over the side, and began the swim to shore. Looking back, he surveyed the ship and at the same time found new strength from the effects of the cool water. While the upper decks of the ship were a "scrap heap," Bodine decided that the ship wasn't sinking fast. While he was helping some of the weaker swimmers, four Navy planes came over at low altitude. As the men waved frantically, one plane dipped its wings in what Bodine interpreted as a sign of recognition. Reassured, he swam back to the ship and managed to climb aboard. After retrieving his clothing and shoes he struck out again for shore.

Capt. William E. Chandler, a 26th Cavalry officer, was in the rear hold. He was roused out of a stupor by the explosion of a bomb which seemed to him to have dropped right through the hatch opening. Dazed and shocked by the concussion, Chandler and other survivors crawled and dragged themselves to the deck. There Maj. Thomas J. H. Trapnell, a fellow cavalry-man and friend, gave Chandler sugar, helped him over the side, and swam with him for a while. Chandler, semiconscious and swimming instinctively, later found himself on the sand— naked and exhausted.

By this time hundreds of the POWs were on the narrow beach, in small groups, under the watchful eyes of Japanese sentries posted along a seawall just beyond the shoreline. Soon guards began herding groups of POWs a few hundred yards inland to a small shady grove of trees near a tennis court. There the men stood in a long line for water at a single spigot. For many of the men this was the first water they had been given since they left Manila forty-eight hours before.

This brief solace ended when they were forced into the small area of the tennis court, surrounded by a chicken-wire fence. Part of the space was set aside for about one hundred sick and wounded. The rest of the men did not have enough space to stretch out or lie down. But at least they could breathe.

Two men gained freedom during the sinking of the *Oryoku Maru*. One was D. W. Kadolph, the other, Lt. George Petritz, U.S.N. Kadolph, after helping a friend out of the forward hold, briefly surveyed the chaotic situation and decided to try to escape. He jumped into the water and hung onto a piece of bamboo. After being fired on, he half drifted and half swam, letting the tide carry him away from the ship. He made shore and was assisted by Filipinos to a nearby village. A few hours later Lieutenant Petritz, also successful in escaping from the Japanese, arrived. After deciding to proceed separately, they both managed to evade the enemy and re-join the U.S. forces. Petritz was evacuated by submarine on January 29, 1945. Kadolph escaped to a destroyer, the USS *Fletcher,* a short time afterward.

Meanwhile, on the tennis court the prisoners observed U.S. planes returning to the now burning wreck of *Oryoku Maru*. More bombs were dropped and secondary explosions were seen. Sometime between 3:30 P.M. and 4:15 P.M. the ship sank.

A little later Bodine watched four planes coming over very low, close to the tennis court. He saw several dip their wings toward the POW enclosure, and once again some of the POWs interpreted this as a recognition signal. It was not. The Navy did not find out that the *Oryoku Maru* was a POW ship until they heard it from Petritz and Kadolph weeks later.

As the afternoon wore on, the men wondered when they would get something to eat. It had been nearly two days since their last meal of rice. A few of the stronger and more resourceful men had small amounts of food that they had carried with them from Bilibid or grabbed on the ship. Most had nothing. Lieutenant Colonel Engelhart was able to persuade a guard to take him to Lieutenant Toshino. He asked the officer for food. Toshino answered bitterly that the Japanese Navy was in charge of the installation and had refused to give him anything for his own men, much less for the prisoners. He said that he would have to buy rice with his own money until Manila sent something out.

On the tennis court rosters were called off several times and all persons were told to give any information available on those who were missing. As the prisoners talked to each other they learned that conditions in the rear hold had been the worst on the ship. Many of the deaths in this hold were caused by suffocation in addition to those caused by the direct bomb hit. At the conclusion of the roll calls that day, it was determined that 1,333 of the 1,619 prisoners who had left Manila the day before were still alive.

The next day, December 16, was a scorcher. The POWs, most of them still with no clothing or headgear, baked in the sun on the open tennis court. The men were weakening because of dehydration and lack of food, though water continued to be available on a limited basis. The only encouragement they had was watching Navy planes bombing the nearby Olongapo naval base throughout the day. The Navy bombers hit all around the enclosure, leading some POWs to continue to believe that the Navy fliers recognized their presence. Other prisoners speculated that the heavy attacks were the Navy's attempt to get even for being "tricked" into bombing the *Oryoku Maru.*

During the next several days the POWs continued to suffer from hunger, heat, and cold. The searing heat of the afternoon sun gave way to the dry, cool, almost cold nights normal in the Philippines at that time of year, causing acute discomfort to the weakened men. The Japanese did permit some of the prisoners on a rotation basis to go out of the enclosure to some shade nearby. The big problem, lack of nourishment, was only partly alleviated on the sixteenth of December, when Lieutenant Toshino obtained two 70-pound sacks of rice. He gave one sack to the POWs along with some salt. The other he kept for himself and the guard detail—fewer than ten men. The POWs share provided each of the more than thirteen hundred prisoners with about three tablespoons of raw rice and one-half tablespoon of salt. No cooking facilities were made available, though some Americans observed the guards cooking nearby.

Despite the heat, crowded conditions, and frustrations, the POWs reorganized themselves and tried to make the best of a poor situation. Some cotton shirts and trousers arrived from Manila and were issued to the men who had none. The prisoners waited for a cooked meal and wondered what the Japanese were going to do next.

★ ★ ★ **2** ★ ★ ★

On December 20 the Japanese decided to continue their efforts to get the POWs out of the Philippines. Twenty trucks arrived at noon that day and about half the prisoners were crammed into them. This was the day on which MacArthur had originally planned to launch the invasion of Luzon, landing his troops on the beaches of Lingayen Gulf. For logistical and other reasons he had to postpone the invasion until January 9, 1945. The trucks transported the men from Olongapo thirty-five miles over winding, bumpy roads to the city of San Fernando. Upon arrival the POWs were housed in the provincial jail and were given a cold cooked rice ball apiece—the first decent bit of food in five days. They were fed more rice balls the following day and then issued water, food, and utensils so that they might prepare a limited issue of rice and sweet potatoes for themselves. Three cases of Red Cross medicine arrived from Manila along with some vitamin capsules and a limited quantity of medical dressings.

Meanwhile, for those left at Olongapo the rice ration was increased—50 percent more for half as many men, and even a piece of salted fish! Major Bodine could only ponder the unpredictability of the Japanese.

On December 21 the remaining POWs at Olongapo, under Lieutenant Colonel Beecher as group leader, took the tortuous road to San Fernando and upon arrival were put into a theater building. Here they obtained their first hot meal in a week. Rumors of American troop landings on Luzon, and of Manila's being evacuated, spread among the prisoners.

In the first group, billeted in the jail, the three senior lieutenant colonels decided to appoint Lieutenant Colonel Engelhart as their representative since he spoke Japanese and could probably best serve the POWs in dealing with Lieutenant Toshino. Engelhart accepted this responsibility. Lieutenant Toshino told Engelhart that the POWs were to be moved to Japan soon. He also said he was going to send some of the more badly wounded to Bilibid in Manila. Toshino asked Engelhart to select three men for the transfer from the jail and asked Lieutenant Colonel Beecher to select twelve men from the theater. Tragically, the group leaders did not know that a Lieutenant Urabe from the Manila POW headquarters had ordered Lieutenant Toshino to execute POWs who could not withstand further movement. Toshino ordered his men to dig a mass grave in a cemetery south of San Fernando. At eight-thirty that evening Toshino, with Sergeant Tanoue and a small guard detail brought the fifteen POWs to the cemetery by truck. There Lieutenant Toshino ordered Sergeant Tanoue to decapitate the bound and helpless POWs. Tanoue complied by cutting off the heads of seven POWs with his army sword. Following this, members of the guard detail bayoneted the rest of the men to death. Toshino waited in the cemetery until the grave was covered, then he returned to his quarters, where he reported to Lieutenant Urabe that the executions were completed.

The next day, Christmas Eve, the POWs trudged to the

San Fernando railway station and climbed into boxcars, with only room to stand. To their dismay the train headed north instead of south, to Manila. Hopes of returning to Bilibid were dashed.

The trip lasted eighteen hours and was another stifling and unbearably hot ordeal. The wounded were allowed to ride on top of the cars and the guards urged them to wave if American planes attacked. Inside the cars when men passed out, their comrades transferred them hand to hand to the door to be revived. The train arrived early Christmas morning at the port of San Fernando. The town had become an alternate harbor for the Japanese since Manila was no longer usable. There the men had Christmas dinner: one cup of rice, a piece of camote (sweet potato), and half a cup of water.

The next day the Japanese marched them to the beach, where some had a chance to wash themselves. Then on December 27 the POWs boarded landing craft which took them to two ships anchored in the harbor. Boarding was another ordeal for the tired, weak men. Because the tide was out, each POW had to jump ten feet to the landing craft below. If a man hesitated before jumping, the guards pushed him, resulting in broken ankles and other injuries. While waiting, the POWs saw landing craft unloading soldiers on the beach. The wharf was stacked high with boxes, mostly military supplies and ammunition. Some of the Japanese soldiers looked curiously at the ragged and emaciated men standing on the pier. Soon they would be facing other Americans—these healthy and robust—in the final battle for the Philippines.

The first group of 1,070 men boarded the *Enoura Maru*. The harbormaster then diverted several of the landing craft to a second ship, the *Brazil Maru*. It was loaded with the rest of the officers and men. Immediately after loading, both ships pulled out in a convoy of four ships.

The prisoners on the *Enoura Maru* were confined to one hold with two levels. The conditions were crowded but not so bad as those on the *Oryoku Maru*. A man could lie down by doubling up his legs. The majority of the POWs were placed in the bottom of the hold. The hold was about 40 to 50 feet deep, and about midway up there was another level, a shelf about 15 feet wide which ran across the forward part of the hold. Colonel Beecher and his staff, doctors, patients, corps-men, and about several hundred others were on this level. The ship had been used recently to haul horses. Along with other discomforts the prisoners had to contend with horse refuse and a myriad of flies. Lieutenant Toshino and Mr. Wada were on this ship, but as in the past paid little attention to the conditions of the prisoners.

The prisoners on the *Brazil Maru* shared space with a large number of sick Japanese soldiers. The military patients occu-pied the ship's upper holds and the Americans were crowded below. It was hot on the afternoon that they departed. The Japanese gave the thirsty prisoners no water or food but fed their sick countrymen twice.

During the first twenty-four hours, POWs on both ships heard the sounds of the firing of guns, running about, and shout-ing. But what the Americans assumed to be a submarine or air attack passed without mishap.

Though the men on the two ships were relieved not to have to go through another sinking they found little else to comfort them. On the *Brazil Maru* the food and water situa-tion was extremely bad. During the first two days they got leftovers from the meals of the Formosan guards. This pro-vided about one tablespoon of rice for each prisoner. On the following day each man received about one third of a mess kit of rice. On the fourth day there was no food at all. The prisoners were issued five Japanese rolls per man on the fifth day. The rolls, a type of hardtack, were infested with maggots and moldy but the POWs were glad to get them. They re-ceived almost no water during the entire period. Colonel Harold K. Johnson, who had organized the men in the hold, personally appealed to the guards for more water and food. In reply one Formosan told him, "It is better that you all die." Colonel Johnson continued to plead, but knew that it was useless.

On the *Enoura Maru* food was scarce, but there was a little water and soup available at least once a day. During the trip between San Fernando and Takao, on the island of Formosa, twenty-one men were buried at sea, sixteen from the *Enoura Maru* and five from the *Brazil Maru*. Both ships arrived and dropped anchor at Takao on New Year's Eve 1944.

★ ★ ★ **3** ★ ★ ★

The ships stayed in the harbor for the next six days. Again, hoped-for improvements in food and water supplies, now that the ships were in port, did not materialize. On the *Enoura Maru,* Colonel Beecher and others continually asked Lieutenant Toshino and Mr. Wada for more food and water, but got none. On one occasion Lieutenant Colonel Olson (who had been the POW leader at Davao and who had good relations with Mr. Wada there) shouted up to Wada that the conditions in the hold were terrible and that men were dying of thirst. One additional bucket of water was passed down. Spirits were low and a feeling of hopelessness spread. In the lower hold, in an effort to boost morale, Cmdr. F. J. Bridget, who had commanded a battalion of Navy men fighting as infantry on Bataan, held "fireside talks." He explained that the delay at Takao was because of American air and sea power and Japanese communication and supply difficulties. The listeners' response was that it sounded logical but didn't help the situation.

On the sixth of January prisoners on the *Brazil Maru* were transferred by barge to the *Enoura Maru.* The Americans completed the move by late afternoon and received a meal, which for them was one of the best in many days. Medical corpsman C. J. Peart was assigned to the upper hold with approximately 450 others. Below them in the lower hold were approximately 900 POWs, including Bodine and most of the rest of the *Brazil Maru* contingent. Looking down on them, Peart thought that they looked small and terribly crowded.

He was right. Despite the improvement in rations, Bodine found that the living conditions in the lower hold were terrible. The night of January 7 was another hell. Swearing, kicking, fighting, and indescribable filth pervaded the entire hold.

The next day the Japanese ordered the men in the lower level up on deck so that tons of sugar could be stored there. These POWs had a rare afternoon in the sun gazing at scores of anchored ships which had sought sanctuary from American bombs and torpedoes in the huge horseshoe-shaped bay. At sundown the guards herded the men into a forward hold of the ship which had been filled with coal. About two-thirds of the men had moved down into this hold when the guards on the deck indicated that the other third would have to be absorbed into the upper level of the rear hold with the "hospital" and the other men who had occupied the space since leaving the Philippines. This created a terribly overcrowded condition. Within hours the crowded men would be thankful that they had not joined their comrades in the forward hold.

On January 9 thousands of Americans came ashore in the invasion of Luzon. The landings were on the southern end of Lingayen Gulf. The POWs' convoy had left the northern end of the gulf just two weeks before. In its last air strike in support of the invasion, Task Force 38 dropped over two hundred tons of bombs on Formosa, primarily to destroy enemy airfields and aircraft that might attack the forces that invaded Luzon. They destroyed few planes—the Japanese did not have many left—but did sink or damage a number of ships at anchor. One of these was the *Enoura Maru.*

During the morning meal the POWs heard antiaircraft fire, first from their own ship, then from all the ships in the harbor. Moments later bombs struck the *Enoura Maru.* One hit squarely on the forward hold, striking the big steel crossbeam over the hatch, dropping it into the hold. Another hit somewhere along the edge of the partition between the forward hold and the rear hold. This hit also loosened other crossbeams and these fell on the POWs. A near-miss ripped holes in the hull, spraying POWs with steel fragments.

In the rear hold Medical Corpsman Peart and a friend, who were completing their rice meal, gulped it down in a hurry when a bomb struck, sending the hatch covers tumbling down on them. Peart was struck on the shoulder, buttocks, and head. He thought he was going to die—pinned beneath steel girders. Then he realized it wasn't a steel girder on top of him but a piece of planking and he dragged himself out. His friend was not so lucky. He was struck on the head and abdomen and had gone into a coma. He died later. Bodine saw sparks fly as steel fragments came through the side of the ship. His left arm burned and he knew he had been hit. He got down as low as he could to protect his glasses from future blasts. Major Gard and a friend, Major Kriwanek, had just received their breakfast when the bomb hit. They dove for cover. A second later the place where they had been sitting was crushed by a girder. Their rice was on the deck mixed with dirt and filth blown about by the bombs. Gard, dazed and thankful for being alive, sat and watched another man scoop the mixture off the floor with his hands and eat it.

The medical officers in the rear hold went to work on the wounded immediately. Lacking dressings, they improvised, using the ragged remnants of clothing from the dead. About twenty men were killed outright and seventy-five to one hundred wounded seriously in this hold. Many others had minor wounds like Bodine's and Peart's.

If things were bad in the rear hold they were catastrophic in the forward hold. The beam that had fallen on the hold, and the bomb fragments resulting from the direct hit, killed more than 200 men instantly. About another 150 were wounded. The men in the forward hold called for doctors and medical attention but got no response. The reason was clear. Nearly all of the medical personnel were in the hospital area in the rear hold. One officer attempted to climb a rope ladder and asked a sentry for help. The Japanese ordered the man back into the hold.

Four Army and Navy doctors worked through the day doing their best to help the wounded and dying, while the few men who were physically able stacked the bodies on one side of the hold. That night, as more men died quietly from their wounds, others, dazed and demented, wandered aimlessly about in the dark, adding to the nightmarish scene.

Meanwhile, in the rear hold many feared that the planes would return as they had at Olongapo for a final deathblow to the ship. Father Cummings, the Catholic priest who had prayed and comforted the men during the worst of the *Oryoko Maru* bombing, gave an inspiring talk and prayed that they might be spared. In addition to their pain and fear the POWs had to contend with paralyzing cold. The hatch covers, which would have kept out the weather, had been blown off by the bombs and the wind whistled down into the hold.

The next afternoon, January 10, a group of Japanese medical corpsmen inspected conditions in the rear hold and treated minor wounds. Bodine and Peart had their wounds painted with something that resembled Mercurochome. The Japanese medics ignored the badly wounded men completely. They did not enter the forward hold.

Finally, on the morning of the eleventh, two days after the bombing, the Japanese lowered rope slings into the forward hold and removed dead bodies by crane. When all were out, a rope ladder was lowered and the rest of the POWs climbed out and joined their comrades in the rear hold. One man from the forward hold reported that all four of the doctors who had given so much of themselves had died, apparently from exhaustion.

The last of the nearly three hundred dead were taken out on January 13. American POWs helped in loading the naked corpses on barges for the trip to shore. The Japanese had at first planned to cremate the bodies but later decided to bury them. This was done in one mass grave, 60 feet long, on the beach near a Formosan cemetery.

All surviving POWs were placed in barges and taken to the *Brazil Maru*. On the *Brazil Maru* the POWs occupied one large hold. The wounded and other patients were placed in the center of the hold, while the less sick and others were assigned to bays with the usual double tiers. In some of the bays men found straw mats and life jackets. The Japanese made the POWs give up most of the life jackets. The mats, a relief from lying on the steel floor, were in short supply. There was much bickering and jealousy over the possession of these valuable items.

On the morning of January 14 the *Brazil Maru* left in a small convoy with seven freighters and several destroyers, and proceeded north. The ship carried 1,000 of the 1,619 who had boarded the *Oryoku Maru* exactly one month before.

★ ★ ★ 4 ★ ★ ★

The Americans hoped that they would be able to make the trip to a port in southern Japan in five to six days, the normal time for a ship to make the run proceeding without stops. The voyage was to take nearly three times that, with no bombings but a seemingly endless ordeal of hunger, thirst, disease, cold, and death.

The Japanese continued to issue a rice-and-water ration that would barely support life. Lieutenant Toshino did not increase the meager rice ration even when more rice became available as death reduced the number of prisoners. Constant hunger was bad but the need for water was much worse. The amount of water (sometimes in the form of weak tea) varied from one canteen cup for four men, at the most, to virtually negligible amounts. Often the water was so brackish that it would be undrinkable except for people with terrible thirst. The worst sufferers were the growing number of men whose bodily fluids were being drained by chronic dysentery. Some men sneaked on deck to the steam winches, where they filled their canteens with water drained from the petcocks. The guards, after catching one man doing this and clubbing him down the gangway into the hold, kept a sharp watch on the winches, eliminating this source of water.

There was one prohibition that the Japanese did not enforce. At the start of the trip Wada had announced that anyone caught stealing from the ship's cargo would be punished or shot. This triggered a search of the hold below, where some POWs found bags of sugar. A number of Americans ate the sugar for the remainder of the voyage. (Some later said it was a lifesaver.) They were able to continue without being caught because the guards, repelled by the filth and disease there, did not inspect the POWs' hold.

From the onset conditions resembled a seagoing version of the Zero Ward at Cabanatuan. The injured, mostly wounded from the Takao bombing, and the sick were laid out under the hatch in an improvised hospital area. The doctors and medical corpsmen maintained a semblance of organization but had practically no medical equipment or supplies to work with. Under germ-laden conditions they drained infections and abscesses, sometimes having to use razor blades or scissors for surgical instruments. Dressings ran out, and rags or kapok from stolen life preservers were substituted. The first to die were the seriously wounded, followed by those whose wounds would be considered minor under ordinary conditions. The places of the dead were taken by the sick, mostly dysentery cases caused by the terrible sanitation in the hold—overflowing latrine buckets, unwashed mess kits, bodies, and clothing. Sulfa pills and other drugs would have helped but supplies had long since been exhausted. By the end of the first week the death rate was averaging about twenty-five to thirty a day.

The destination of the *Brazil Maru* was Moji, a port on Kyushu, the southernmost of the Japanese main islands. To avoid U.S. submarines and planes the Japanese convoy followed a circuitous route off the coast of China, anchoring frequently in island harbors and bays. The convoy was further slowed by the necessity to tow damaged ships or those with engine problems. By the end of the first week—when under normal conditions they would have reached Moji—the ships were still only halfway, roughly east of the port of Shanghai.

At this time the captain of the *Oryoku Maru,* Kajiyama, advised the convoy commander that conditions on the *Brazil Maru* were so bad that if they were to continue the voyage to Moji he feared that all of the prisoners would die. He asked for permission to enter Shanghai harbor, provided that Toshino agreed. When approached by Kajiyama, Toshino objected, claiming that there was no place in Shanghai to quarter the prisoners and that the death rate was gradually going down. He told Kajiyama that he was following international law in handling the prisoners so there was "nothing to worry about." Toshino's view prevailed and the *Brazil Maru* remained with the convoy as it slowly made its way north.

As the ship moved into colder latitudes, snow began to fall. Below, the prisoners huddled and slept together to draw warmth from one another's bodies. Any material available— grass mats, life preservers, sugar bags, rags—was used for protection from the frigid air. But with all body fat gone and caloric intake at starvation levels, cold and exposure increasingly sapped men's energy and diminished their will to live.

Morale and regard for human dignity, already very low at the beginning of the voyage, continued to deteriorate throughout the trip. Previously cherished possessions—gold wedding bands, West Point and Annapolis rings—were eagerly exchanged with Japanese crewmen for a small amount of water or food. The modicum of organization and discipline which had served the POWs so well in the early part of the long journey gave way to survival of the fittest. Stealing, cheating, and conniving over clothing, mats, water, and food were rampant.

Despite this some men were able to draw inspiration and hope from chaplains and others who shared their strength of spirit. Father Cummings was one of these. He prayed and talked with his fellow prisoners each evening. At the beginning of the voyage the chaplains went on deck and performed a brief service as the bodies were dropped over the side. Soon the bitter-cold winds forced the last rites below. Toward the end, with most of the chaplains dead or exhausted, the bodies were dumped into the sea without ceremony.

For the rest of the voyage most of the living hung on the very edge of their existence. Immobilized by loss of strength and energy, they huddled together in small groups. Many passed the time dreaming and talking about their families, food, experiences, and even plans for the future. But for some the future was short and, usually at night, they would drift into death. Frequently, men died so peacefully that their companions sleeping alongside did not know it until their bodies grew cold. Others found death far from painless.

During this period Bodine wrote in his diary: "Had count of men by Japs and then roll call by Colonel Beecher. . . . Hope it means end is near. . . . Only 630 left of 1,619 . . . Terrible . . . Unbelievable . . . Father Cummings died . . . about 40 died last night, not buried today . . . hope ends soon. . . ."

Finally, on the twenty-ninth of January, the *Brazil Maru* pulled into the harbor at Moji, Japan. The first Japanese aboard were medical personnel, who looked aghast at the emaciated Americans and the corpses stretched out under the hatch, and hurriedly departed. Later that day the ship was boarded by Colonel Odashima, the officer who the previous March had recommended the evacuation of all prisoners of war in the Philippines. The *Brazil Maru* carried the last of them—about 500 of the 1,619 who had started from Manila forty-eight days before. Of this number over 100 were so weak and unhealthy that they died within the next few weeks. Fewer than 300 survived to be liberated when the war ended.

PART IV

Victory and Liberation

January–September 1945

13

"I'M A LITTLE LATE,
BUT WE FINALLY
CAME"

January–February 1945
The Philippines

★ ★ ★ 1 ★ ★ ★

As the *Brazil Maru* was slowly making its way to Japan, Gen. Walter Krueger's Sixth Army troops were moving south from Lingayen Gulf toward Manila. Months before, MacArthur, ever the optimist, had predicted that Manila would not be defended and could be occupied in two weeks. On the twelfth of January, three days after the troop landings, MacArthur held a conference with General Krueger and other top commanders aboard the cruiser *Boise*. He pressed for a speedy advance. In addition to the military importance of seizing Manila, MacArthur stressed the importance of freeing Allied prisoners and internees held there.

General Krueger had hoped to capture Manila by MacArthur's sixty-fifth birthday, the twenty-sixth of January. The Japanese destruction of bridges, railroads, and roads plus the Sixth Army's lack of experience in large overland movement made the going much slower than he had expected. On the twenty-sixth, Sixth Army forces were still fifty miles north of Manila. After passing a deserted Camp O'Donnell, one forward element was heavily engaged at Clark Field. Other Americans occupied the town of Guimba, twenty-five miles north of Cabanatuan, where 516 POWs languished.

Once again American POWs found themselves caught up in the tides of war. The Japanese needed to hold Cabanatuan and the towns to the north along Route 5 to keep this major road open to move troops and supplies from Manila to northern Luzon, where General Yamashita was preparing his final defense line. American troops were pressing forward against the same towns to deny them to the enemy and to protect the exposed Sixth Army flank. The POWs at Cabanatuan were in sort of a limbo—neither POWs nor free men.

Their strange new status had begun three weeks before, when the POWs noticed the Japanese guards making preparations to leave. Soon thereafter the American senior officer passed on orders from the Japanese camp commander. For the convenience of the imperial government, the commandant said, the men at Cabanatuan were no longer POWs. They were to receive a thirty-day supply of food and remain inside the camp area. Later the Japanese guard detachment fell in and left the camp. That night, as far as the POWs were able to determine, there were no Japanese guarding the camp. This was the first implementation of a directive by General Yamashita in mid-December to release American POWs "in the event of an American landing on Luzon." Strangely, the Japanese commander released the POWs two days before the first Americans hit the beach at Lingayen.

The next morning POWs, looking in several storage buildings, found hundreds of sacks of rice, five hundred cans of milk, and assorted other foodstuffs. The POWs moved all of these supplies into the prisoners' compound, which occupied the northeast corner of the total camp area. In the next few days enterprising POWs found and slaughtered two carabao. With this meat and the supplies that had been left, they had a very adequate ration. Nearly everyone in the camp began gaining weight.

After the POWs had been unguarded for a day or two, some Japanese soldiers arrived but did not enter the POW compound. Now fully concerned with their own death struggle, the Japanese had little interest in the American POWs. From that time on, the major use of the camp at Cabanatuan, exclusive of the POW section, was for quartering Japanese troops on the move to northern Luzon.

If the POWs were no longer of Japanese concern, they were very much a concern of the Americans. Two guerrilla leaders—one an American, Capt. Robert Lapham, and the other a Filipino, Capt. Juan Pajota—had been watching the POW camp at Cabanatuan for over two years. They had previously developed plans for liberating the prisoners but never obtained approval by radio from U.S. headquarters to carry out their plans. Now with the U.S. forces approaching, Lapham and Pajota met with Sixth Army intelligence officers, expressed fear for the safety of the POWs, and recommended a rescue mission. The Sixth Army staff officers immediately accepted the idea and obtained General Krueger's approval. A company of the U.S. Sixth Ranger Battalion along with two teams of the Sixth Army's "Alamo Scouts" was assigned to carry out the mission. Fashioned after the commando and ranger units first used in the European theater, the Sixth Ranger Battalion had trained hard and had seen some action in the Leyte invasion. The Alamo Scouts consisted of a number of small intelligence teams with previous experience in penetrating enemy lines.

The rescue operation was scheduled for January 29. This left less than two days to plan and organize a very high-risk mission requiring surprise and split-second timing. With Lapham's knowledge of the camp and surrounding area, and maps and an aerial photo of the prison compound, the American officers were able to develop an overall plan for the raid in a matter of hours. The plan called for the Rangers to execute a night march of twenty-five miles through enemy territory to a point near the POW compound. The Filipino guerrillas were responsible for setting up roadblocks on the road northeast and southwest of the camp. Then the Rangers, on signal and under cover of darkness, would assault the camp and free the POWs. Only on the return march would the raiding force be able to call for air cover. The Alamo Scout teams were to proceed ahead of the Rangers and obtain specific information on the camp and troop movements around it. With this information the final detailed plans would be developed and the raid conducted.

At 5 A.M. on the twenty-eighth of January, 1945, the rescue force—consisting of Lt. Col. Henry Mucci, battalion commander, and Company C of the Sixth Rangers, commanded by Capt. Robert W. Prince, reinforced by a platoon of Company F of the Sixth Rangers, commanded by Lt. John P. Murphy— left their camp in a truck convoy and proceeded to Guimba. At 2 P.M. that afternoon the Ranger force moved cross-country to the guerrilla headquarters, where Capt. Eduardo Joson and his 80 men attached themselves to the Rangers. The American-Filipino force marched through the night, forded the Talavera River, and arrived without incident at the village of Balangkare at 6 A.M. on the twenty-ninth of June. Here they met Captain Pajota, the guerrilla commander in the area. His force of 90 armed men and 160 unarmed men were attached to the raiding group. During the day while their men were resting, Colonel Mucci and Captain Prince discussed the operation with Captain Pajota and carefully worked out the important responsibilities that the guerrillas would have in the operation. Pajota agreed that the security of the area would be the responsibility of the guerrillas. This meant that all civilians in the area north of the road linking Cabanatuan and Cabu, a small town northeast of the POW camp, would remain there; and any persons entering the area would be held and not be permitted to leave until the mission was accomplished. Chickens were to be penned up and dogs to be tied and muzzled in areas through which the raiding party would pass. The Filipino leaders agreed to organize an oxcart train to haul 200 men and provide food for 650 men, to be distributed along the route of return.

Late that afternoon Mucci ordered the Rangers to the jump-off point at Platero. There they received a disappointing report from the Alamo Scout team. The Scouts were not able to get close enough to the camp to get new information on the situation there. They did hear reports of a very large group of Japanese soldiers moving north from Cabanatuan up the road by the camp and of a Japanese battalion at the Cabu Bridge, east of the POW compound. Because of the unfavorable enemy situation and lack of information, Mucci postponed the operation for twenty-four hours.

On the following day the Alamo Scouts, with a guerrilla lieutenant named Tombo, spent the day carefully observing and sketching the layout of the camp. By midafternoon final reports were in, and Prince and his officers went over the detailed operations with their men. At 5 P.M. the raiding group left Platero and crossed the Pampanga River. There Captain Joson's men split off south toward Cabanatuan, and Captain Pajota and his detachment moved north to the vicinity of the Cabu Bridge. After crossing the river the Rangers entered flat rice fields. To avoid detection they crawled most of the two miles—to the highway just north of the POW stockade. By 7:30 P.M., as it was becoming dark, two Ranger platoons had taken positions in a ditch twenty yards from the front (north) gate of the camp. The other platoon, Lieutenant Murphy's, had circled the camp and concealed itself at the southern end. All was quiet in the camp.

At 7:45 P.M. Murphy's platoon opened fire. This was the prearranged signal for all units to carry out their assigned missions. As men at both ends of the camp cut the telephone wires to the camp, Murphy's men sliced their way through the barbed wire and entered the compound. With their fire they pinned down the Japanese and prevented them from moving to the northeast corner, where most of the POWs were quartered. Meanwhile, Lt. William J. O'Connell and his platoon forced the front gate, killed the guards there, and then, moving down the center road of the camp, swept the whole western half with withering fire. They killed or wounded most of the two hundred men quartered there, destroyed four tanks, and set afire two truckloads of Japanese soldiers waiting to leave the camp. Within minutes Lt. Melville H. Schmidt and his platoon, covered by fire from the other two platoons, began moving the first confused POWs out of the front gate and across the road to an assembly point.

The attack had completely surprised both the Japanese and the POWs. With a combination of extraordinary skill and luck the attacking Rangers, firing rapidly and in semidarkness but aided by a full moon, killed or wounded virtually all of the Japanese in the camp without hitting a single POW. The unharmed POWs were not sure what was going on. Some, hearing the firing, thought that a mass execution was in progress. Others thought that the attack was by guerrillas and did not know whether to seize the opportunity to escape or to remain in the camp.

At the south end of the POW compound Lt. Raymond Bliss ran to the POW senior officer's hut to see what he could find out. The hut was empty. Then he ran to the hospital area near the north end of the camp and found it empty also. It was here that he met a Ranger who gave him chewing gum and headed him out the front gate. By this time many of the able-bodied as well as the sick and disabled were being helped or carried up the center road of the camp to the main gate. All made it except one POW, who, while being carried piggyback to the gate, suffered a heart attack and died fifty feet short of the main gate and freedom.

The skill and grit of the Rangers were shared by the Filipinos under Captain Pajota at the Cabu Bridge. When they heard the shots at the POW camp, they opened fire on the Japanese on the opposite side of the river and set off charges which destroyed a section of the bridge. As the Rangers had, the guerrillas achieved complete surprise and inflicted heavy casualties on resting Japanese troops who were settling down for the night and on groups who charged to the bridge and found it blown. Pajota's intrepid Filipinos caused more havoc when with their newly acquired American bazooka (an antitank rocket-firing weapon), they first disabled a truck, which caught fire and illuminated the whole area, and then hit two Japanese tanks.

Back at the camp, as more POWs crossed the road, the Rangers suffered their first casualties. Among the wounded one was serious, Capt. James Fisher, the battalion surgeon. The evacuation continued with the Rangers escorting or carrying POWs across the rice fields to the Pampanga River, where waiting Filipinos with carts drawn by carabao hauled those unable to make it across the river. At 8:15 P.M. Captain Prince, after searching the POW area twice and finding no POW's,* fired a flare into the sky, signaling all Ranger units to withdraw to the Pampanga River. In the withdrawal one Ranger, Cpl. Roy Sweezy, was killed by enemy fire. (Captain Fisher later died of his wounds.) At 9:15 P.M., an hour and a half after the raid had begun, Captain Prince, satisfied that everyone was across the river and in or on the way to Platero, fired a second red flare. This one signaled Captains Pajota and Joson to withdraw. Captain Joson did so but Captain Pajota and his men fought on for an hour longer to protect the retiring

---

* He missed one British POW in a latrine, who was found later by Captain Joson's guerrillas and was conducted by them to freedom.

raiding party and the ex-POWs. In the entire action Pajota's men suffered only minor wounds while inflicting hundreds of casualties on the Japanese across the river.

Later that night, after leaving Platero, the rescue column reached Balangkare. Here they regrouped, rested, and around midnight pushed on for another two hours to another village, where more carts were obtained. The column of fifty-one carts stretched nearly one and a half miles. A final hazard was the crossing of the Japanese-held Rizal Road. This they safely negotiated at 4:30 A.M. By 8 A.M. on January 31 the column reached the town of Sibul, where the Filipinos provided more water, food, and carts. The cart total now was more than seventy. Radio contact was established with Guimba base headquarters. Sixth Army officers, hearing of the success of the mission, were overjoyed. Mucci requested ambulances for the litter cases and trucks for the rest of the men. The vehicles met the long oxcart caravan at about midday and transported the former POWs to the 92nd Evacuation Hospital. Later that evening the Alamo Scouts along with two ex-POWs, Lts. Merle Musselman and Hugh Kennedy,* reached American lines.

The raid was in all respects a success. The rescue, which cost the lives of two Americans, was achieved without the loss of a single POW from enemy action and, amazingly, with no Filipinos killed. Soon after the raid General MacArthur announced that all the raiding party would receive decorations and commented that "no incident of the campaign has given me such personal satisfaction."

After a short stay at the hospital, all except the sick were moved to a replacement camp and then to the island of Leyte. From Leyte most of the POWs returned to the United States by ship and a few by air.

★ ★ ★ 2 ★ ★ ★

On the day after the liberation of the POWs at Cabanatuan the final thrust for Manila began. Two days earlier General MacArthur had made a personal reconnaissance of 37th Division units south of Clark Field and had observed that the troops demonstrated "a noticeable lack of drive and aggressive initia-

---

* Musselman, a doctor, and Kennedy, a chaplain, had stayed behind to minister to the dying Captain Fisher.

tive. . . ." With this pressure from MacArthur and two newly arrived divisions under his control, General Krueger renewed his drive on that up-to-now elusive objective, while Gen. Robert L. Eichelberger's Eighth Army attacked the city from the south.

The Sixth Army drive amounted to a race down Luzon's major north–south roads between two divisions: one the 37th Division, which MacArthur had criticized; the other the 1st Cavalry Division, which was being committed for the first time in the Luzon area. General Krueger sent a message through to the 37th to "advance aggressively southward." MacArthur, visiting the 1st Cavalry Division assembly point near Guimba, told the division commander to tell his men: "Go to Manila. Go around the Nips, bounce off the Nips, but go to Manila. Free the internees at Santo Tomas, take Malacañan Palace and the Legislative Building." There was little question which was MacArthur's favorite in the race.

Unaware that MacArthur had failed to include their prison in his liberation objectives,* the prisoners at Bilibid were desperately hungry and hopeful that their ordeal would soon end. The camp population had grown in late December when about five hundred civilian internees, most from the northern Luzon city of Baguio, were brought in and put in a part of the big compound separate from the military prisoners. The movement of the civilians would be cited after the war by General Muto, General Yamashita's deputy, with some justification as a humane action, since Yamashita had ordered that Manila be evacuated and expected that the fight in northern Luzon around Baguio (Yamashita's headquarters) would be to the death.

The already deplorable food supply situation was worsened by the additional civilians. It became still worse in early January when 400 POWs were transferred to Bilibid from Fort McKinley, in south Manila. The Bilibid population now stood at about 828 POWs and 500 internees. The ration of between 200 and 300 grams—about seven to ten ounces of rice, corn, and soybeans per day—was not enough to sustain life over an

---

* General MacArthur's omission, which is baffling, was compounded by the lack of knowledge of the use of Bilibid Prison on the part of the commanders of the 37th and 1st Cavalry divisions. As the reader is aware, Bilibid was one of the oldest permanent POW camps in the Philippines. It was marked on aerial photo maps as such, and was carefully avoided by Army and Navy fliers in the bombings in late 1944.

extended period. American camp authorities at the time warned the POWs of the dangers of food poisoning, which might result from stealing and eating garbage from the few remaining pigs in the Japanese pigpen—but some men persisted.

During the last days of January and the first of February, the Bilibid prisoners, with a secret radio still in operation, were aware of U.S. landings and the Sixth Army movement toward Manila. The men drew encouragement from the still distant but increasing sound of gunfire north of the city. (Some of this was the sound of the Japanese blowing up military supplies.) Then, just after 7 P.M. on February 3, the sound of tanks and machine-gun fire became unmistakable to the ears of the veterans of Bataan and Corregidor. The Yanks and tanks were near.

The sounds came from units of the 1st Cavalry Division, official winners of the race to Manila. Leading units of the division had crossed the city limits a little after 6 P.M. and moved down Quezon Boulevard to Santo Tomas University (only one third of a mile northeast of Bilibid) about an hour later. After a brief fight at the front gate of the university they liberated about 3,700 American and Allied civilian internees. Another 220 were held hostage by the Japanese guard force until the following morning and then released. Meanwhile, other troopers of the 1st Cavalry Division moved down Quezon Boulevard against stiffening resistance until they were halted by heavy machine-gun and rifle fire coming from in front of them and from the Far Eastern University building on their left. Bilibid Prison, looming on their right, appeared deserted. After fighting awhile against the first stubborn resistance they had encountered so far, the cavalrymen moved back up Quezon Boulevard to positions near Santo Tomas University. Other 1st Cavalry units, moving through side streets and guided by guerrillas, had secured Malacañan Palace (another of MacArthur's objectives), about a mile southeast of Santo Tomas, by late that night.

If the U.S. soldiers who had been fighting just over the wall were unaware of their countrymen inside Bilibid, the POWs and their captors were very much aware of the American troops. At roll call that night some of the Japanese sentries had said that it would be the last one they would be holding in Bilibid. As the POWs sat outside as usual until just before dark, the heavy rumble of tanks and shooting caused the Japanese to order all prisoners into their buildings. Some Japanese troops arrived and took up positions to defend the prison compound. Huddled inside their barracks, the American POWs listened with some satisfaction to the firing of .50-caliber machine guns, the rumble of tanks, and the sound of cannon firing. Peering through the windows, some POWs watched the sky redden over the Japanese headquarters of the Far Eastern University building, leading them to think that the building, under heavy fire from the Americans, was burning. As the shooting died down late that night those prisoners who could fell asleep wondering what the next morning would bring.

The sentries of the night before had been wrong. At 8 A.M. the Japanese were still there and held yet another roll call—their last. Later that morning, as the firing outside the walls renewed, the Japanese commandant called the senior American medical officer, Maj. Warren A. Wilson, and the civilian in charge of the internees to his office and after a brief conference handed them the following proclamation:

1. The Japanese Army is now going to release all the prisoners-of-war and internees here on its own accord.
2. We are assigned to another duty and shall be here no more.
3. You are at liberty to act as free persons, but you must be aware of probable dangers if you go out.
4. We shall leave here foodstuffs, medicines, and other necessities of which you may avail yourselves for the time being.
5. We have arranged to put up signboard at the front gate, bearing the following content:
    "Lawfully released Prisoners-of-War and Internees are quartered here. Please do not molest them unless they make positive resistance."

Shortly after noon the Japanese guards marched through the gates and the Americans were, technically speaking, free. Like their fellows' at Cabanatuan, their delight was tinged with some apprehension over what would happen next. Excited and expectant, they talked and waited.

That afternoon elements of the 37th Infantry Division entered Manila with the 2nd Battalion, 148th Infantry, under

Lt. Col. Herbert Radcliffe, moving south down Rizal Avenue. This was a major city street just four blocks west of and parallel to Quezon Boulevard, the road being used as the axis of advance by the 1st Cavalry Division. The Americans encountered no resistance—only the cheers, gifts, and encouragement of the Filipinos along the way. Sometime after 3 P.M. the leading company encountered enemy fire about four hundred yards north of Bilibid. The company commander sent a platoon to reconnoiter. When it did not return he dispatched a squad of nine men under Sgt. Rayford Anderson to locate the missing platoon.

As they moved down Rizal Avenue, Anderson and his men were informed by friendly Filipinos that the big walled building ahead was a prison with many Americans and Japanese in it. Anderson's patrol approached the huge enclosure cautiously, concerned about the absence of people and the ominous quiet in the area. After observing the front gate,* they decided to enter a door on the west side. Inside, they found themselves in a large, long storage room separated from the prison proper by a thick wall with high boarded windows and a locked gate. One of the Americans pried a board off one of the windows and, peering through, saw about fifty men huddled in an open courtyard. The soldier yelled at the men, asking them to open the gate, but got no response. In the gathering darkness—it was now after seven o'clock—the ever-cautious POWs were suspicious of the men on the other side of the wall. Finally one of the POWs courageously ventured forward and picked up a pack of Philip Morris cigarettes which a soldier had thrown through the window. This did the trick. Shouting, "By Jesus, it's the Yanks," he summoned the others, and laughing, cheering, and crying together they opened the gates, inundating Anderson and his men with congratulations and questions. Anderson sent word of his discovery back to his commander. Not long after, Colonel Radcliffe moved his battalion to the vicinity of the prison. After sizing up the situation Radcliffe requested food, trucks, doctors, and medical supplies for the thirteen hundred people in Bilibid. Guards were posted and Major Wendt, 2nd Battalion executive officer, spoke to a group of assembled POWs, reassuring them that they were now safe

* If the sign that the Japanese posted was in English as well as Japanese, the Americans were probably not close enough to read it.

under the U.S. flag. His talk was received with great enthusi-asm. One of the listeners, Navy pharmacist mate R. W. Kenner, before retiring that night recorded in his diary words that prob-ably reflected the thoughts of most of his comrades: "This would be the most unforgettable day of all our lives."

The next morning, while sporadic fighting continued outside the walls, American soldiers inside the compound visited with the ex-POWs and gave them cigarettes and some of the food they carried with them. However, because supply lines were stretched to the limit, the hoped-for bulk food for the liberated Americans could not be made available at once. The ex-POWs, reveling in their freedom, understood. They were more than delighted with their own food supply, which, with the remain-ing rations the Japanese had left, provided heaping servings of rice and thick soup made meaty with soybeans and mangoes. Most important, seconds were available and, for some, thirds. No food was wasted.

As the afternoon wore on, the Japanese intensified their demolition work. This created huge fires, particularly to the south and west of the prison. As fighting continued, the Ameri-cans took their first Japanese prisoners in the area and brought them into the compound. The newly liberated Americans looked on with little pity as Bilibid, after only a brief respite, again became a POW enclosure. Late in the day the winds shifted, blowing sparks and debris directly toward Bilibid. Senior officers among the ex-POWs and their rescuers became concerned that the approaching flames might ignite a Japanese fuel-and-ammunition warehouse next to the prison. Later the 37th Division's assistant division commander, after a personal assessment of the situation, ordered the immediate evacuation of the POWs and internees. Col. Lawrence K. White, the regi-mental commander, sent three of his staff* to the prison along with a quickly assembled group of medical aid men, litter bear-ers, clerks, communications personnel—just about anyone who could be rounded up who was not committed to fighting. About ten that night the rescue team began moving the first of those who could walk out of the gate and up Rizal Avenue. A few protested leaving their meager possessions behind, but most

* Lt. Col. Delbert E. Schultz; Maj. John J. Gallen, the regimental surgeon; and Capt. Stanley A. Frankel.

understood the urgency and marched off with what they could easily carry in their weakened condition. At the beginning of the evacuation there were not enough trucks and litters for the nearly three hundred former POWs and internees who could not walk. But as the flames illuminated the area, more trucks began to arrive. By midnight the last of the nonwalking were loaded, and later trucks began picking up the weary ex-POWs who were trudging up Rizal. After assuring himself that all were evacuated, the battalion commander ordered his battalion to withdraw to the north, fully expecting that Bilibid would soon be engulfed by fire. By midnight the last of the liberated Americans were trucked into the Ang Tibay shoe factory six miles north of the prison with no loss of life despite sporadic sniper fire. Hot tea was served and the exhausted ex-POWs settled down for a night's sleep.

On the following day General MacArthur announced to the world press that "our forces are rapidly clearing the enemy from Manila. Our converging columns . . . entered the city and surrounded the Jap defenders. Their complete destruction is imminent." MacArthur's announcement was premature. It would take another month of bitter fighting before Manila was cleared of the enemy. But on that day the rescued Americans at the shoe factory were more concerned with food than the war situation and were savoring such gourmet delicacies as Vienna sausage, sauerkraut, and, best of all, chocolate bars, the sweets that American palates craved.

On the following day, with Bilibid no longer in danger from the flames or the Japanese, the ambulatory ex-POWs and internees were moved back to their old compound. The litter cases were taken to an Army hospital which by now had been set up at Santo Tomas University. The ex-POWs had just arrived at Bilibid and were straightening out their pitiful belongings (which had been strewn about by some not-so-compassionate Filipino looters) when word was passed that General MacArthur had entered the compound. As members of his old command stood by their cots in a semblance of attention, the five-star general went down the line, greeting each briefly. When he came to Lieutenant Colonel Hardee, who had been pronounced physically unfit to go with his many companions from Davao when they left on the ill-fated *Oryoku*

Maru, the general's words were particularly warm and personal. Recalling that he had sent Hardee to Bataan to make "infantry out of the Air Corps," he added that he had received word from Mrs. Hardee that all was well at home. The mention of his family was too much for Hardee and he began to cry, regaining his composure only after MacArthur had passed on and one of his assistants whom Hardee knew well struck up a friendly conversation. The visit to Bilibid that day made a deep impression on MacArthur himself. Years later he would write:

> Here was all that was left of my men of Bataan and Corregidor. The only sound was the occasional sniffle of a grown man who could not fight back the tears. As I passed slowly down the scrawny, suffering column, a murmur accompanied me as each man, barely speaking above a whisper, said, "You're back," or "You made it," or "God bless you." I could only reply, "I'm a little late, but we finally came." I passed on out of the barracks compound and looked around at the debris that was no longer important to those inside: the tin cans they had eaten from; the dirty old bottles they had drunk from. It made me ill just to look at them.

The liberated Americans stayed at Bilibid for a couple of more days while arrangements were being made for their disposition. By now, good Army hot chow was being served three times a day and mail from home was delivered to many eager recipients. The American public got a look at the ex-POWs in newsreel footage which showed Lt. Homer Hutchison* demonstrating how he had assembled the last secret radio used in Bilibid and concealed it in the top of a stool; while another ingenious ex-POW amputee, Maj. W. J. Hinkle, opened up his wooden leg for the cameraman to show where he had hidden his diary.

Later all of those who could make the trip were driven north to a replacement center near Lingayen Gulf. Here each man was outfitted with two suits of khaki, two suits of jungle-weight fatigues, a field jacket, underwear, socks, handkerchiefs, shoes, towels, and a cap. To Commander McCracken it seemed

---

* He had operated the radio at Cabanatuan for over two years.

a tremendous wardrobe. At the time he wondered what he would do with all those clothes.

Soon all of the Americans freed in the Philippines (except the most seriously ill) were on their way home. But for the threadbare, hungry POWs still in Japanese hands, the war was far from over.

14

DOWN THE STRETCH

January–July 1945
Japan—China—Thailand—Manchuria

★ ★ ★ 1 ★ ★ ★

For the over five thousand POWs from the Philippines who
had survived the seaborne movements to Japan of the previous
summer and fall, the winter of 1944–1945—the coldest in over
a half century—was their first outside a tropical climate. Now,
along with Americans arriving earlier in the war, they found
themselves, hungry and shivering, in over thirty camps stretching from the northern to the southern reaches of the Japanese
home islands.

In northern Honshu at Hanawa, Sendai 6, the five hundred
men who had arrived on the *Noto Maru* in September got
some relief from the subzero weather largely through the efforts of Capt. Dan Golenterek, Army Medical Corps.
Golenterek was assigned to Hanawa from Tokyo after his
predecessor had been relieved for trying to keep too many
men on the sick list. He was an excellent physician and, more
important, a master diplomat in his relations with the Japanese.
Shortly after he arrived, during the worst of the winter weather,
he succeeded in keeping nearly three hundred men on the
quarters list and giving them some medical attention—this
without being overruled by the Japanese. Another great help
to the men at Hanawa that winter was the issue (on an individual item basis) of the equivalent of four Red Cross packages
per man through the winter. These were part of the Vladivos-

tok stockpile which had had such a spotty distribution after delivery to Japan in November 1944.

Three hundred miles southwest at a camp near Hosakura, 230 Americans who had arrived in January 1945 in poor physical condition from the rugged trip on the *Benjo Maru* were less successful in contending with harsh conditions in their new camp. Between forced labor in lead and zinc mines and the subzero cold at the 2,500-foot elevation, many died of pneumonia and other diseases. In the first month alone eight men died, more than the total deaths during the entire winter at Hanawa.

In the Osaka area even those POWs like Martin Boyle and his fellow Marines who were ending their third winter in Japan found the weather exceptional. Boyle would later recall snowdrifts piled near the top of telephone poles. Nearby at the Yodogawa steel mill, Al Costello, another Marine, and four men on detail with him got a break from the cold and hard labor when his smelting machine broke down and could not be repaired. Instead of turning Costello and the other men back to the labor pool to be reassigned to other work, their Japanese supervisor let them go to the inoperable equipment daily for most of the winter. After arriving there the five men would proceed to a deserted shed which they had discovered under a water tower. There with smuggled charcoal and anything else that would burn they kept a fire going and whiled away the day in comparative comfort while their fellow POWs labored in the windy, cold steel plant.

★ ★ ★ 2 ★ ★ ★

American POWs in camps in Manchuria and China shared to some degree with those in Japan the discomforts of cold weather, while survivors of the Burma–Thailand railroad sweated in their camps in tropical zones. But cold or hot, Americans in all camps were seeing an increase in American air activity. As it had before, the increased American air action brought cheer to many Americans but death and suffering to some. At Mukden, Manchuria, the B-29's had returned again in late December, after the deadly raid earlier that month, but this time no bombs fell in the prison compound. In the Kiangwan camp near Shanghai, five men were punished severely when they cheered low-flying P-51 fighters in a brief strafing mission of nearby airfields. This was their second sighting of American planes. The first, with the usual thrill to the POWs, had been an overflight of bombers in November. At the big POW camps at Kanburi and Tamarkan, west of Bangkok in Thailand, attacks by American Liberator bombers had begun in the fall, followed later by B-29's. Casualties in one raid were heavy—forty-one Allied POWs were killed, but no Americans were among them.

The luck of some of the pilots in the stepped-up air action was not as good as that of the men in the POW camps. In the February bombings of the Bonins (a small cluster of islands north of Iwo Jima, which had been invaded that month by the U.S. Marines) some American aircraft had been shot down and eight airmen captured. Four of them were executed, leaving the others to await a decision as to their fate. Anticipating invasion of one of the islands, Chichi Jima, at any time, the commanding general of the forces there told his subordinates that he expected a battle to the death. With no hope of resupply, food and ammunition would eventually run out. Under these circumstances, he said, men might have to eat the flesh of their own comrades or their enemies. Soon after this meeting but prior to an American landing on the island, the four captured fliers were executed. Then, contrary to Western mores and probably most Asian mores as well, the flesh of these men was cooked and consumed by their captors. Both Gen. Yushio Tachibana, the commanding general, and Adm. Kunizo Mori, the senior naval officer on the island, partook of the meal as did other officers and enlisted men of the island garrison.

Though the U.S. Army Air Force employed large numbers of B-29's in precision bombing of industrial targets in Japan during January and February of 1944, the results were not satisfactory. Beginning in March the Air Force adopted a radically different strategy: the use of incendiary bombs against Japanese cities. The decision to carry out relatively indiscriminate bombing of Japanese major industrial cities would lead to extremely heavy loss of life among the Japanese people. Inexplicably, at least in the initial phases of the bombing, casualties among the POWs, many of whom were held in the target cities, were relatively small.

The first firebombing raid, against Toyko on March 10,

burned over 200,000 buildings and killed more than 80,000 people.* It would rank as one of the most destructive single air attacks of World War II. But despite the severity of the raid no damage was done at the Tokyo camp at Omori, which was situated on a small island, or to the Shinagawa POW hospital south of Tokyo. After the bombing, Japanese civilian casualties were brought to both camps and Red Cross supplies stored there were used to treat them. A POW observer at the time, Navy lieutenant J. K. Davis, saw no objection to this but did object to pilfering by Japanese camp personnel from the medical stores for their own use. As a result of the destruction from this massive air attack Dr. F. W. Bilfinger, an International Red Cross representative, was forced to make his report of inspection concerning one of the Tokyo area camps from memory. This was necessary since his home and all his papers were burned on the night of the raid. In an obvious reaction to his personal experience and observations Bilfinger recommended to the Japanese Prisoner of War Bureau that air raid shelters and steel helmets be provided to POWs in the Tokyo camps.

Twentieth Air Force bombers hit Nagoya on the night following the Tokyo raid, and two days later, Osaka. Here 274 B-29's in successive formations dropped 1,732 tons of bombs for about three hours. The Osaka Marine stevedores had a ringside seat. As they peered out of their small windows, they thought that the whole city would be destroyed and themselves with it. Their luck held. Eight square miles of the commercial district was wiped out but their waterfront buildings were spared. The American POWs at two other Osaka camps, the Yodogawa steel mill and the Umeda railroad yards, also came through unscathed. At Umeda bombs fell just two blocks away but the fires created by them did not spread. The March fire blitz concluded with raids on Kobe, across the bay from Osaka, and another strike on Nagoya, both cities with POW camps in or around them. But as in Osaka, apparently few if any Americans lost their lives while thousands of Japanese perished. The reason for the lack of POW casualties amidst such intensive destruction and loss of life in the first months of firebombing

* As noted later, this was a greater death toll than that resulting from the atomic bombs dropped on Hiroshima or Nagasaki.

must be attributed to chance. POWs would not escape death in later bombings.

After assessing the results of the five firebombing raids Air Force headquarters in Washington concluded that continuation of the new tactics would substantially contribute to the accomplishment of the Twentieth Air Force's mission, which was to dislocate Japanese military, industrial, and economic systems and to undermine the morale of the Japanese people to a point where their capacity and will to wage war would be decisively weakened.

With the devastating bombing of cities in progress, the Japanese imperial headquarters staff had another concern. The U.S. invasion of Okinawa—the last Japanese island south of the home islands—was imminent. Preparing for the worst, the Japanese included in their contingency planning Secret Order 2257, entitled "Outline for Disposal of Prisoners of War According to the Change of Situation." Essentially it called for moving the POWs out of areas under air attack and away from locations which might be threatened by attacking Allied land forces. In addition to its vague title, the directive contained other ambiguities. In one section it permitted commanders to set POWs free and in the same section also authorized "emergency measures" to be taken against those with antagonistic attitudes. Though the Japanese would later point to the humanitarian motives of the directive, its main purpose was to retain as many POWs as possible as part of the labor force. Implementation of the order would not begin for another month. In the meantime the actions of a U.S. submarine would once more affect the lives of American POWs.

★ ★ ★ 3 ★ ★ ★

After distributing some of the Red Cross shipment from Vladivostok to Allied POWs in Japan in the fall of 1944, a substantial quantity of the supplies intended for POWs in the Philippines, Formosa, China, Malaya, and Indonesia remained in storage in Japan. The supplies could not be transported farther because of the lack of shipping and the submarine blockade. The United States, aware of this and acting on behalf of all

Allied POWs, requested shipment of the supplies and guaranteed safe passage for the ship transporting them. After some
delay, in February 1945 the Japanese agreed. On the seven-
teenth of that month the *Awa Maru*, a large cargo-passenger
vessel, left Moji, Japan, bound for Singapore and Indonesian
ports with a return trip via Hong Kong and Takao, Formosa.
In addition to two thousand tons of Red Cross supplies, the
ship probably carried a much larger cargo of military and other
supplies needed by the Japanese forces in the south. The
United States had agreed that there would be no restrictions
on what the *Awa Maru* could carry, either on the outgoing
or return voyage. The ship had special markings—white
crosses on each side of her hull and lighted white crosses at
night. The vessel made its outgoing trip without mishap, dropping off the Red Cross supplies and loading nearly two thousand
Japanese passengers and a cargo of scarce raw rubber. As in
the case of the *Gripsholm* diplomatic exchanges, the safe return
of the *Awa Maru* would have been of benefit to both the United
States and Japan.

This was not to be. On the night of April 1 an American
submarine skipper in a heavy fog, using radar, sank the *Awa
Maru*. The submarine picked up a survivor and from him
determined the identity of the ship. Informed of the sinking,
the Navy Department, obviously aware of the potentially adverse effects the sinking would have on U.S.-Japanese relationships concerning POWs, ordered the submarine to port and
directed that its commanding officer be tried by general court-
martial.

The Navy had good reason. The sinking came at a time
when the U.S. State Department was receiving and digesting
reports from hundreds of American POWs liberated in the Philippines and from survivors of POW ship sinkings. This wealth
of information on Japanese mistreatment of POWs was the basis
for renewed protests to the Japanese government. Though
the Japanese had ignored most of the U.S. protests submitted
to them previously, they now had a legitimate countercharge.
As the chief of the Prisoner of War Bureau later put it, regarding
one U.S. protest: "Such is the sly way of covering up its own
inhumane conduct. The Imperial Government will not give
a reply to the U.S. as long as we do not receive a reply to all
our requests concerning the sinking of the *Awa Maru*."

★ ★ ★ **4** ★ ★ ★

Meanwhile, the B-29 raids against populated areas had been reduced during April as the Twentieth Air Force turned its attention to airfields in Kyushu to help stop hundreds of kamikaze (suicide) bombings, which were raising havoc with U.S. Navy ships supporting the invasion of Okinawa, which had begun on April 1. Late that month the Prisoner of War Bureau began issuing orders implementing Secret Order 2257. Movements of POWs in accordance with this order would take place in Japan, China, and Manchuria over the next several months.

In Japan the Prisoner of War Bureau transferred the Americans in the Osaka camps—the Yodogawa steelworkers and the Umeda rail freight handlers—from the much-bombed city to towns on the north coast. These moves were done in compliance with the provisions of the order calling for POWs to be taken out of bombing target areas, rather than with the other criterion, which was to remove them from areas where enemy ground action was expected. Left behind until later—even though they now had few ships to load and unload—were the Marine stevedores at the docks. The POWs at the Omori and Shinagawa camps in the Tokyo area, the Twentieth Air Force's highest-priority target, would remain where they were until the war's end. This was done in the face of U.S. protests through the Swiss minister stating that the location of these camps placed the POWs there at extreme hazard and in violation of Article IX of the Geneva Convention.

The Japanese kept POWs hard at work at their new locations. Men from Yodogawa went to Oeyama, those from Umeda to Tsuruga, towns on the north coast of Japan above Osaka and an area which up to now had not been targeted by American bombers. At their new camp the Yodogawa men were put to work in a nickel mine. The Umeda group were told that they were being moved to Tsuruga because it was safer, but as one man would recall, as soon as they saw the docks and the ships that they would be unloading they knew that they would probably be bombed again. Their predictions were well founded. Tsuruga was bombed later and two thirds of its area destroyed.

Besides shifting POWs out of bombed cities, the Japanese transferred some Americans because they were in areas that the Japanese expected to have to defend. After the loss of the Mariana Islands the Japanese defense line included Okinawa, Formosa, Korea, and Shanghai. In May the Japanese moved the large group of prisoners of war at the POW camp near Shanghai north by train to a new camp at Fengtai, outside of Peking. During the trip four Marine officers and a former pilot with the Flying Tigers escaped and, after a forty-four-day trek by foot, horse, and boat, rejoined American forces.* The five would add their names to those of Commanders Smith and Woolley and Corporal Storey, who the previous fall on their second try had escaped from Kiangwan and had made their way over six hundred miles to gain their freedom.

Fengtai was just a stopover for the Americans. After a month they took another long train ride across north China and down the Korean peninsula, ferried across to southern Honshu, and again rode by train to northern Japan. Some of the men went to work in iron mines at Sendai 11 while others dug coal at two camps in Japan's northernmost island, Hokkaido. That the Japanese Army would use scarce rail transport (major railheads had been bombed continually and many engines and cars had been destroyed) to move the POWs such a long distance demonstrated the Japanese nation's lack of manpower and desperate need for coal and steel to support their dying industry.

★ ★ ★ 5 ★ ★ ★

Blasting away again at Japan's remaining factories was the Twentieth Air Force. Orders to resume the massive firebomb attacks came on the heels of Germany's surrender on May 8. In mid-May, Nagoya was bombed twice with more than five hundred planes in each mission. After the second bombing, the city was crossed off as target.

Beginning with the big March raids, the Japanese had captured and held an increasing number of B-29 flight crews who had survived after their planes were shot down. Given the terrible human casualties that the bombs inflicted, it is surpris-

* The officers were James D. McBrayer, Richard Huizenga, John F. Kinney, John A. McAlister, and Louis S. Bishop.

ing that more American airmen were not killed by civilians. The fact that in most cases the crews were turned over alive by civilians who captured them must be attributed to the discipline of the people.

On its part the Japanese Army segregated downed American fliers from other POWs. One of the reasons for this was that they did not want longtime POWs to learn how badly the war was going for Japan. This was despite the fact that many POWs had by this time seen for themselves ample evidence of the destruction of Japan's cities and its effects on the nation. After the fliers were captured, the Japanese went through the motions of interrogation. There was not a great deal that the Japanese could learn from the pilots that would blunt the overwhelming power of the B-29's. It was on this same premise that the American Air Force changed its policy from permitting a captured person to give the enemy only his name, rank, and serial number to letting him tell the Japanese whatever would keep him from being tortured or killed.

After interrogation Japanese military laws and regulations for "Punishment of Enemy Plane Flight Personnel" required that except for those bombing a purely military target (few if any of the later B-29 raids had this objective) all crew members would be charged with inhumane and indiscriminate bombing and tried by a military court. The sentence for those found guilty was execution.

Death came without trial for one large group of downed American fliers. With Nagoya out of the way, the Twentieth Air Force had turned to Tokyo for a final one-two knockout blow. On the nights of May 23 and May 25 there were two attacks of greater than five hundred planes each. The area laid waste by fire in the second of these raids was even greater than in the March raid. One of the buildings destroyed that night was part of a Tokyo military prison where sixty-two U.S. airmen were being held along with Japanese military prisoners. All of the airmen were burned to death. Captain Tashiro, commander of the prison, later claimed that the Americans died because in the intensity of the attack and the confusion the guards got to the American section of the building too late to free them. None of the over four hundred Japanese prisoners held in the same building died.

During the same raid antiaircraft fire was the heaviest yet

encountered. Twenty-six B-29's were lost. Following the raid, a number of American air crewmen from the downed planes were brought into the military police headquarters in Tokyo. Sgt. Michael J. Robertson was one of these. Robertson lost consciousness after bailing out of his stricken B-29. When he came to, he was being attacked by a mob of Japanese men and women. The mob beat him with rocks, sticks, and their fists until they were dispersed by the Japanese military police. After he was brought into the Japanese headquarters, he was beaten, interrogated, and then placed in a small cell with eighteen other prisoners. Conditions in the cell were primitive, discipline was strict, and rations were three bowls of rice per day. Robertson received no medical treatment for a broken leg and shrapnel wounds. But except for one man, all the Americans survived. This was probably because of their excellent physical condition when captured. In another B-29 that crashed that night all the crew except one were killed. The commander of the Japanese military unit that later found this plane, after determining that the man was seriously wounded, ordered one of his sergeants to carry out *kiashaku* (a Bushido term for "a sympathetic and merciful act to stop pain and hasten death"). The act, death by beheading, was carried out on the spot.

Less merciful was the death of eight men of a twelve-man B-29 crew shot down over Kyushu. Under guise of medical research, on four occasions during May and early June the Japanese jailers turned over their American prisoners to members of the medical school of the Kyushu Imperial University for vivisection. None of the Americans survived the surgical experimentation, which was observed by a number of the staff and students of the university.

After the two Tokyo raids and an attack on Yokohama, the Twentieth Air Force turned to Osaka, already heavily damaged in March. This time Osaka POW Camp 1, near the docks, was not spared. Though no POWs were killed a number suffered severe burns and the building in which they slept was destroyed. On the day after the raid the men were trucked to new locations. Most went to Notogawa, about forty miles northeast of Osaka, where they dug canals and built dikes for the irrigation of rice fields. After the work on the docks, which they had become used to, the POWs found their days in the

rice field monotonous and taxing, but the knowledge that liberation was not far off kept their morale up. Later nearby Kobe
was again bombed. The POW hospital there was hit, killing
five POWs of undisclosed nationality.

By this time Japan's major industrial cities—Tokyo, Kawasaki, Yokohama, Nagoya, Osaka, and Kobe—were in ruins.
Still fearful of more bombings, the Japanese moved POWs from
the Tokyo area. Kawasaki POW Camp 23-D men moved to
Niigata, on the north coast of Honshu, in early June. The move
was probably unnecessary. The Twentieth Air Force, considering the large cities finished, except for certain specific industrial
plants that were targeted, next turned to the smaller cities.

In this new phase twenty-five cities were scheduled for firebombing, but eventually the list would exceed fifty. On the
first day of these bombings, June 17, two cities with POWs in
their vicinity were hit—Omuta and Yokkaichi. No bomb casualties occurred among the mine and foundry workers at Fukuoka 17, outside of Omuta. The men at the camp near
Yokkaichi, some distance from the city itself, also came through
unharmed. Two days later the city of Fukuoka was hit. Here
again no POWs in the camp near the city were killed, but
eight fliers from a B-29 downed in the raid were executed
without trial the following day. This was because some staff
officers of the western military district, headquartered at Fukuoka, became incensed over the destruction inflicted on the
city. A week later for similar reasons officers at the Eastern
Sea military district headquarters decided to forgo time-con-
suming military court proceedings and had eleven American
airmen who had bombed Nagoya in May executed in the mountains east of that city. In the weeks that followed, bombing
missions against the less-populated cities averaged two per
week, with three to four cities bombed on each night. By
the end of the following month, July, forty-six of the smaller
cities had been bombed, eleven of which had POW camps
nearby. The Japanese would later report that about fifty POWs
were killed and twenty-one injured as a result of these bombings. Though the exact number will never be known, it is
reasonable to assume that some of them were Americans.

Meanwhile, the execution of captured airmen continued.
On July 14 sixteen men were executed without trial at the
rear of the headquarters of the Eastern Sea military district,

which included the Tokyo area. In another instance, after a long delay two airmen who had been held since the March raids on Osaka and Kobe were tried by military court and executed by a firing squad on the same day as their trial. Thirty-eight other men who had participated in later bombings of Osaka and Kobe were not provided even this hollow privilege of trial and during July and into August, in several groups, were taken to a maneuver area and a rifle range near Osaka and executed. Though records are incomplete and sometimes conflicting, it is probable that well over two hundred American fliers were executed or killed after capture by the Japanese military.

The Japanese had by now little or no economic war potential. All transportation, the lifeline of this island nation, was severely crippled. Most factories were destroyed or had ceased to operate. Food supplies were at minimum levels. Keeping the Japanese Army fed had the highest priority. Sustenance of Japanese civilians and POWs was provided, in that order, after the needs of the Army were met. Most of the city dwellers who had seen and lived through the bombings believed that their nation would lose the war. The people were losing faith in their military and civilian leadership and had grown to distrust government propaganda. Pessimism spread as more Japanese evacuated the bombed cities and moved to other parts of the nation.

★ ★ ★ 6 ★ ★ ★

If the civilian populace was losing heart, their military leaders, with the tenacity and fatalism they had shown throughout the war, were not. With the fall of Okinawa in late June, the Japanese imperial staff turned its full attention to the defense of Japan proper. *Ketsu-go*, the plan for defense of the homeland, called for an all-out effort to defeat the invaders. Civilians—the elderly, the young—would be armed and be expected to fight as guerrillas if Japanese military forces were overrun. Under such circumstances there can be little doubt as to what the fate of POWs in Japan might have been.

In the United States, President Truman, though faced with decisions which would shape the world for decades to come, found time soon after taking office to express his feelings on the fate of POWs. At a White House press conference he said, "The welfare of these men [the POWs] is a matter of deep concern to me and I am determined to do everything possible to help them and to bring about their release as soon as possible." On the same day as the President spoke, Secretary of War Stimson was chairman of a meeting of top-level military and State Department officials and scientists who had been convened to determine how to employ the first atomic bombs. Various methods of demonstrating the power of the weapon were discussed short of dropping it on a Japanese city. One of these was to issue a warning to the Japanese and then explode a bomb in or over an uninhabited section of Japan. The President's representative, James Byrnes, expressed the fear that the Japanese if forewarned might assemble a group of Americans and other POWs to stand as viewers and possible victims at such a demonstration. Later the group voted against any kind of demonstration and recommended that the bomb be used for military purposes.

Then, on July 26 at Potsdam, Germany, the United States and Great Britain issued an ultimatum to Japan (the Potsdam Declaration) to surrender unconditionally or suffer "prompt and utter destruction." Included in the Declaration was this statement: "We do not intend that the Japanese shall be enslaved as a race or destroyed as a nation, but stern justice shall be meted out to all war criminals, including those who have visited cruelties upon our prisoners."

On his way back to the United States from Potsdam, President Truman, convinced that his action would speed the end of the war and save hundreds of thousands of American and Japanese lives, ordered atomic bombs to be dropped on two Japanese cities. By the beginning of August the Air Force had selected the cities and issued orders for the delivery of two atomic bombs, one to be used on Hiroshima and the other on Nagasaki. Hiroshima would be first.

15

LIBERATION
August–September 1945
Japan—Manchuria—Korea—Thailand

★ ★ ★ 1 ★ ★ ★

The Japanese government, undecided, did not respond to the Potsdam Declaration. Then on August 6, a B-29, the *Enola Gay*, released the first operational atomic weapon on Hiroshima, in southern Honshu. It devastated that hitherto unbombed city and killed nearly eighty thousand Japanese people. Twenty-three American POWs may have been among the dead. They were probably downed American fliers held at an army headquarters known to have been located close to the bomb's center of impact, which was completely destroyed.

Two days later, with still no response from the Japanese, a second atomic bomb was released by another B-29, *Bock's Car*. It detonated at 3:40 P.M. above Nagasaki, a port city on the west coast of the island of Kyushu. Melvin Routt, at Fukuoka Camp 17, was on a farming detail that day. Looking west across the bay, Routt and his companions saw a mushroom cloud. Then they heard and felt what seemed to them to be two explosions and watched a varicolored cloud arise in the vicinity of Nagasaki, over thirty miles away. The men continued work, mystified at what they had observed. Their puzzlement only increased when later an acrid odor carried by westerly winds reached them.

At another POW camp, Fukuoka Camp 24 near Senryu, Lt. Julien Goodman was glancing out of a storeroom door when he observed vapor trails in the sky and simultaneously heard and sensed a loud roar like a "myriad of sixteen-inch naval batteries fired in unison." He and a companion dove for the floor as the building shook with earthquake force, after which there was an ominous quiet. After brushing themselves off they found that no one had been hurt, but for the rest of the day Goodman wondered what had happened. That evening the radio in Japanese headquarters was on continuously. The POWs sensed that something terrible had happened at Nagasaki. Later the Japanese informed the POW senior officer that when the next shift came out of the mine no more would go down. Though the reason for this generosity was still obscure, the POWs concluded that whatever the cause, the end of their forced servitude was not far off.

Over thirty-five thousand Japanese lost their lives in the Nagasaki bombing. Some Allied POWs died in the blast that day but no Americans were known to have been among them.

While *Bock's Car* was returning from its deadly mission and Japanese authorities in Tokyo were receiving word of this second catastrophic use of an atomic weapon, the U.S.S.R. declared war on Japan.

★ ★ ★ 2 ★ ★ ★

The Soviet entry into the war, on top of the news of the atomic bombs, made a Japanese decision on the Potsdam Declaration most urgent. For forty-eight hours Premier Kantaro Suzuki and his cabinet ministers debated whether conditions should be attached to Japan's acceptance of the Declaration. Among the conditions considered, probably a reaction to the Declaration's stern announcement, was that the Japanese government be allowed to prosecute all war criminals. However, in the Japanese government's statement transmitted on August 10 only one condition, aimed at preserving the prerogatives of the emperor, was included. On the twelfth of August the Japanese read the short, five-paragraph Allied response to their message. It left the role of the emperor unclear but was very specific, demonstrating the importance that Allied leaders placed upon the matter, in reference to POW and civilian internees. They were to be transported to places of safety where they could be placed aboard Allied transports.

After two days of agonizing discussions about the role of the emperor and with the assent of the emperor himself, the Japanese finally informed the Allies that would accept the surrender terms. The emperor decided to announce the decision personally to the people on the following day.

The government alerted the country to stand by at noon on August 15 for an important announcement which many of the people thought might be an exhortation to fight to the death. Others believed it might be a declaration of war on Russia. As it turned out, the listeners, many weeping, had a double shock. First they heard the voice of the emperor. His spoken words had never been broadcast before. Second, they learned that their country had surrendered on the enemy's terms. Following the broadcast, war plants were closed and workers dismissed. Millions of Japanese, both the general populace and the military, accepted and moved toward full compliance with their emperor's decree.

There were some exceptions. A few diehards urged that the country fight on, but nothing resulted from this. However, for some American POWs the emperor's decree brought death. At western army headquarters at Fukuoka, where eight American fliers had been executed earlier, Japanese officers, concerned that the remaining captives would testify against them, sentenced the prisoners to death. Later that day the sixteen Americans, unaware that the war was over, were trucked to the same site—Aburayama—as their companions had been taken to. This time the Japanese soldiers led the bound Americans in groups of two or three into the trees and hacked them to death with swords. The butchery over, the mutilated corpses were shoved into a hastily dug grave.

Meanwhile, on the day before the emperor's broadcast and continuing through that day the War Ministry had been busy notifying the various headquarters to cease hostilities and, in addition, it instructed them to destroy all "confidential documents." At POW camps such documents included orders for harsh treatment and records of punishment and execution. U.S. attempts to assemble such documents later would show that the Japanese camp personnel did a thorough job of destruction.

On August 16 the United States notified the Japanese government that its surrender was accepted and ordered the Japanese to send a delegation to the Philippines to meet with representatives of General MacArthur to arrange for the formal surrender and occupation of Japan. The code name for the plan for occupation, which had been under preparation since May of that year, was "Blacklist." One of the major missions of Blacklist was to locate POWs and internees and to provide them with adequate food, shelter, and clothing and medical care, and subsequently to evacuate them.

★ ★ ★ 3 ★ ★ ★

Except for the few camps without radio communication, POW camp commanders soon learned of the nation's capitulation either from the emperor's broadcast or through military channels, or both. They then faced a difficult task—communicating the new state of affairs to the men in the camp, men for whom the Japanese were still responsible but who were no longer POWs. Few commanders found it possible to announce the surrender immediately. To avoid or defer the anguish and loss of face in admitting defeat, many delayed telling this momentous news to the POWs. This compelled them to resort to various ruses to explain the releases from work and improved treatment which occurred in virtually all camps soon after August 15.

Most of the POWs saw through the silence and flimsy excuses. Such was the case for Sgt. Walter Bowsher and some of the Wake Island Marines working in the copper mines in the mountains of Japan's northernmost island, Hokkaido. Just a few days before the emperor's announcement, four impatient POWs had, in Bowsher's words, "gone over the hill." Two were caught the following day but the others were still at large on August 15. Around noon Bowsher and others not working in the mine that day heard the local camp radio being played loudly for a group of Japanese camp personnel. Later that afternoon they saw a newspaper delivered to camp headquarters with what one man described as headlines two inches high. The men noted an immediate change in the guards' attitudes toward them and knew something big had happened. When the Japanese called off the night shift for the mine detail (still not telling the POWs of the surrender announcement) and declared a four-day holiday, the POWs became confident that the war was over. Soon the rumor was going around that American troops had landed and seized seven of Japan's largest cities. At the officers' camp not far away, work was also called off. The Japanese interpreter explained that it was to protect the POWs from a typhus epidemic in a nearby city.

South on Honshu, high in the mountains near the town of Rokuroshi, 360 officer POWs were held in an isolated location. By strange coincidence—such attempts were rare in Japan—here also two Americans had escaped but both were captured a few days before Japan's surrender announcement. It was only by then that the news of the atomic bombs had reached the Japanese commander. The camp had no radio and its only connection with the outside world was a single telephone line. Soon after this the Americans noticed that camp officials became very surly, and finally got a guard to tell them the reason. Then on August 17 the phone rang again. In the stillness of the remote surroundings everyone knew when it rang, which was seldom. After the call the commandant left the camp and the Japanese announced that there would be no work for a few days. The guards' attitude changed radically. Some of the officers accepted offers to be taken in small groups for walks in the forest. Meanwhile, the camp waited expectantly for the commandant to return.

Farther south at Notogawa, Martin Boyle and his fellow Marines, on a morning soon after the emperor's announcement, had finished their rice and soup and were waiting for the work whistle to blow as it had for hundreds of mornings in the past. It didn't blow that day. After waiting for nearly an hour, some of the men discovered that the sentry boxes of the inner compound were unoccupied. The absence of work and guards was sufficient to convince some of them that the end was near. Later in the day one of the guards came into the compound, and in answer to a direct question of whether the war was over, he answered with a nod. Even after this confirmation, in contrast to the enthusiasm found in some camps, the men at Notogawa were relatively unmoved by the news. There were no shouts and cheers, just, as Boyle remembered it, a "dog-tired feeling of relief." West at Hirohata on the fifteenth the Japanese camp officials told the senior POW there that because of a lack of raw materials all men would be excused from work at the factory that day. Later an interpreter told the senior POW the truth.

On the island of Kyushu, at big Fukuoka Camp 17 with its seventeen hundred American and Allied POWs, all POW work had been called off after the dropping of the Nagasaki atomic bomb with no explanation given. No announcements were made on the fifteenth, but on the following day a Dutch chaplain held a memorial service for the dead in the camp, attended by a large number of the POWs, and spoke of freedom to come. The new leniency of their captors and the fact that the chaplain was permitted to speak openly led many POWs to conclude that the end of their captivity was not far off.

At Camp 14, Senryu, where work had also stopped after the explosion of the bomb, the commandant was more straightforward. On August 16 he read an announcement which was translated as follows: "The order has been given to stop the fight. You are all staying in the camp from this time and should wait for further instructions. In the future as well as before, the camp commandant will take responsibilities for your rest, food, clothing, and the necessary means for security. Each prisoner is expected to carry on his daily life as regularly as before." A moment after the commandant had turned and reentered his headquarters the men gave a great cheer. This was followed by dancing and backslapping and much rejoicing.

Across the Korean Strait at Jinsen, Korea, Major Bodine and other survivors of the *Oryoku Maru* and the ships that followed did not get to relish a public admission of Japan's defeat by their captors. Instead, on August 17 the commandant notified the prisoner-of-war senior officer that the war was over and released a Red Cross package to each man.

On August 16 at Nakhon Nayok, in Thailand, Ben Dunn and his comrades were surprised when on their way to work as usual, the guards abruptly turned the column around and with glum looks marched them back to the camp. For the rest of the day the men discussed and speculated on what was going on. The next morning the men were formed on the parade ground and "Mother" Stimson, a British warrant officer and the senior POW there, climbed on a box and announced in a booming voice that the war was officially at an end. After a few moments of stunned silence the men, some twenty-five thousand British, Australians, and Americans, gave vent to their pent-up feelings with cheers, shouting, and backslapping. This spontaneous reaction was followed by individual national groups singing their respective anthems. The Americans substituted "God Bless America" for "The Star-Spangled Banner" because, in Dunn's view, it more appropriately expressed their gratitude to their country and their feelings at that time.

★ ★ ★ 4 ★ ★ ★

Unlike their countrymen in Japan, Korea, and Thailand, the POWs at Mukden, Manchuria, the largest single group of Americans held in the Far East at the time, would be liberated relatively quickly after a succession of dramatic events.

The first came on the morning of August 16 (the Japanese had called off work the previous day) when some of the idle POWs saw six parachutists jumping from a plane south of the camp. The six were an Office of Strategic Services team sent by Gen. A. C. Wedemeyer, commander of the China theater of operations, to effect the prompt and safe release of POWs at Mukden.*

The team, equipped with radio and other gear, landed safely in a field of vegetables and, after meeting a friendly Chinese who volunteered to guide them, started walking toward the POW camp. On the way they were captured by a Japanese military police detachment who did not seem to know the war was over. After they had been blindfolded, threatened, and handled roughly for over four hours their captors belatedly received news of the surrender. After apologizing the military police drove them to the POW camp, where they were received cordially later that afternoon by the commandant, Colonel Matsuda. Despite protests by Major Hennessy, Colonel Matsuda would allow no contact with the Americans in the camp until he had a chance to cable Tokyo for instructions. After some discussion Matsuda promised to begin moving his men out of the prison compound and to turn over administration to the POWs as soon as possible.

* The six were Maj. J. P. Hennessy and Maj. Robert F. Lamar; three noncommissioned officers, Edward Starz, Harold Leith, and Fumio Kido (a nisei); and Maj. Cheng-Shi-Wu (a Nationalist Chinese).

Some of the POWs, watching from a distance, saw the strangers arrive but were mystified as to the identity of four Occidentals and two Asians in strange uniforms. (The uniforms were of a design and color developed for the U.S. forces after the capture of the POWs in 1941–1942.) As the word spread through the camp most agreed that these men certainly must be important emissaries of some kind—how else would they enter and leave the commandant's office wearing their side arms? That night few slept. Nearly all by now were convinced that the next day would bring some big news.

They were right. After breakfast on August 17, Colonel Matsuda called the three senior POW officers to his office. A half hour later they returned and each made an announcement to the POWs of his nationality. Maj. Gen. George Parker's statement was brief. He told the listening Americans that an armistice had been declared between Japan and the United States, Great Britain, and China but that fighting between Japan and Russia continued. He told them that for the present the Japanese were still in control, and since they had the guns, the Americans should be careful about creating any disturbance.

Later that day General Parker assembled some of the senior American officers and introduced the Office of Strategic Services team. Hennessy told his eager listeners that plans were being made to evacuate them as soon as possible and brought them up to date on the progress of the war. On the following day the Japanese held their last roll call. The POWs, though still confined to their compound, were technically free men.

Meanwhile, two of the rescue team, Major Lamar and Sergeant Leith, had reached Sian, where they cheered General Wainwright with the news that he was an American hero and had been written up in *Time* magazine. On the following morning, after breakfasting with the Allied officers, Lamar returned to Mukden to secure vehicles to bring the men south.

At Mukden after supper on August 20 most of the former POWs gathered for an outdoor concert by the camp's small orchestra. Following a medley of national anthems, some popular tunes, and group singing, the concert was interrupted by the announcement that all men would assemble on the north side of the hospital building. Upon arrival they found two Russian officers standing on the steps with General Parker and the other two Allied senior officers. Off to the side stood Colonel Matsuda and his staff. As one of the Russian officers, a captain, stepped forward the group cheered and then fell quiet. As an American interpreter translated, the Soviet officer announced that the Russians had occupied Mukden that day and loudly proclaimed in Russian—under the circumstances the statement hardly needed translation—"From this hour, all American, British, and other Allied war prisoners in this camp are free."

This statement drew great cheering, shouting, and some tears of happiness from the former POWs. Among them were survivors of the Death March, Camp O'Donnell, Bilibid, Cabanatuan, Davao, Formosa,* Japanese camps, the *Oryoku Maru* and other death ships; even some downed B-29 fliers who had been brought in by the Japanese a few days before. For all of them this was a crowning moment.

When the din subsided, the captain proudly told his listeners that the Russian troops, a mechanized unit, had traveled over one thousand kilometers in less than ten days to capture Mukden. In the name of the Soviet government, he congratulated the Allies for their victory over Japanese imperialism. After each statement by the captain the POWs cheered lustily. Colonel Matsuda and other officers looked downcast. Lieutenant Oki, a medical officer who had consistently tried to treat POWs fairly, wept. The Russians asked where General Wainwright was and seemed concerned that he was not present. Finally, the captain stated that the Japanese camp guards would be disarmed and that he was going into conference with the senior Allied officers to arrange for the early departure of all POWs to their homes. General Parker stepped forward and expressed, on behalf of all, his thanks and appreciation to the Russian Army and congratulated them on their great victory. That ended the meeting, and most of the joyous crowd returned to the concert or elsewhere.

A now hilarious group of officers and men had hardly resumed the singing of "California Here I Come" and "Happy Days Are Here Again" when a number of them were called back and asked to line up on one side of the prison compound. Then as the men looked on, the Russian officers had the Japa-

---

* The senior officers at Chen Chia Tung had been transferred to Mukden in May.

nese officers and men march out into the center of the quadrangle and lay down their arms. The officer of the day, Lieutenant Levie, led a guard detail which picked up the rifles. The Russians presented a Japanese pistol to General Parker. The proceedings were now in semidarkness and not easy to see but were being announced by an American interpreter. The last translation was "The Russian officer has directed that the Japanese be paraded before you and marched out of this compound forever."

Out they went under the American guards and with the former POWs watching, satisfied that finally things were as they should be. After leaving the quadrangle the guard detail confined the Japanese enlisted men to the guardhouse and the officers to a room in another building. Soon after this, General Parker moved into Colonel Matsuda's office. The turnover was complete.

★ ★ ★ 5 ★ ★ ★

In Japan and Korea the rest of the now "free" Americans would have to await the arrival of Allied forces before tasting the full fruits of liberation. Planning for that event was proceeding.

In Manila a Japanese military delegation met with General MacArthur's representatives and agreed to return Allied military personnel and civilian internees immediately and designated the ports for their evacuation. In Tokyo officials of the POW Bureau were working hard on arrangements for returning the former POWs to Allied control.

Some of the work was self-serving. General Tamura, the Bureau chief, sent a letter to camp commanders asking them to treat their prisoners well, quoting an Allied message which said that such treatment could influence coming peace negotiations. Two days later another Tokyo message, clearly demonstrating the Prisoner of War Bureau's awareness of the situation in POW camps, went out to major commanders and camp commandants. The message read: "Personnel who mistreated prisoners of war and internees or who are held in extremely bad sentiment by them are permitted to take care of it by immediately transferring or by fleeing without a trace. Moreover documents which would be unfavorable for us in the hands of the enemy are to be treated in the same way as

secret documents and destroyed when finished with." At Notogawa and Fukuoka Camp 17, and probably many other camps,
the message merely put an official blessing on a *fait accom-
pli*. In these camps guards known for their brutality disappeared on the day the emperor announced the Japanese
surrender.

While awaiting the arrival of the U.S. forces, POWs found
themselves possessed of varying degrees of freedom. At the
officer camp at Rokuroshi the men had yet to hear the surrender
news on August 22. Consequently, they anxiously watched
as their camp commandant's car wound its way slowly back
up the mountain that day. Upon arrival the commandant immediately went to the room of the U.S. senior officer, Lt. Col.
Marion D. Unruh, and told him that the war was over. Soon
thereafter, Unruh made the announcement to a rejoicing group
of officers. Later the Americans held a surrender ceremony.
With a group of American officers in formation and at attention, the Japanese commandant turned over his sword to Colonel Unruh. (The guards had already turned over their arms
and ammunition.) Then a color guard lowered the giant-sized
Japanese flag from its tall pole and raised a small U.S. flag.
The flag was one that had been smuggled through the years
of captivity at great risk by an American officer. After a salute
the colonel ordered the troops dismissed. As Captain Coleman,
one of the officers in charge of the American detail, turned
to dismiss his men, he noticed tears streaming down the faces
of many of them. But the tears dried quickly as rejoicing took
over and lasted into the night.

The next few days were exciting ones. The men painted
large "POW" signs on the roofs of the buildings and tore down
the compound fence. Hoarded food was consumed and the
Japanese commandant arranged for grapes and other extra rations to be brought in by the villagers nearby.

Though turning over control was in most cases less formal,
transfers similar to that which occurred at Rokuroshi were hap-
pening in dozens of camps in Japan where Americans were
located. The Japanese camp personnel, meanwhile, were generally keeping themselves at a safe distance in or near the
camps. Most of the camp commanders, apprehensive as to
their fate when the Allied forces arrived, and obedient to the
orders of their emperor, were highly solicitous in their dealings

with the men in their charge. An extreme in conciliation attempts might have been illustrated in the closing paragraph of an announcement of "peace" (no mention of surrender) made by the commandant of Hakodate POW Camp 2—delayed until nine days after the emperor's broadcast. It read in part:

> As the war came to an end, so let it be with Enmity, if any of you happens to hold a grudge against any particular man of the staff or sentries, let us shake hands and forget the dark hours for the sake of peace and love.
>   Lastly the commandant, with good grace, has prepared to drink a toast to your health and happiness. Are you all going to accept this invitation? Yes? Very well.
>
> Congratulations to each of you.
Lieutenant Jiro Tendo

Few accepted Lieutenant Tendo's invitation.

The Japanese POW officials had ample reason to be concerned about their former charges' attitudes toward them. Many American officers and enlisted men had vowed to punish or kill their oppressors when the opportunity came. Fortunately little of this occurred. One reason was that some of the worst guards had fled. Even where they remained, a vindictive former POW had to consider the fact that U.S. military might was still hundreds of miles and days or weeks away and might not help him in a conflict with his former captors. For most POWs the elation of their newly gained freedom overcame their desire for retribution. Some of the Americans noted this psychological phenomenon in themselves at the time and were surprised by it.

In contrast, a few men did what they could to see that deserving Japanese camp personnel would be protected from later punishment by Allied forces. Lt. Col. Guy H. Stubbs, a man who had shouldered POW responsibilities in several camps in Luzon, Mindanao, and finally at Toyama in Japan, was one among a small number of former POWs who wrote letters commending guards for fair treatment. Such letters were given to individuals to show to occupation forces when they arrived.

Relationships with civilians in the vicinity of the camps were surprisingly good. Though the Japanese camp commandants had warned the men against going out of the camps (they were concerned that any trouble would reflect on them), most of the American senior officers either permitted the men in their camps to leave or were unable or unwilling to prevent them from doing so. Consequently many men took advantage of the opportunity to see what the world looked like on the other side of the fence.

Excursions outside took a variety of forms. At the Nishi Ashibetsu camp in Hokkaido, Captain White, Major Devereaux, and five other officers were guests of the Mitsui Mining Company at the company's private club. The meal was sumptuous—ten separate dishes combining fowl or seafood with various types of vegetables and sauces, along with wine, beer, and whisky. At Rokuroshi, Lieutenant Emerson was out by himself exploring a neighboring village and saw an old lady hanging out some kimonos. He said that he would like to buy one and the Japanese woman, at first reluctant, finally agreed not to sell it but to trade it for a G.I. raincoat, which Emerson had bought from a friend in the barracks. At Notogawa some of the more rambunctious Marines grew restive and decided to go to Osaka to get some medical supplies. After commandeering a police car they headed south but, after reaching Kyoto, stopped over at the plush Miyako Hotel, where other ex-POWs were enjoying the food and accommodations. They finally did get to Osaka, picked up the supplies, and returned to Notogawa. Men at the big Fukuoka 17 camp, also impatient, left the camp and headed north and south, some visiting other camps and others proceeding by train to some of the port cities, hoping to find passage on ships that they expected to dock there. These self-initiated POW movements would increase in numbers on both Honshu and Kyushu as the days passed and were a concern only to Japanese and American officers who wanted to maintain order in a time of much confusion.

Meanwhile, the men at Mukden were also enjoying their liberty; and some were starting home. On the same day as the first of these, thirty-two hospital patients, left on two B-24's for China, General Parker lifted a ban he had imposed on visits to the city of Mukden. He felt the Russians now were present in sufficient strength to make it safe. Daily thereafter officers and men on foot, in pony carts, on bicycles, and in rickshas roamed through the city, seeing the sights, drinking, and souvenir-hunting. The items brought back to camp ranged from Japanese sabers, field glasses, rifles, helmets, cameras, kimonos, and bicycles to—unique case—a saddle horse. It was not long before someone located a brewery. From then on there was a steady stream of men, using a variety of conveyances, returning to the camp with cases of beer.

On August 27 General Wainwright and others from Sian arrived at the Mukden main camp. Major Lamar had been unsuccessful in getting transportation for them so they had come on their own. First with a Russian motorized column and then by commandeering rail transport, the top-ranking Allied officers finally arrived, worn out, in Mukden just in time for Wainwright to board a plane that would take him to American headquarters in China. This flight was followed by a fairly regular air shuttle every other day, taking sick and disabled men first and later on some senior officers.

Meanwhile, with a bit of luck—they were neither sick nor high-ranking—Ben Dunn and some other Americans at Nakhon Nayok had been flown out of Thailand. They arrived in Calcutta, India, a major American military headquarters, on August 27.

★ ★ ★ 6 ★ ★ ★

On that same day the Twentieth Air Force, its bombing over, had begun a new mission, supplying food and clothing to ex-POWs. Though supplies had been air-dropped to some camps before, with an accurate list of the camps and their locations now available Air Force B-29's from the Marianas began a large-scale program of air supply to all known camps. Within five days most of the camps received their initial deliveries of clothing, medicine, and a three-day stock of food consisting of soups, fruit juices, staples, vitamins, and other items. A second drop followed, consisting of a seven-day supply of rations. Thereafter, for those camps that not yet been reached by a ground party, more supplies of foodstuffs would be continued until the camps were evacuated.

Of the supplies the food was the most welcome. Warnings by medical officers to avoid overindulgence fell mostly on deaf ears. It was not unusual for a man to receive the equivalent of a bushel basket of canned food. After the drops eating was a round-the-clock activity. At nearly any time of the day, men could be found eating, talking, playing cards, and walking off the effects of their frequent meals. Though acute problems from overeating were common, few suffered chronically from the massive change in diet. Medicine and vitamins brought new vigor to the ill and most debilitated men. The clothing that was part of the air drops would have been appreciated more if it had been received in the freezing weather of the previous winter. As it was, Captain Hewlett and some of his fellows at Fukuoka Camp 17 were a bit disappointed to open a huge carton only to find it full of long winter underwear. The temperature in Kyushu at the time was in the nineties, with high humidity. At Omine Machi, the grateful ex-POWs even found use for recovered red-white-and-blue parachutes. From them they fashioned American and British flags, which once completed were raised over the camp, replacing the Japanese colors.

Though aerial resupply was highly successful it was not without cost. Of the over nine hundred planes which were airborne on POW supply missions eight were lost, with seventy-seven casualties. The bounty brought with it some misfortune for the recipients also. The supplies were dropped from very low altitudes and parachutes malfunctioned occasionally. Since most of the supplies were packed in 55-gallon steel drums, those that fell free were in effect lethal projectiles.

At Jinsen, Korea, Bodine watched the first B-29's, three of them, reach his camp, drop their supplies, and return for a second run. On this run Bodine was shocked to see part of one of the drums that had split upon impact hit a good friend and companion from the *Oryoku Maru* voyage, Capt. Oliver W. Orson. The piece of the drum broke both of Orson's legs as well as his knee. After this mishap the POWs briefly tried to anticipate where the drops were going to occur and then ran away from that area. Finally, in desperation the Japanese ordered the camp evacuated until the American planes had left.

Most of the aerial supply missions were without incident, and as a result of these missions the years of hunger of the men in the camps were over. With this need satisfied, some Americans turned to fretting about when Allied troops would arrive to liberate them. Some did not have long to wait.

★ ★ ★ 7 ★ ★ ★

The evacuation of ex-POWs was scheduled to begin after representatives of the Japanese government signed the formal surrender documents on September 2 and American troops arrived on the mainland of Japan. However, after getting clearance from MacArthur's headquarters, a U.S. Navy rescue task force proceeded in landing craft to Omori on Tokyo Bay. The ex-POWs there, after spotting the oncoming rescuers, crowded cheering onto the docks. Some even leaped into the water and swam out to the boats. At Omori the Navy rescue team learned of other men at the Shinagawa hospital camp and went there. On the morning of August 30 all of the men from both camps were taken aboard the hospital ship *Benevolence*, where they were able to bathe and receive medical exams and new clothing. While enjoying good meals and clean beds, they filled out questionnaires on camp conditions. They were asked to furnish detailed information on cases of atrocities and brutality.

While the Navy was freeing the men at Omori and Shinagawa, an armada of transport aircraft was beginning to ferry U.S. Army troops to Japan. On the thirtieth, while the ex-POWs from Omori and Shinagawa were relaxing in Tokyo Bay on the *Benevolence*, not many miles away Gen. Douglas MacArthur walked down the ramp of his plane, the *Bataan*, at Atsugi Airport outside Tokyo. From there he and his party moved by motorcade to the Grand Hotel, where he took up residence. Part of the advance echelon with MacArthur was the recovered-personnel section, made up of twenty-eight teams each comprised of one officer and three enlisted men. Eighth Army staff officers and representatives of the International Red Cross, in consultation with General Tamura, chief of the Prisoner of War Bureau, immediately began making plans for contacting and evacuating Allied personnel.

On the following day a haggard General Wainwright, clad in an ill-fitting uniform and walking with the aid of a cane, arrived in Tokyo and was immediately taken to the Grand Hotel, where General MacArthur warmly greeted him in an emotion-charged reunion. Two days later Wainwright, along with more than a score of other high-ranking military officers, stood on the deck of the battleship *Missouri*. After placing his signature on the surrender document ending World War II, General MacArthur handed the first pen used to Wainwright. In far-off Mukden and some of the other camps lucky enough to have radios, ex-POWs listened with deep emotion as the announcer described the historic ceremony.

Now rescue efforts got into gear. On September 3, the U.S. Army 42nd General Hospital, with the hospital ship *Marigold* standing by, set up processing facilities on the Yokohama docks. On the following day the first men began moving through as recovery teams and medical personnel fanned out over the Japanese islands. Within five days more than seven thousand men from thirteen camps in the Kobe/Osaka area had been located and were en route to Yokohama. During the same period another thirty-eight hundred were recovered in the Nagoya area, and about three thousand from the Sendai group of camps in northern Honshu began moving south by rail. Ex-POWs in the extreme northern and southern islands, Hokkaido and Kyushu, had to wait a little longer for the recovery teams to arrive.

Americans at Yokkaichi in the Nagoya group of camps were among the first to join their countrymen. On September 3 (a Red Cross team had arrived at the camp earlier) they traveled by train to Hamamatsu. From there, in Navy landing craft that had been designed and built since their capture, they rode out to a hospital ship anchored offshore. They remained on the ship until transported to Atsugi Airport to await a flight to Okinawa.

One group of ex-POWs en route from a northern camp to Yokohama made the Japanese newspaper *Asahi Shimbun*. The newspaper, in a report headlined "A Good Deed by U.S. POW's," told of a railroad accident on September 6 in which some Japanese civilians were injured. Just after the accident a train bearing eighty American ex-POWs arrived at the station where the accident had occurred. About a dozen ex-POWs, upon learning of the accident, got out of their train and began giving first aid to the civilians with medical supplies they had with them. In the meantime other men opened their canned goods and gave them to the injured, also offering blankets and other comfort to the stricken Japanese. When the train carrying the ex-POWs pulled out, the men were still tossing canned goods out the windows to the Japanese involved in the accident.

In sharp contrast, a few days later, Boyle and his companions from the camp near Notogawa were waiting in a station for one of the special trains which had started in southern Honshu and were picking up men along the way. When they suddenly spotted one of their most brutal and sadistic guards, nicknamed "Sadie," they immediately swung into action. Well fortified with beer from a warehouse that they had discovered that morning, the men at first were intent on hanging the now cringing, terror-stricken Japanese. But cooler heads prevailed and Sadie's punishment was a brutal beating administered by one of the Americans. The Japanese guard's ordeal ended when the train arrived and the Americans rushed to climb aboard.

More trains followed, hauling thousands of ex-POWs from the Osaka/Kobe area as well as camps northwest of those cities to Yokohama, where by this time processing and evacuation activities were proceeding at a rapid pace. On one day alone over sixteen hundred men were flown from Atsugi Airport to Okinawa and then on to Manila.

Other recovery teams were contacting camps on the coast north of Nagoya—nearly four hundred Americans each at Oe-yama and Tsuruga. A team also reached the 365 officers at nearby Rokuroshi, but only after impatient officers there sent Maj. William Orr and another officer to see if they could find the teams that they had heard about on their radio. After Orr's return a recovery team consisting of a small detachment of soldiers from the 1st Cavalry Division, two Army doctors, and two Army nurses arrived at the camp. The team members had hardly gotten out of their vehicles before eager and curious officers swarmed around them, quizzing them about the war, their equipment, and a variety of other subjects. On the following day the freed prisoners rode down the mountain in Japanese trucks, and for the first time in years there was plenty of room in each vehicle. They were astounded (as were many other ex-POWs leaving camps throughout Japan) at the devastation done by the B-29 raids. When they stopped in the rail center of Fukui, they found it almost completely in ruins. In the railroad station, one of the two or three large buildings left standing, members of the Japanese Red Cross—this was the

first time any of the ex-POWs had seen members of this organization—served them tea. After a comfortable overnight ride
on a special train the group arrived the following morning in
Yokohama, where they were greeted by the commanding general of the Eighth Army, Gen. Robert L. Eichelberger, and
other senior officers while an Army band played "California
Here I Come." The men were taken to the dock area, where
they bathed and put on new uniforms, and then they rode
out to a waiting ship which carried them to the Philippines,
the place where most of them had started their long period
of enforced servitude.

Men from Toyama and Niigata and other camps in the Tokyo
group were also moving through Yokohama, and after a brief
stay they traveled on to the Philippines by ship or plane.

Men in the more remote camps to the north were among
the last to begin their journeys to freedom. From Hanawa,
at the northern end of Honshu, Charles Williams, a New Mexico
National Guardsman, and nearly five hundred other Americans
rode a train to the port city of Sendai, where they boarded
either a hospital ship or a transport depending on their physical
condition, which carried them to Yokohama and later southward. On the northernmost island, Hokkaido, the men in the
three camps north of Sapporo (mostly Marines from Shanghai
along with a smaller number of Army, Navy, and merchant
seamen) were still waiting when on September 9, at one of
the camps near Akahira, the Navy decided to make one more
supply drop.

Captain White, recently assigned as senior officer there, and
roughly 130 men in the camp were delighted with the prospect
of more food and quickly cleared an area previously marked
for B-29's to drop supplies. As the last carrier plane made
its pass, three Americans, one Marine and two Army men, were
out chasing some Korean road workers away from the dropped
items and failed to hit the ground in time. One of the last
drums hit near them and some of its contents of five-pound
cans flew through the air, striking all three men and killing
two of them—a tragic end to their short-lived freedom.
Recovery teams arrived at all three camps shortly after this
accident and the ex-POWs took a train to an airfield north of
Sapporo, where they were loaded on U.S. Army Air Corps

C-47 transport planes. The last of them left on September 15 and flew to Atsugi Airport for subsequent movement by ship or plane.

Far to the south, U.S. forces had arranged to evacuate the men in the camps at the southern end of Honshu and on the island Kyushu through two ports, Wakanoura on Honshu, and Nagasaki on Kyushu. It wasn't until September 15 that Benson Guyton and the men from Omine Machi entrained, arriving at Wakanoura on the sixteenth. Among the last of more than two thousand men to move through this port, they boarded the hospital ship *Sanctuary,* which took them to Okinawa to await transport to the Philippines. By mid-September nearly half of the men at Fukuoka Camp 17 on Kyushu had left the camp, some going north and others going south to Kanoya Airfield, where they were able to gain passage on American military aircraft leaving the island. A recovery team finally arrived and the men remaining at Fukuoka 17 traveled by train to Nagasaki. When they got to the outskirts of the city the train moved at a crawl. The Americans viewed with awe and amazement the tremendous damage done by the second atomic bomb, which had fallen a little over a month before. Joe Smulewicz was particularly impressed by two huge steel oil-storage tanks. Each looked to him as if it had been smashed by a giant fist from the sky. The bomb damage abruptly stopped short of the dock area. Here the hospital ship *Haven* was tied up. It provided medical treatment, hot water, general utilities, and food to arriving ex-POWs. After a short time on the docks the men boarded American and British ships which carried them to Okinawa. Many of the returning prisoners of war would wait a week or more there for a flight or a ship to the Philippines, but it was a pleasant stay. The food was good and there was plenty of it.

Earlier, on September 7, near the Jinsen camp in Korea, the American Seventh Division had landed. After a day of shopping for some new eyeglasses, Major Bodine watched, fascinated, from a tower as scores of ships stood offshore and four lines of landing craft brought in thousands of soldiers with their equipment. He returned to camp just in time to climb into a truck along with his friends and ride to the beach. As they boarded landing craft to take them to waiting transports Bodine noticed their Japanese camp commander, an elderly colonel and a fair man overall, standing forlornly watching the proceedings. Sympathetic, Bodine and a few others went over and said good-bye. After a long wet ride on the landing craft the men boarded the hospital ship *Relief.* After a delousing and a bath Bodine relaxed in clean pajamas on a bed with an innerspring mattress and, following a meal of ham and eggs, ate ice cream for the first time in over three years.

The *Relief* next sailed to Dairen, Manchuria, south of Mukden, where the last 750 ex-POWs from that camp boarded. Immediately thereafter all were served a steak dinner. Like Bodine, Colonel Quinn was delighted with the new comforts even though the ship was loaded at over twice its capacity. On September 16 the men on the *Relief* arrived at Okinawa, where they joined others awaiting transportation to the Philippines.

By the end of the third week in September virtually all the ex-POWs, including more than twelve thousand Americans, had been evacuated from Japan, Manchuria, and Korea. While the liberated Americans would follow different routes home, for most the 29th Replacement Depot, south of Manila, was their last stop before leaving the Far East. Here many of the men's long-unmet needs—adequate medical attention, back pay, new uniforms, entertainment, food, letters and cablegrams to and from home—were met. They were also asked to fill out more questionnaires concerning their imprisonment and identification of Japanese who might be subject to trial as war criminals. Then as transport ships and planes became available they journeyed homeward across the Pacific, leaving behind their less fortunate comrades who

—first felt the deadly wrath of the victor after the fall of Guam and Wake;

—suffered humiliation and died on the march out of Bataan;

—succumbed to dysentery, malaria, malnutrition, and despondency at Camp O'Donnell;

—continued to expire in even greater numbers at Cabanatuan;

—died of exposure, malnutrition, and disease during their first winters in Manchuria and Japan;

—were victims of overwork and cruel neglect on the Burma–Thailand railway;

—were executed en masse on Wake Island;

—perished in the sinking and bloody aftermath of the *Shinyo Maru;*

—drowned in the sinking of the *Arisan Maru;*

—were massacred on the islands of Guam and Palawan;

—suffered and died on the *Oryoku Maru, Enoura Maru,* and *Brazil Maru;*

—were executed or died in the closing days of the war.

Over ten thousand of their number did not return—two out of every five of those who had begun the uphill struggle for survival after the guns were still.

AFTERMATH

1945–1984
The Far East—The United States

★ ★ ★ 1 ★ ★ ★

As thousands of ex-POWs were enjoying reunions with family and friends, General MacArthur's headquarters, Supreme Command Allied Powers (SCAP), began a long legal process which over the next few years in accordance with the Potsdam Declaration brought hundreds of Japanese war criminals to trial.

SCAP placed the Japanese accused of war crimes into two categories. One was made up of high-ranking government civilian and military officials charged with planning and waging a war of aggression in violation of international law. Tojo and twenty-seven others were in this category. A larger group, over two thousand persons, included those charged with atrocities or inhuman acts committed against POWs, civilian populations, or particular races or groups in violation of accepted laws and rules of warfare. Generals Homma and Yamashita were the most prominent in the latter category.

Yamashita and Homma were tried by U.S. military commissions and convicted before the trials of Tojo and other high-ranking officials had begun. Yamashita was found guilty of permitting brutal atrocities and other high crimes against Americans and Filipinos at the end of the war in the Philippines. Among the major charges against him were responsibility for the brutalities at Pasay School and the Palawan massacre as well as widespread slaughter of Filipino men and women in

Manila. Homma was charged for failing in his responsibilities for Japanese actions at the beginning of the war—the Bataan Death March and Camp O'Donnell. Both men were found guilty and sentenced to death. Yamashita was hanged in February 1946. Homma died in front of a firing squad in April of that year.

, The following month General MacArthur established the International Military Tribunal for the Far East, and the trials of the twenty-eight major war criminals began. Like the Nuremberg trials in Germany these proceedings were complicated and lengthy, stretching over nearly two years. Tojo's trial was the most prominent. Included in the charges against him was his failure to act responsibly regarding the treatment of POWs—the Bataan Death March and the Burma–Thailand railroad were cited. The tribunal found Tojo guilty and sentenced him to death. It rendered the same verdict and sentence for four other generals who had command responsibility which included POWs. M. Shigemitsu, who as foreign minister was charged with failure to investigate mistreatment of POWs, was found guilty but received a light sentence, seven years, because unlike the others he was not involved in the actual waging of a war of aggression.

While the trials of the twenty-eight major war criminals before the International Military Tribunal were under way, large numbers of individuals charged with mistreatment and atrocities against POWs were being apprehended and tried by U.S. military commissions in Japan, the Philippines, China, the Pacific Ocean area, and India. The bulk of the trials were held in Yokohama and Manila. Among those tried were many of the Japanese officers and soldiers (and to a much lesser extent Koreans and Formosans) who are mentioned in this book.

Accused of war crimes in the Philippines, General Kawane and Colonel Hirano received death sentences for responsibility for the Bataan Death March. The commandants of Camp O'Donnell, Cabanatuan, Davao Penal Colony, and Bilibid during particular periods when Americans were held in these camps were given sentences ranging from twenty-five years to life. A number of the junior officers and Japanese and Formosan guards who actually mistreated and brutalized the POWs at these camps were sentenced to terms in prison. The sentences for these men were sometimes lighter than those of the camp commanders because the commissions often took into consideration that the accused were obeying the orders of their superiors. A harsher sentence—death—went to General Kou for command responsibility for the brutality at Pasay School, the killing of survivors in the sinking of *Shinyo Maru,* and other brutalities and mistreatment. Only one of the men who brutalized the Americans at Pasay School was found. He was in an institution for the permanently insane and was never tried. The others are presumed to have died in the final battles in the Philippines. Others who never came to trial for the same reason were two of the officers in charge of the prisoners on the *Shinyo Maru* and the commandant at Palawan at the time of the massacre there. For their responsibility for the inhumane treatment on the *Oryoku Maru* and following ships, Lieutenant Toshino received a death sentence and the interpreter Wada got life.

Elsewhere in the Pacific area, the executioners on the *Nitta Maru* received life sentences but their commander escaped trial by committing suicide. Found guilty by a British military commission, the two senior officers of the camps on the Burma–Thailand railroad were hanged in Changi Prison. The interpreters at Mukden and Kiangwan received twenty years and life respectively. Far across the Pacific a military commission found Admiral Sakaibara guilty of ordering a mass execution of ninety-six American construction workers on Wake Island and sentenced him to death. The general who authorized the execution and subsequent cannibalism of the Americans at Chichi Jima received the same punishment.

In contrast to the prison terms of their counterparts in the three big camps in the Philippines, the two successive commandants at Fukuoka 17 on Kyushu, Japan, received death sentences. Most of the officers found responsible for the deaths of American fliers during the last nine months of the war were given life or long prison terms. Strangely, a commission sentenced General Tamura, head of the Prisoner of War Bureau during the last year of the war, to only eight years. Also, for reasons which cannot be determined, his deputy Colonel Odashima, who was the general overseer of POW operations during most of the war and who some members of the Prisoner of War Bureau referred to as the most influential officer in that bureau, never came to trial at all.

The trials concluded in the fall of 1949.   Liberal clemency and parole policies reduced the number of prisoners serving sentences in the years that followed.   By 1956 the total population of Sugamo Prison, where most of the war criminals were incarcerated, was down from a high of 2,000 to only 383.   These were the long-term prisoners, guilty of some of the most serious offenses.   Meanwhile, a number of the freed war criminals were back in the mainstream of Japanese business and politics.   The durable Shigemitsu, given a relatively light sentence by the International Tribunal for his acts as wartime foreign minister, eventually was appointed to this office for a second time.

The status of Japanese war criminals was of little worldwide interest until December 31, 1958.   On that day the *New York Times* reported: "United States authorities finally freed today the last group of war criminals held in Sugamo Prison here. The United States informed the foreign minister of Japan it was terminating the sentences of eighty-three prisoners. Sugamo thus ceases to be a prison for war criminals."

So as the U.S. and Allied war crimes process ended—except for those condemned to death—the severest punishment, even for those found guilty for the most cruel and savage acts, was thirteen years in prison.   Virtually all were freed in a far shorter time.   The retribution strongly voiced in the Potsdam Declaration had run a short course.

★ ★ ★ **2** ★ ★ ★

While their former captors were serving terms in prison, American ex-POWs were returning to work and family life.   Among the millions of war veterans created by World War II, they were, as a group and as individuals, hardly distinguishable. A few, like General Wainwright, got a hero's welcome.   Most unobtrusively began to readjust to their new world of freedom. The difficulty of their readjustment varied widely from individual to individual.

In 1948 the U.S. government recognized that ex-POWs had had a more arduous experience than the average veteran and awarded each ex-POW one dollar a day for every day he was deprived of adequate food rations in violation of the Geneva Convention.   Two years later an additional dollar and a half per day was authorized as reparation for enforced labor and inhumane treatment.

The lump-sum payments, while welcome, would do little to compensate for the physical and mental residuals of Japanese imprisonment from which many would suffer over the years. Among the ravages of the prison camp, beriberi and malnutrition left many Pacific ex-POWs with heart and liver problems, visual impairment, and an assortment of neurological complications. With no records to validate that their ailments derived from their POW days, some men would have great difficulty in obtaining treatment in Veterans Administration hospitals and still others would not obtain any treatment at all.

The psychological effects of being a POW were probably more pervasive than the physical ones. The Pacific POW underwent an experience unlike that of his millions of fellow veterans. The harshness, cruelty, and barrenness of their prison lives had forced these men to look at themselves and their fellow prisoners stripped of the veneer of modern society. It made them see how they and others reacted when tested to the limits of endurance. It revealed the worst and the best in themselves, their comrades, and their captors. Many of them consciously or unconsciously shoved their wartime experience into the furthest reaches of their minds. A smaller number chose to talk and in particular to write about their life in prison camp. But whether they were tight-lipped or open, over time their experience left its mark on nearly every POW. Some men would draw from their prison days a deeper understanding of themselves and others and build this into their philosophy of life. Others would derive from the same introspection a more guarded and cynical attitude. Differences would also exist among the ex-POWs in their attitude toward their former captors. As time passed, a growing number of men lost most of the deep-seated hatred that they had had for the Japanese during their prison life. A smaller number have never forgotten or forgiven the acts of the Japanese despite the fact that the United States and Japan are now international allies.

Unfortunately, the long-term effects of prison camp went much further than creating different attitudes toward life. Some men would suffer permanent mental scars and would be plagued with persistent anxieties, depressions, neuroses, and, in rare cases, suicidal tendencies. As with physical infirmities, private and Veterans Administration doctors treated the men with little understanding of the causal factors.

For a handful their deeds, not just their memories, came back to haunt them. As might be expected, some men bore grudges against their fellow POWs for collaborating with the Japanese to the detriment of other POWs. Most of these feelings got no further than an occasional conversation at an ex-POW convention. In a few instances a moral indictment might be shared by a substantial number of ex-POWs, but rarely did such sentiments end up as formal charges. One such case (already mentioned) was that of Lieutenant Little, the mess officer at Fukuoka 17, who was eventually cleared of charges against him.

The most serious charges against an ex-POW after World War II were made against John D. Provoo. In October 1952 the U.S. government accused him of treasonable acts which included offering his services to the Japanese Army after the capture of Corregidor, helping to cause the execution of Captain Thompson on that island, and participating in wartime Japanese propaganda broadcasts. In early 1953, after a lengthy trial at which a number of ex-POWs and some Japanese testified, a jury found Provoo guilty and the judge sentenced him to life imprisonment. However, in August 1954 the U.S. Circuit Court of Appeals of New York declared the trial invalid because of the introduction of irrelevant and prejudicial allegations pertaining to Provoo's homosexuality and, in addition, declared that the case was tried in the wrong court jurisdiction. While federal prosecutors were preparing to try the case again, a U.S. district judge ordered that all proceedings against Provoo cease on the grounds that he had been denied the right of a speedy trial within the meaning of the Sixth Amendment to the Constitution. The U.S. Supreme Court subsequently upheld this ruling and in the fall of 1955 Provoo was a free man.

★ ★ ★ 3 ★ ★ ★

Soon after the war former POWs, like other war veterans, formed organizations, primarily at first for communicating and socializing, but later for more substantive purposes. The Amer-

ican Defenders of Bataan and Corregidor is the overall organization for former prisoners of the Japanese in the Pacific. Many
of these men also belong to the American Ex-Prisoners of War,
open to former POWs of all U.S. wars and conflicts. In some
cases the camaraderie of individual groups and camps caused
the formation of other organizations. The large number of
ex-POWs in the state of New Mexico organized the Bataan
Veterans Organization. Wake Island defenders keep up with
one another through a newsletter called *The Wigwag*. Other
ex-POWs, such as the men at Zentsuji (mostly officers) and those
captured on and around Java, maintain rosters and communication.

The two major POW organizations—American Ex-Prisoners
of War and The American Defenders of Bataan and Corregidor—are more than social organizations. The motto of the
American Ex-Prisoners of War, "We exist to help those who
cannot help themselves," is put into practice when men in
both of these organizations annually convene. Member com-
mittees report on their review of national and state legislation
concerning the health and welfare of ex-POWs. States and
localities in which the number of men who became POWs is
large have erected monuments and named roads and bridges
in honor of departed comrades.

In recent years the size and the activities of ex-POW organizations have increased. Reticence has given way to nostalgia.
More and more men want to share their experiences with old
buddies and—for those who never did so before—with their
families and friends.

★ ★ ★ **4** ★ ★ ★

For some with the time and the money this nostalgia has im-
pelled them to return once again to the camps and countryside
that had been the setting for events which deeply affected
their lives. Most of them returned to the Philippines. On
Bataan markers have been placed on the route of the Death
March, and on Mount Samat a huge and impressive monument
dominates the surrounding terrain. But beyond the monuments and markers there is little to remind the returning American of the former battleground. The dense jungle trees and
foliage are gone, stripped for timber, industry, and cultivation.

At Camp O'Donnell and Cabanatuan the returning POW finds a similar situation. The barracks and barbed wire are gone. Monuments alone remind him of the camps' locations, and only recently was a monument erected at Cabanatuan. Bilibid Prison is a different matter. Almost abandoned decades ago, it is still in service, housing a new generation of Filipino convicts after a brief use to detain Japanese POWs in 1945. It is on Corregidor that the returning American can indulge his nostalgia. Cared for by the Philippine government, this famous bastion retains much of its past appearance.

The adventuresome American who journeys to Japan or other locations will find few if any commemorative markers. If his memory is sharp he may find an old building or an abandoned site that for him has a meaning which it has for no one else.

Etched on the minds of many are memories of the ships that carried them to various parts of the Japanese empire. Virtually all were sunk and their hulks are resting in ill-defined locations in the waters stretching from Japan to the southern Philippines. The location of one, the *Oryoku Maru*, is known. On the afternoon of December 15, 1983, after earlier dedicating a plaque in the memory of their departed comrades on the ill-fated ship, a small delegation of survivors boarded a launch at the U.S. Naval Station at Olongapo, Philippine Islands. The launch carried them to a location above the coral-caked remains of the submerged *Oryoku Maru*. Here, in a brief ceremony, they cast a floral wreath on the water's surface where, thirty-nine years before, nearly three hundred of their fellow POWs had ended their journey.

ACKNOWLEDGMENTS

Most of all I am grateful to the men who shared with me the memories of their personal experiences as POWs. Without them this book could not have been written. Their contributions came to me in the form of published books, unpublished memoirs and diaries, personal interviews, and correspondence. I have recognized in my *Sources* and *Notes* those whose contributions are directly reflected in the text. For the scores of others not mentioned—those with whom I've had spot conversations by phone or in person or corresponded with to check a fact or pursue a lead—my thanks. A number of their accounts were fascinating and might well have been included except for space limitations and the necessity for selectivity.

Some former POWs deserve special mention. Early in my research two members of the American Defenders of Bataan and Corregidor organization expressed interest in my project. Art Bressi provided a comprehensive list of books written by POWs; Benson Guyton, in letters and on the telephone, generously shared with me his knowledge of sources of information. Mel Routt, active in American Ex-Prisoners of War activities, first introduced me to the people and the publication of this fine organization. Also in the early stages, recognition of the value of a book about American POWs of the Japanese by Generals Thomas J. H. Trapnell and Harold K. Johnson was most encouraging. Later, Colonel John R. Vance, a longtime friend, reviewed the entire manuscript draft with an experienced and careful eye.

A number of other individuals were helpful. Charles B. McDonald provided valuable advice on improving the presentation of the material, as did Irene Elmer. Frances W. Lipe, in addition to providing me with her excellent published map locating POW camps, gave freely of advice on source material. Credits also go to Mark Montgomery for the map work; Christine Van Noy, Barbara Schneider, Janet Stearns, and Irene McKim for typing the successive manuscript drafts; and Norwood Allen and June Gilmartin for their interest and assistance.

Men and women of libraries and other public institutions deserve thanks for their cooperation. Among these were: the Washington National Records Center (George Chalou for advice, and Greg Bradshear, William Getchell, Fred Purnell, Ellie Melemed, and others for retrieving countless boxes of documents from the bowels of this enormous archival mine); the Naval Historical Center (Dean Allard); the Center for Military History (Hannah M. Zeidlik); the United States Military Academy Library (Marie T. Capps); the University of California, Berkeley, Library (personnel of the Government Documents Section); the Defense Audio-Visual Agency (Virginia Horrell); the Office of the Adjutant General (personnel of the Recovered Records Section); the Saint Mary's College Library, Moraga, California (Patricia Reitz and Antonia Friedman); the National Archives (personnel of the Still Pictures Branch).

I owe much to the two persons whose confidence and efforts led to the publication of my work: Dora Williams, my agent, and Howard Cady, senior editor of William Morrow; my thanks to both.

Finally, a word for my friend John Harper, whose commitment to the successful completion of this book was second only to mine. In our many discussions of the manuscript, his interest, enthusiasm, and the value of his counsel never diminished. His was a major contribution, for which I am grateful.

NOTES

In the notes that follow I have identified the sources for each numbered section within a chapter by particular reference to the subject matter within that section. For quotations, the page numbers of the source document are usually provided. Citations throughout are in shorthand form. Complete citations are included in the Sources.

PROLOGUE

–1– Hull's statement is found in Herbert Feis's *The Road to Pearl Harbor*, p. 201. The war plans summary was developed from Lewis Morton's benchmark work *The Fall of the Philippines* and supplemented by his *Strategy and Command: The First Two Years*. The prewar status of Guam, Wake, and Midway is from Samuel Eliot Morison's *The Rising Sun in the Pacific*. Coverage of the abortive reinforcement of the Philippines is based on Morton's two works previously cited. –2– For the account of the San Francisco School Board actions and their impact, I drew on William L. Neumann's *America Encounters Japan: From Perry to MacArthur* and on Hugh Borton's *Japan's Modern Century*. The sketch of the stereotypical Japanese is from Neumann. Japanese actions at the Paris Peace Conference and the United States Exclusion Act of 1924 are covered by Borton. Sidney L. Gulick's *Toward Understanding the Japanese* was also useful. The events and outcome of the 1929 Geneva Convention were drawn from Supreme Commander Allied Powers (SCAP) *History of Non-Military Ac-*

tivities of the Occupation of Japan, Monograph 5 (hereafter referred to as SCAP Monograph 5). Lord Russell of Liverpool's *Knights of Bushido* and International Military Tribunal for the Far East (IMTFE) transcript of proceedings pages (hereafter designated by the letter T) 27179–27182. –3– For the events surrounding the seizure of Manchuria and the 1937 attack on China, I tapped Burton's and Neumann's books as previously cited, as well as Robert J. C. Butow's book *Tojo and the Coming of the War.* Insights on Japanese ideology came from Hugh Byas's *Government by Assassination. The Washington Post* headline quotes were extracted from Neumann. United States' misconceptions about the Japanese were found in Neumann and also in Edwin O. Reischauer's *The United States and Japan.* My description of the Japanese army and the individual soldiers came from two revealing pre-World War II books, Captain M. D. Kennedy's *The Military Side of Japanese Life* and Hillis Lory's *Japan's Military Masters: The Army in Japanese Life.*

ONE. FIRST CAPTIVES

–1– My basic source on the circumstances of surrender at Shanghai (and Guam and Wake in the following section) was Samuel Eliot Morison's *The Rising Sun in the Pacific.* Additional information came from W. S. Cunningham's *Wake Island Command* and American Prisoner of War Information Bureau (APWIB) report "Naval Prisoner of War Camp, Shanghai, China." Particulars on the situation at Tientsin and Peking were drawn from John A. White's memoir, *The United States Marines in North China.* –2– The description of the Guam incident is from a telephone interview with John Podelesny. Conditions at Wake draw on the different perspectives of Cunningham's *Wake Island Command* and James P. S. Devereaux's *The Story of Wake Island.* For Japanese organization for POW administration see IMTFE, T 14440–14446 and Exhibits (hereafter designated as EX) 1469 and 1493. –3– The journey from Guam to Zentsuji is taken from Hugh N. Meyer's *Prisoner of War, World War II.* "Regulations for Prisoners" are as quoted in IMTFE, EX 1640. Wake to Shanghai and Woosung is from Cunningham's *Wake Island Command.* Quotes on the Japanese position on the Geneva Convention are from IMTFE, EX

1469, 1493, and 2038. –4– The U.S.S. *Houston* sinking after-math is from an interview with Gene Crispi. Makassar survivor estimates are based on statements by P. A. Donovan, H. N. Netter, and A. D. Eaton, all in Record Group (RG) 153 at the Washington National Records Center (WNRC), Suitland, Mary-land. Surrender of the 2nd Battalion, 131st Field Artillery came from an interview with Edward Fung and from Creighton R. Gordon's "Lost Battalion." –5– The account of the Woosung escape attempt is from Cunningham's *Wake Island Command.* –6– The War Ministry POW administrative actions are found in IMTFE, T 27695–27700 and T 14443–14445.

TWO. BATAAN TO O'DONNELL

–1– and –2– As general sources on the surrender of Bataan and the aftermath, I drew on Louis Morton's excellent *The Fall of the Philippines* and Stanley Falk's *The March of Death,* with additional insights from Donald Knox's oral history, *Death March.* –3– His personal experience came from John D. Gam-ble's personal diary (extract sent to me by Roger Farquhar); Dyess's is based on *The Dyess Story,* the earliest book-length revelation of Japanese atrocities to be published in the United States. Earl Dodson's trials on the Death March are based on interviews and his written account. David L. Hardee's thoughtful and insightful "Memoirs of a Jap POW" record his recollections of the trek. –4– A basic source on conditions of Camp O'Donnell and the actions of the camp commandant was the Record of Trial "United States of America vs. Yoshio Tsuneyoshi," WNRC, RG 153. The quote "you are our ene-mies . . ." is from E. B. Miller's *Bataan Uncensored,* p. 233. The description of disease and death at the camp came from Wibb E. Cooper's "Report on Medical Activities in the Philip-pines 1941–May 6, 1942" and from statements by Merle M. Musselman, Charles S. Lawrence, and Charles C. Johnston, WNRC, RG 153. –5– Sources for the situation on the "Bicycle Camp" were Rohan Rivett's *Behind Bamboo* and Benjamin Dunn's *The Bamboo Express.* Antrim's heroic act is described in the *Congressional Medal of Honor Roll Book.* Life at Woosung is drawn from White's *U.S. Marines in North China* and from Devereaux's *The Story of Wake Island.*

THREE. CORREGIDOR TO CABANATUAN

–1– For description of the Corregidor surrender, I relied on Morton's *Fall of the Philippines* as well as on Duane Schultz's *Hero of Bataan*. John R. Vance's *Doomed Garrison* and interviews with him provided much valuable material for this and subsequent sections' treating of men captured on Corregidor. S. M. Mellnik's *Philippine Diary* was another fruitful source concerning the fate of men captured there. The actions of John E. Provoo are taken from Clark Lee's "The Case of the Coward," *Cosmopolitan*. John H. McGee's *Rice and Salt* and E. S. Northway's diary provided information on the days at Malybaly. –2– For the move from Corregidor to Bilibid, I relied on Vance's and Mellnik's books mentioned in Section –1– as well as in Albert Svihra's diary. The description of Bilibid prison derives from Charles T. Brown's *Bilibid Prison: "The Devil's Cauldron, A Fragment from That Devil's Mosaic."* –3– For movements out of Bilibid, I used once more Mellnik's account plus Alan McCracken's *Very Soon Now, Joe* and Vance's *Doomed Garrison*.

FOUR. "NO WORK—NO FOOD"

–1– Tojo's speech at Zentsuji is quoted in IMTFE, EX 1960, while the Prisoner of War Bureau's actions were taken from IMTFE, T 14414–14415 and 14505 through 14508. –2– Levy's experience was from an interview. Wohlfeld's anecdote is from a typed account of his story narrated in November 1944 to Capt. Harold A. Rosenquist, who was then an intelligence agent operating in the southern Philippines. I found a sketch of the unusual assignment of the POWs on Corregidor in James H. and William M. Belote's *Corregidor, the Saga of a Fortress*. Dodson's written and oral statements were used for the Calumpit Bridge account, IMTFE, EX 1460 and 1456 for what happened at Gapan and Tayabas, and the statement of Theodore Bigger in Donald Knox's *Death March* was the source for the executions south of Laguna de Bay. –3– The account of the important meeting of POW camp commanders came from IMTFE, T 27232–27239 and EX 1964–A. Tojo's address and the policy on officer prisoners were excerpted from IMTFE,

EX 1962 and 1961, respectively. –4– I am indebted to Arthur Robinson's excellent monograph, "Relief to Prisoners of War in WWII," for most of the information for my account of the first *Gripsholm* exchange and for relief actions described later. Some additional details came from the International Committee of the Red Cross *Relief Activities,* Vol. 3 and various issues of the American Red Cross Prisoners of War Bulletin.

FIVE. ZERO WARD

–1– I drew here, in 2 and in later chapters, on Calvin Chunn's *Of Rice and Men,* a unique book, primarily focused on POW life at Cabanatuan, consisting of contributions made by certain POWs at that camp and buried when they left. Most of the contributors later died, but the manuscript was recovered in the U.S. Rangers' daring liberation of the camp. It was subsequently edited and published in 1946. The exact figures for deaths at Cabanatuan here and later were from the Cabanatuan Death Report, a carefully kept record ending in March 1944, which contained the name, rank, and serial number of each man who died with the cause of his death when known. For my portrayal of "Zero Ward" and the conditions of the time, I drew on Eugene C. Jacob's "From Guerrilla to POW in the Philippines" in *Medical Opinion and Review;* Roy L. Bodine, Jr.'s monograph, "Bataan and the Jap Prison Camps"; and Godfrey Ames's and Robert Field's diaries. –2– The "Regulations for Concentration Camp, May 1942" were found in WNRC, RG 153. For my descriptions of lack of food, "quan," disease, entertainment, religion, and morale, in addition to Chunn and other sources in –1–, I used Hardee's "Memoirs," E. R. Fendall's diary, and A. C. Oliver's statement, the latter two in WNRC, RG 153. Other references here were Dyess's *Dyess Story* and Ralph E. Hibb's "Beri Beri in Japanese Prison Camp" in the *Annals of Internal Medicine.* –3– Benson Guyton's diary published in *Of Rice and Men* furnished most of the material for life at Cabanatuan Camp No. 3. –4– The scenes at Tarlac were taken from Vance's book, already cited, and from J. M. Wainwright's *General Wainwright's Story* and William C. Braly's *The Hard Way Home.* The poignant quote is from Michael A. Quinn's *Love Letters to Mike,* p. 25. –5– The registration procedures were from Hardee's "Memoirs."

The Japanese plans for future use of POWs as industrial workers in Japan are contained in IMTFE, EX 1971–A.

SIX. ON THE MOVE

–1– The senior officers' and officials' journey to Formosa is derived from the books by Vance, Wainwright, and Quinn cited above. –2– For the escape incidents, I turned once more to Hardee's "Memoirs" and to Field's diary, supplemented by M. H. McCoy and Steve Mellnik's *Ten Escape from Tojo* and by an interview with Kermit Lay. I found the information on the fate of the nine Marines in Benis M. Frank, Jr.'s and Henry I. Shaw, Jr.'s *History of USMC Operations in WWII, Victory and Occupation,* Vol. 5 and IMTFE, T 15018–15019 and 15029. I obtained information on the POWs' voyage on the *Tottori Maru* to Pusan, Korea, from an interview with David Levy. The quote on the "technician shortage" is from IMTFE, EX 1970–A. The continued trip of the *Tottori Maru* to Japan and the fate of the men left at Pusan came from a report by Jack W. Scwartz, WNRC, RG 153 and from Malcom V. Fortier's *Life of a POW Under the Japanese.* –3– The account of the American POWs in the early days on the Burma–Thailand railroad is from interviews from Edward Fung and from Rivett's *Behind Bamboo.* Colonel Nagatomo's speech is found on pages 122–123 of *Behind Bamboo.* – –4– For the trip to Davao, I leaned on Hardee's "Memoirs" and the previously cited books by Mellnik and McCracken. –5– Events on the *Nagato Maru* voyage to Osaka were taken from E. B. Miller's *Bataan Uncensored.* Particulars on POW food and clothing allowances and reactions of the Japanese to POWs in Japan were found in IMTFE, T 10591 and EX 1969, respectively. For the work assignments at the locations in or near Osaka, I used J. S. Coleman's *Bataan and Beyond;* APWIB's "Report on Umeda Bonshu"; statements of John H. Marshall and Charles E. Maurer, contained in IMTFE, EX 1946 and 1947, respectively; K. C. Emerson's *Guest of the Emperor;* and E. B. Miller's above-cited book. –6– Initial conditions at the Pasay Camp came from a statement by H. H. Herzog, WNRC, RG 153, and the discussion of the death rate at Cabanatuan was derived from the "Cabanatuan Death Report." The estimated number of POWs held in the various locations is based on information found in diaries, published and unpublished memoirs, camp strength records, and death reports, most of which have been cited above.

SEVEN. RELIEF AT LAST

–1– Details of the *Gripsholm*'s cargo is taken from Robinson's monograph. Receipt of Red Cross supplies at Cabanatuan is from Eugene Forquer's and K. E. Ranson's diaries and from Chunn's *Of Rice and Men*. The sketch about Father Cummings and Bilibid is from a letter from Sister Maura Shaun to Sister Mary Joseph, dated June 1946. Christmas and New Years at Davao was based on McCracken's book, previously cited. For distribution of the Singapore shipment, I turned to Dunn and to Fung's interview. –2– The lack of Red Cross supplies for the men at Mukden and Karenko was as described in the Levy interviews and in Vance's book, while the traditional Christmas dinner at Kiangwan is from a description by White in his *U.S. Marines in North China* and Bill Marvel's article "He-e-e-ere's Jimmy!" in the *Dallas Times-Herald,* November 2, 1980. –3– Descriptions of the varying circumstances surrounding the receipt of Red Cross supplies in Japan were found in the APWIB report "Zentsuji Headquarters Camp on the Island of Shikoku, Japan"; Martin Boyle's *Yanks Don't Cry;* Emerson, Coleman, and Myers's previously cited works; and IMTFE, EX 1936.

EIGHT. TROPICAL TOIL

–1– For my characterization of POW life at Davao, I leaned on Hardee's "Memoirs" and McCracken's book, supplemented by Jack Hawkins's *Never Say Die,* and interviews with Charles Brown. –2– In my account of the successful escape from the penal colony, I made use of the books by Mellnik, Dyess, McCoy and Mellnik, and Hawkins. For the aftermath, I tapped McGee and Hardee. –3– Rivett's and Dunn's books contain vivid descriptions of labor on the Burma–Thailand railroad. Interviews with Fung provided additional information. –4– Sources for picturing Americans under the yoke at Cabanatuan were Fendall, Guyton, and Forquer diaries. The account of the two underground groups is taken from the fascinating books by the leaders of the groups, Margaret Utinsky's *Miss U* and Claire

Phillip's *Manila Espionage;* additional sources for the section were Chunn, and Thomas H. Haye's diary. –5– Information on conditions at Pasay/Nichols Field was gathered from statements by J. E. Strawthorn in IMTFE, EX 1453, and by H. H. Herzog's and L. G. Williams's in WNRC, RG 153, and the legal section of the Supreme Commander for the Allied Forces (SCAP) report of investigation re: "Pasay Elementary School Prison Camp, Luzon, PI," dated 27 May 1946. The description of the use of POWs at Nielson and Clark fields came from "History of Nielson Field" and a statement by James C. Kent, both in WNRC, RG 153. For work and escapes on Palawan, I relied on the statements of G. W. McDole and D. W. Bogue, in WNRC, RG 153. The information on Lipa is in a statement by O. B. Kittleson in the same record group. Earl Dodson provided a written account of Los Pinas. The APWIB report "Manila Port Area Work Detail," November 19, 1945, told of work at this location. –6– Robinson's monograph was the major source for the second *Gripsholm* relief mission. Events surrounding the receipt of supplies at Bilibid and Cabanatuan are from diaries of Hayes, Fendall, and Forquer. The former POW quote is by Benson Guyton in *Quan,* a publication of the American Defenders of Bataan and Corregidor. The clandestine radio at Davao story came from interviews with C. Brown and R. J. Hutchinson (the operator of the radio). Other information at this camp came from McCracken and Hardee and from a statement by Austin J. Montgomery in WNRC, RG 153. My recounting of the suppression of the Dyess story and the ultimate U.S. release of information on Japanese atrocities came from a series of memoranda between Roosevelt and his secretaries of War and Navy, subject "Japanese Atrocities—Reports of Escaped Prisoners," September 9, 1941–December 30, 1943, and IMTFE, EX 1977, 1488, and 1479. The quotation from the Vice Minister's instruction was taken from EX 3051.

NINE. IN COLDER CLIMES

–1– I am indebted to interviews with Thurman Matthews and Yoshio Kai, as well as Levy, for my narrative on American workers at the Manchuria Machine Tool Company. The escape story was reconstructed from statements by J. R. Brumley and C. E. Evans in WNRC, RG 153, and IMTFE, EX 1998. The sequence on Noda is from a statement from Fred A. Anderson and also the review of trial of Noda, both in RG 153. The Red Cross Inspection Report, WNRC, EX 385, RG 331, and the Matthews's interview provided information on the new barracks and the Red Cross supplies. –2– Vance and Quinn were the basic sources for this section with some details supplied by C. H. Stringer in IMTFE, EX 1629–A, and Duane Schultz's *Hero of Bataan*. –3– The "Mount Fuji" episode and other details came from Cunningham, White, and Devereaux. Information on the camp radios was obtained from White and from John F. Kinney's "POW Radio" in *Combat Illustrated* (Winter 1979). The massacre at Wake is narrated in Lord Russell of Liverpool's *Knights of Bushido*, while the "water cure" incident at Kiang Wan is found in a statement by R. M. Brown in IMTFE, EX 1986–A.

TEN. UNDER THE RISING SUN

–1– The APWIB report on Umeda Bonshu, 31 July 1946; Coleman's and Emerson's books, before cited; William Spizziro's interview; and P. E. Sanders's statement in IMTFE, EX 1936 all tell of the hardships of the American POWs' first winter in Japan. For particulars on relief of Sgt. Tanaka and the machinations of Col. Murata, I made use of W. B. Reardon's statement in WNRC, RG 153 and the legal review of the case of the *United States* v. *Murata*, et al., RG 331. Conversion of Zentsuji to an officers' camp and conditions there were drawn from the APWIB report; Coleman's and Emerson's books, all previously cited; and a statement by J. S. Combs in WNRC, RG 153; copies of the American Red Cross *Prisoners of War Bulletin*, Vols. 1 and 2; and a biographical statement of H. J. VanPeenen, Naval Historical Division, Washington, D.C. –2– The Shinagawa POW hospital and the Omori headquarters camp are well described by A. W. Weinstein in *Barbed Wire Surgeon*, and by J. R. Davis's, E. J. Brown's, and A. J. Spilak's statements, all in WNRC, RG 153. Conditions at Kawasaki came from statements by R. H. Gilbert, T. P. Pierce, and J. B. Schwartz, RG 153. Stefan A. Nyarady told of his ordeal at Ofuna in his statement in RG 153. The quote from a Japanese soldier's diary was found in WNRC, RG 407. –3– Information and insightful interviews with J. R. Mamerow, T. H. Hewlett, M. Ruba,

J. Smulewicz, and M. Routt, along with a synopsis of evidence
in the case of the *United States* v. *Yamauchi and Fukuhara*,
both in WNRC, RG 331; the APWIB report on Fukuoka, No.
17, undated; and T. H. Hewlett's article "Di Ju Nana Bunshyo—
Nightmare Revisited," December 1978, provided the grist for
my recounting of life in this POW mining camp. The glimpses
of Hirohata, Sakurajima, and Niigata came from interviews with
H. A. Lovato, H. E. Steen, and W. Bigelow and from the APWIB
report on Sakurajima Divisional Camp, 31 July 1946. –4–
POW reactions to Christmas 1943 Red Cross supplies at the
several camps came from previously cited sources for each
camp. I based my account on visits to POW camps on the
Red Cross, *International Committee Report on Activities During the Second World War*, Vol. III; a list of POW camps inspected from 1942 to 1945, IMTFE Document 2214 and T
14729–14743; and a review of Vols. 1 and 2 of the American
Red Cross *Prisoner of War Bulletin*. Bishop Marella's quote
was found in a transcript of Radio Tokyo, June 1943, WNRC.
I turned again to the American Red Cross *Prisoners of War
Bulletins* and to Norman Greunzer's *Postal History of American POWs: WWII, Korea, Viet Nam* to tell about POW mail.
Walter Odlin's thoughtful memoir, *A POW's War*, disclosed
the story of "Humanity Calls." Col. Odashima's inspection trip
was described by him in a statement contained in WNRC,
RG 153.

ELEVEN. VOYAGES NORTH AND DISASTER

    –1– My information on the escape came from Wohlfeld's
statement previously cited. For the Davao to Manila trip, I
relied on Hardee's "Memoirs" and on an account by S. A.
Bowes, WNRC, RG 331; also on W. J. Hinckle's "POW Hell-
Ship" in the *Ex-POW Bulletin;* McGee's book; and Kent Biffle's
article on D. A. Wills in the *Dallas News*. The American intelligence agent's arrival at the Davao Penal Colony is from Mellnik's *Philippine Diary*. *Canadian Inventor* and *Nissyo Maru*,
dates of ship departures and arrivals here and later, were taken
from a listing in "General Matters re: Improper Transportation
of PWs," WNRC, RG 153 and from cross-checks with statements
with men on the ships. For the end of the underground, I

turned to Utinsky's and Philip's books, previously cited, and Calvin Chunn's diary as reproduced in his book *Of Rice and Men;* also consulted was Weinstein's *Barbed Wire Surgeon.* Identification of the final destinations of the men on the *Nissyo Maru* came from an analysis of the APWIB reports on the camps mentioned. For the experience of the men on the *Canadian Inventor,* I drew on a detailed account furnished me by Benson Guyton as well as on interviews with Saul Rubenstein and Mel Routt. –2– Sources for my story of the torpedoing of the *Shinyo Maru* were B. H. Nowell's report "USS *Paddle* (SS263)— Report of War Patrol Five" to the Commander in Chief, United States Fleet, 25 September 1944, Naval Historical Division, Washington, D.C.; a letter from M. L. Shoss to W. H. Bartsch, published in *Quan,* November 1978; and statements by C. B. Claiborne, O. A. Schoenborne, T. L. Pflueger, C. C. Johnstone, all in WNRC, RG 153, and W. P. Cain, in RG 331. –3– The description of the first dramatic air strikes on Luzon and the aftermath came from J. M. Goodman's *MD-POW* and Hardee's "Memoirs" as well as from Fendall's and Forquer's diaries; also useful was F. S. Conaty's diary. Information on the *Haru Maru* was from a written account provided by E. C. Dodson and from Goodman's book. –4– For my reconstruction of the events surrounding the sinking of the *Arisan Maru,* I drew on statements by C. R. Graef, P. Brodsky, A. E. Wilber, D. E. Myer, G. S. Oliver, and M. Binder, all in WNRC, RG 153. Also useful were C. R. Graef's "We Pray to Die" in *Cosmopolitan;* Robert S. Overbeck's "Escape in the China Sea," recorded by the MIS-X Section (date unknown); and a statement by M. Binder contained in an APWIB report, 31 July 1946. The note on the responsibility for the sinking is taken from a letter from D. C. Allard, Naval Historical Division, to L. R. Guthrie, 4 December 1975. –5– I relied heavily on Morison's *Rising Sun* and W. Craven and J. Cate's, eds., *Army Air Forces in WWII,* Vol V, for U.S. naval and air actions described here and later. Muto's quote and the ration-reduction statement by him are in WNRC, RG 331. *Hakusan Maru* information came from the American Red Cross *Prisoners of War Bulletin,* Vol. III, No. 5. The Mukden bombing was from the Matthews's interview; a statement by M. G. Herbst, WNRC, RG 153; and a statement from H. Hall, IMTFE, EX 1913–A. –6– The account of the massacre on Palawan is based on the Record of Trial of S. Terada et al., and statements by D. W. Bogue, J. Barta, and E. A. Petry, all in WNRC, RG 153. Additional information came from a report of the War Crimes Branch on atrocities, IMTFE, EX 1455.

TWELVE. LAST OF THE DEATH SHIPS

–1– No single record equals Roy L. Bodine's "Diary of a Prisoner of War of Japan in the Philippines, Japan and Korea (19 Oct. 1944–8 Sept. 1945)" as a chronicle of the arduous journey of the men who boarded the *Oryoku Maru*. It was my major source throughout this chapter. Other basic references were the statements of charges; testimony and findings contained in the Record of Trial of Junsaburo Toshino, et al. by a military commission at Yokohama (hereafter referred to as the Toshino Trial); and the legal section, Supreme Commander for the Allied Powers, Public Relations Informational Summary, 25 February 1947, both RG 153. Also referred to throughout was the E. Carl Engelhart memoir. Information on the United States Navy's air attacks were taken from Action Reports, U.S.S. *Hornet*, 14–16 December 1944, Naval Historical Center. Personal experiences of the POWs on the ill-fated ship were taken from interviews with William E. Chandler, Harold K. Johnson, Melvin H. Rosen, and Thomas J. H. Trapnell, and also from statements by James E. Alsobrook, and J. W. Schwartz, Toshino Trial. Dwight Gard's account came from his memoir, "Our Boat Trips." The escape sequence is from Darnell W. Kadolph's "The Hell Ships" in *Argosy*. –2– Additional sources tapped for the survivors' continued journey after the sinking were a written account furnished to me by H. K. Johnson and the statement of S. Tanoue, Toshino Trial. –3– In addition to Bodine's and Gard's records of their experience in the Takao bombing, I made use of C. J. Peart's "Journal—Bilibid Prison to Manchukuo," National Archives, RG 389. –4– For the final phase of the journey, I leaned on Bodine, and on H. K. Johnson's written accounts and interviews supplemented by Peart's and Engelhart's accounts. The exchange between Toshino and the ship's captain is taken from a statement by S. Kajiyama, Toshino Trial.

THIRTEEN. "I'M A LITTLE LATE, BUT WE FINALLY CAME"

−1− I drew on Samuel Eliot Morison's *Liberation of the Philippines* and on Robert R. Smith's *Triumph in the Philippines* for the historical backdrop for this and the following chapter. My major source for the Ranger raid was Forrest Johnson's *Hour of Redemption,* a detailed chronicle of this unique military operation; also helpful was the commander of the 6th Ranger Battalion report to G-3 Sixth Army, undated: "Ranger Mission at the Pangatian Prison Camp." Additional POW experience was found in the Mis-X Section Report, "Liberation from Cabanatuan, Philippines, 1st Lieutenant Raymond W. Bliss Jr." MacArthur's quote concerning the raid is from Johnson, page 347. −2− MacArthur's statements in the first and second paragraphs are from Smith, page 212, and from Morison, page 194, respectively. For the situation in Bilibid Prison as it developed, I relied on Hardee, McCracken, and Kentner; on a letter from W. A. Wilson to the author, 3 September 1981; and on an interview and correspondence with W. J. Hinckle. For the details of the rescue action, I am indebted to S. Frankel's "Rescue at Bilibid Prison" in the *37th Division Veterans News.* The commandant's proclamation is from McCracken. The MacArthur quote on his visit to Bilibid is taken from his *Reminiscences,* page 248.

FOURTEEN. DOWN THE STRETCH

−1− The Hanawa and Hosakura experiences came from statements from C. J. Jackson and J. F. Lawrence, IMTFE, EX 3137, and from Document 8029. For conditions in the Osaka area, I drew on Boyle and on an interview with Al Costello. −2− Details on the U.S. Army Air Force actions in this section and the rest of this chapter were extracted from Craven and Cate's history. The Matthews interview and White's and Rivett's books provided the POW side of the story. Major Matoba's statement in IMTFE, EX 2056–A disclosed the cannibalism on Chichi Jima. The personal reactions to the Tokyo bombings were drawn from statements by J. R. Davis, WNRC, RG 153, and F. W. Bilfinger, IMTFE, EX 375. Secret Order 2257 was found in IMTFE, EX 1978. –3– I used Clay Blair's *Silent Victory* for the *Awa Maru* episode along with the *Far East Prisoners of War Bulletin*, Vol. I, No. 1. The quote "such is the sly way . . ." is from a message from the chief of the Prisoner of War Bureau to Foreign Minister Suzuki contained in IMTFE, EX 274. –4– For events at Yodogawa and Umeda, I drew on the APWIB reports on these camps. The trip to Fengtai and Sendai was as described in Frank and Shaw's *U.S. Marine Corp History* and augmented by White's book. –5– I obtained facts on the American fliers during the Tokyo, Kyushu, and Osaka raids from a statement by H. Hoda, EX 429; *U.S.A.* v. *Tamura*, WNRC, RG 331; SCAP Monograph 5; review of trial, *U.S.A.* v. *Tashiro et al.*, WNRC, RG 331; statement by M. J. Robertson, IMTFE, EX 1953; and Boyle's book. The execution of airmen after June 17 was extracted from three reports by the Japanese Central Investigation Committee Relating to POWs, "The Treatment of Allied Air Force Personnel, 1946," IMTFE, EX 1921, 1922, and 1924. –6– The "Ketsu-Go" plan is described in Part II of *Reports of General MacArthur*, Vol. II, edited by Charles A. Willoughby. The account of Secretary Stimson's meeting is from a report by the Interim Committee on the Atomic Bomb. Quotes from the Potsdam Declaration are from *Foreign Relations of the United States, Conference at Berlin and Potsdam, 1945*, Vol. II, pages 1474–1476.

FIFTEEN. LIBERATION

United States air operations throughout this chapter come from Craven and Cate. –1– The reference to Americans who may have died in Hiroshima is from an article in *Quan*. The Nagasaki bombing descriptions were drawn from an interview with Mel Routt and from Goodman's book. –2– For the events surrounding Japan's surrender, I used Willoughby's *Reports of General MacArthur* and William Craig's *The Fall of Japan*, supplemented by IMTFE, EX 2001. –3– The reactions to the surrenders at the POW camps were described in a written account furnished to me by W. Bowsher; the books of Emerson, Boyle, and Dunn; Hewlett's article; and the Bodine diary, all previously cited. The quoted Senryu announcement is from page 202 of Goodman's book. –4– For the dramatic events at Mukden, I turned to Craig, Vance, and Quinn and the Matthews's interview. The quote "the Russian officer . . ." is from William Braley's *The Hard Way Home*, page 254. –5– For the situations at the camps while POWs awaited liberation, I turned again to the books of Coleman, White, Boyle, Quinn, and Dunn. The sources for the message "personnel who mistreated prisoners . . ." was IMTFE, EX 2011, while the information from letter by Col. Stubbs and others came from EX 3139. –6– POW receipt of air-drop supplies was taken from descriptions by Hewlett, Guyton, and Bodine. –7– Willoughby's *Reports of General MacArthur* furnished the backdrop for the rescue and evacuation activities. Individual camp stories were from Craig, Boyle, Emerson, White, Guyton, and Bodine, plus interviews with Joe Smulewicz and Saul Rubenstein.

AFTERMATH

–1– In summarizing the trial proceedings, I drew on John Mendelsohn's monograph, "The United States and the Problem of Clemency for Japanese War Criminals," undated; on SCAP Monograph 5, previously cited; and on the General Headquarters, SCAP "Final Report on War Crimes Activities," 21 June 1946. Specific sentences for individual convicted war criminals were taken from trial proceedings contained in WNRC, RG 153 and RG 331; from the National Archives Microfilm Publications pamphlet *Reviews of Yokohama Class B and Class C War Crimes Trials by the U.S. Eighth Army Judge Advocate, 1946– 1949*, 1981; and supplemented by Russell's *Knights of Bushido*. –2– The experience of ex-POWs is based on the Veterans Administration report *POW, Study of Former Prisoners of War*, 1980. The Provoo trial information came from Clark Lee's article and from R. M. Brown's *I Solemnly Swear, the Story of a GI Named Brown*. –3– The summary of POW organizations came from the publications *Quan, The Ex-POW Bulletin, The Wig Wag*, and others. –4– The description of the World War II Philippine POW camps is based on the author's observations in 1977. Charles Brown told me about the 1983 *Oryoku Maru* memorial ceremony.

SOURCES

BOOKS AND ARTICLES

It is fortunate that during World War II and in each decade since, books written by former POWs have found their way into print. Their memoirs, along with unpublished diaries, each presenting a distinctly individual view of POW life, were my basic sources for describing the collective experience of these men. For historical perspective, the relationships between the governments and the people of the United States and Japan prior to World War II and for the actions of the opposing military forces during the war itself, I turned to the excellent histories and other writings on the two periods.

Abraham, Abie, *Ghost of Bataan Speaks.* New York: Vantage Press, 1971.

Beloti, James H. and William M., *Corregidor, Saga of a Fortress.* New York: Harper and Row, 1967.

Benedict, Ruth, *The Chrysanthemum and the Sword.* Boston: Houghton Mifflin, 1946.

Bergamini, David, *Japan's Imperial Conspiracy.* New York: William Morrow, 1971.

Blair, Clay, Jr., *Silent Victory: The United States Submarine War Against Japan.* 2 vols. Philadelphia: J. B. Lippincott, 1975.

Borton, Hugh, *Japan's Modern Century.* New York: The Ronald Press, 1955.

Boyle, Martin, *Yanks Don't Cry.* New York: Random House, 1963.

Braly, William C., *The Hard Way Home.* Washington, D.C.: Infantry Journal Press, 1947.

Brougher, William E., *The Long Dark Road.* Privately published, 1946.

_____, *South to Bataan, North to Mukden.* Athens, Georgia: University of Georgia Press, 1971.

320 SURRENDER AND SURVIVAL

Brown, Charles T., *Bilibid Prison: "The Devil's Cauldron, a Fragment from That Mosaic."* San Antonio, Texas: Naylor Company, 1957.
Brown, R. M., and D. Parmenter, *I Solemnly Swear: The Story of a G.I. Named Brown.* New York: Vantage Press, 1957.
Butow, Robert J. C., *Tojo and the Coming of the War.* Princeton, New Jersey: Princeton University Press, 1961.
Byas, Hugh, *Government by Assassination.* New York: Knopf, 1942.
Chunn, Calvin E., *Of Rice and Men.* Los Angeles: Veteran's Publishing Company, 1946.
Chynoweth, Bradford G., *Bellamy Park.* Hicksville, New York: Exposition Press, 1975.
Coleman, J. S., *Bataan and Beyond.* College Station, Texas: Texas A & M Press, 1978.
Craig, William, *The Fall of Japan.* New York: Dial Press, 1967.
Craigie, Sir Robert, *Behind the Japanese Mask.* London: Hutchinson, 1945.
Craven, W. F., and J. L. Cate, eds., *The Pacific—Matterhorn to Nagasaki,* Vol. V, *The Army Air Forces in World War II.* Chicago: University of Chicago Press, 1953.
Cunningham, W. S. with Lydel Sims, *Wake Island Command.* Boston: Little, Brown, 1961.
Department of State, *Foreign Relations of the United States, Conference at Berlin and Potsdam, 1945.* Washington, D.C.: Government Printing Office, 1947.
Devereaux, James P. S., *The Story of Wake Island.* New York: J. B. Lippincott, 1947.
Dull, Paul S., and Michael T. Umemura, *The Tokyo Trials: A Functional Index to the Proceedings of the International Military Tribunal for the Far East.* Ann Arbor, Michigan: University of Michigan Press, 1957.
Dunn, Benjamin, *The Bamboo Express.* Chicago: Adams Press, 1979.
Dyess, William E., *The Dyess Story.* New York: C. P. Putnam's Sons, 1944.
Eads, Lyle, *Survival Amidst the Ashes.* New York: Carlton Press, 1978.
Eichelberger, Robert L., *Our Jungle Road to Tokyo.* New York: Viking Press, 1950.
Emerson, K. C., *Guest of the Emperor.* Privately published, 1977.
Falk, Stanley, *Bataan: The March of Death.* New York: W. W. Norton, 1962.
Feis, Herbert, *The Road to Pearl Harbor.* Princeton, New Jersey: Princeton University Press, 1950.
Fortier, Malcom V., *Life of a POW Under the Japanese.* Spokane,

Washington: G. W. Hill Printing Company, 1946.

Frank, Benis M., and Henry I. Shaw, Jr., *Victory and Occupation,* Vol. V, *History of U.S.M.C. Operations in World War II.* Washington, D.C.: Government Printing Office, 1968.

Goodman, J. M., *MD—POW.* New York: Exposition Press, 1972.

Greunzer, Norman, *Postal History of American POWs: World War II, Korea, Vietnam.* State College, Pennsylvania: American Philatelic Society, 1979.

Gulick, Sidney, L., *Toward Understanding the Japanese.* New York: The Macmillan Company, 1935.

Hawkins, Jack, *Never Say Die.* Philadelphia: Dorrance and Company, 1961.

Ienaga, Saburo, *The Pacific War.* New York: Random House, 1978.

Ingle, Don, *Fall Forward, My Son.* New York: Carlton Press, 1974.

International Committee of the Red Cross, *Report of the International Committee of the Red Cross on Its Activities During the Second World War.* 3 vols. Geneva: International Committee of the Red Cross, 1948.

Johnson, Forrest B., *Hour of Redemption: The Ranger Raid on Cabanatuan.* New York: Manor Books, 1978.

Keith, Billy, *Days of Anguish, Days of Hope.* New York: Doubleday, 1972.

Kent-Hughes, W. S., *Slaves of the Samurai.* Melbourne, Australia: Ramsey Ware Publishing, Ltd., 1946.

Kennedy, Captain M. D., *The Military Side of Japanese Life.* Boston: Houghton Mifflin, 1923.

Knox, Donald, *Death March.* New York: Harcourt Brace Jovanovich, 1981.

Lory, Hillis, *Japan's Military Masters: The Army in Japanese Life.* New York: Viking, 1943.

MacArthur, Douglas, *Reminiscences.* New York: McGraw-Hill, 1964.

Matloff, Maurice, and Edwin Snell, *Strategic Planning for Coalition Warfare: 1941–1942.* U.S. Army in World War II, Washington, D.C.: Government Printing Office, 1953.

McCoy, Melvin H., Steve Mellnik, and Wellborn Kelley, *Ten Escape from Tojo.* New York: Farrar and Rinehart, 1944.

McCracken, Alan, *Very Soon Now, Joe.* New York: Hobson Book Press, 1947.

McGee, John H., *Rice and Salt.* San Antonio, Texas: Naylor Company, 1962.

Mellnik, S. M., *Philippine Diary.* New York: Van Nostrand, Reinhold, 1969.

Mendelsohn, John, "The United States and the Problem of Clemency for Japanese War Criminals." National Archives Monograph, undated.

Miller, Ernest B., *Bataan Uncensored.* Long Prairie, Minnesota: Hart Publications, 1949.

Moody, Samuel B., *Reprieve from Hell.* New York: Pageant Press, 1961.

Morison, Samuel Eliot, *The Rising Sun in the Pacific,* Vol. III. History of the United States Naval Operations in World War II. Boston: Little, Brown, 1948.

————, *Leyte.* Vol. XII, 1958.

————, *The Liberation of the Philippines.* Vol. XIII, 1959.

————, *Victory in the Pacific.* Vol. XIV, 1960.

Morton, Louis, *The Fall of the Philippines.* U.S. Army in World War II, Washington, D.C.: Government Printing Office, 1953.

————, *Strategy and Command: The First Two Years.* 1962.

Myers, Hugh N., *Prisoner of War, World War II.* Portland, Oregon: Metropolitan Press, 1965.

National Archives, *Reviews of Yokohama Class B and Class C War Crimes Trials by the U.S. Eighth Army Judge Advocate, 1946–1949.* Microfilm publications pamphlet, Washington, D.C.: Government Printing Office, 1981.

Neumann, William L., *America Encounters Japan: From Perry to MacArthur.* Baltimore: The Johns Hopkins Press, 1963.

Phillips, Claire, *Manila Espionage.* Portland, Oregon: Binford and Morts, 1947.

Quinn, Michael, A., *Love Letters to Mike.* New York: Vantage Press, 1977.

Reischauer, Edwin O., *The United States and Japan.* Cambridge, Massachusetts: Harvard University Press, 1957.

Rivett, Rohan D., *Behind Bamboo.* Sydney, Australia: Argus and Robertson, 1946.

Robinson, Arthur, "Relief to Prisoners of War in World War II." Department of State monograph, undated.

Russell, Lord, of Liverpool, *Knights of Bushido.* London: Cassell and Company, Ltd., 1958.

Schultz, Duane, *Hero of Bataan: The Story of General Jonathan M. Wainwright.* New York: St. Martin's Press, 1981.

Smith, Robert R., *Triumph in the Philippines.* U.S. Army in World War II, Washington, D.C.: Government Printing Office, 1963.

Stewart, Sidney, *Give Us This Day.* New York: W. W. Norton Company, 1957.

Tasaki, Hanama, *Long the Imperial Way.* Boston: Houghton Mifflin, 1950.

Thompson, Paul W., et al., *How the Jap Army Fights.* Washington, D.C.: Infantry Journal Press, 1942.

Toland, John, *But Not in Shame.* New York: Random House, 1961.

———, *The Rising Sun: The Decline and Fall of the Japanese Empire, 1936–1945.* New York: Random House, 1970.

Utinsky, Margaret, *Miss "U."* San Antonio, Texas: Naylor Company, 1948.

Vance, John R., *Doomed Garrison—The Philippines (A POW Story).* Ashland, Oregon: Cascade House, 1974.

Van der Post, Laurens, *The Prisoner and the Bomb.* New York: Morrow, 1971.

Veterans Administration, *POW—Study of Former Prisoners of War.* Washington, D.C.: Government Printing Office, 1980.

Wainwright, Jonathan, *General Wainwright's Story,* ed. Robert Considine. Garden City, New York: Doubleday, 1946.

Watson, Mark S., *Chief of Staff: Prewar Plans and Preparations: 1941–1942.* U.S. Army in World War II, Washington, D.C.: Government Printing Office, 1950.

Weinstein, A. M., *Barbed Wire Surgeon.* New York: The Macmillan Company, 1948.

Willoughby, Charles A., ed., *Reports of General MacArthur.* (5 vols. in 4 parts). Washington, D.C.: Department of the Army, 1966.

UNPUBLISHED DIARIES, MEMOIRS, AND OTHER DOCUMENTS

Unpublished diaries, journals or records written at or close to the time events occurred were important sources. Also valuable were a number of fine memoirs that have not yet found a publisher. Copies or excerpts of all items shown are in the author's files.

DIARIES AND JOURNALS
(with titles, if any, and the sources indicated)

Ames, Godfrey R.	Recovered Records, RCPAC,* Office of the Adjutant General, St. Louis, MO
Conaty, F. S.	Recovered Records, RCPAC, Office of the Adjutant General, St. Louis, MO
Fendall, E. R.	Recovered Records, RCPAC, Office of the Adjutant General, St. Louis, MO
Fields, Albert	Recovered Records, RCPAC, Office of the Adjutant General, St. Louis, MO

* Reserve Components Personnel and Administration Center.

Northway, Edward S. Recovered Records, RCPAC, Office of the Adjutant General, St. Louis, MO

Oliver, William P. Recovered Records, RCPAC, Office of the Adjutant General, St. Louis, MO

Ranson, Kenneth E. Recovered Records, RCPAC, Office of the Adjutant General, St. Louis, MO

Chunn, Calvin Printed in Calvin Chunn's *Of Rice and Men*

Guyton, Benson Printed in Calvin Chunn's *Of Rice and Men*

Forquer, Eugene Washington National Records Center, Record Group 153

Hayes, Thomas H. Washington National Records Center, Record Group 153

Peart, C. J. "Journal—Bilibid Prison to Manchukuo," National Archives, Record Group 389

Bodine, Roy L., Jr. "Diary of a Prison of War of Japan in the Philippines, Japan and Korea (19 October 1944–8 September 1945)," The Writer

Gamble, John S. "Notes" (Written while aboard the *Oryoku Enoura Maru*), Colonel J. R. Vance

Svihra, Albert West Point Library

MEMOIRS

Bodine, Roy L., Jr. "Bataan and the Jap Prison Camps (an object lesson in military preparedness)," The Writer

Engelhart, Carl E. The Writer

Gard, Dwight "Our Boat Trips" Colonel J. R. Vance

Hardee, David L. "Memoirs of a Jap Prison of War," Colonel J. R. Vance

Odlin, Walter "A POW's War" The Writer

OTHER

Death Reports— Colonel J. R. Vance
Cabanatuan

INTERVIEWS

Even after nearly four decades, I found the memory of some men vivid and the precision of their recall truly remarkable. Interviews and correspondence with such men from 1979 to 1983 provided a better grasp of the feelings and emotions of the POW and often provided information unavailable in written accounts.

N. A. Albertsen

W. Bigelow

Roy L. Bodine

Walter A. Bowsher

Art Bressi

Charles M. Brown

William E. Chandler

Robert M. Costello

T. A. Cressner

Gene Crispi

Earl C. Dodson

E. Carl Engelhart

Thomas Essaf

J. C. Finch

Stanley Frankel

H. C. Freuler

Edward Fung

Crayton R. Gordon

Benson Guyton

T. H. Hewlett

W. J. Hinkle

R. J. Hutchinson

Harold K. Johnson

Yoshio Kai

J. F. Kinney

Manny Lawton

Kermit Lay

David Levy

H. A. Lovato

J. R. Mamerow

Thurman Matthews

Lewis Moldenhauer

Walter Odlin

John Podelesny

L. E. Poulin

R. F. Riera

Melvin H. Rosen

Mel Routt

Matt Ruba

Saul Rubenstein

Joe Smulewicz

William Spizziro

H. E. Steen

Charles A. Stenger

Jack Stevenson

J. B. Tracy

Thomas J. H. Trapnell

John R. Vance

J. A. White

W. A. Wilson

Warren Wilson

Walter C. Winslow

Jack Winterholler

OFFICIAL SOURCES

An account of the POW experience would be incomplete without a description of the policies, attitudes, and actions of the Japanese captors. The records of sworn testimony and supporting evidence resulting from the trials of accused war criminals were the major source of information for this. In using the legal records I, as did the members of the tribunals, courts, and commissions before me, had to do my best to determine what was fact and what was not. The statements of Americans contain varying amounts of emotional upwelling, vengefulness, and exaggeration. The responses of the accused—many with their very lives at stake—were often laden with self-serving accounts of events. Despite these deficiencies, the testimony provided a vast store house of information provided nowhere else. Also of great value were investigative reports prepared by Americans as part of the legal process. Finally, the trial proceedings yielded copies of Japanese directives, messages, and minutes of meetings prepared during the war that pertained to POWs. Unfortunately, the number of these documents is not great because of both deliberate and accidental destruction.

The legal proceedings I used were found in two collections. One is that of the International Military Tribunal for the Far East (IMTFE). This tribunal sat in judgment of the sixteen so-called Class A war criminals—those accused of being involved in the planning, initiation, or waging of wars of aggression. The accused included the war minister, Hideki Tojo, and other top government officials and military officers, some of whom were directly or indirectly involved with POW matters. The voluminous proceedings, thousands of pages of testimony and supporting documents, can be found in about a dozen locations in the United States. One of the more complete sets, which I made use of, is in the University of California, Berkeley library.

The second collection, actually two separate groups of records, is in the Washington National Records Center (WNRC) located in Suitland, Maryland, and is part of the National Archives. The first group, assembled by the legal section, Headquarters, Supreme Commander Allied Powers (SCAP), is Record Group (RG) 331. It consists of about 100 boxes of documents on the Japanese war crimes trials that at the time of my research were stored essentially as they were received by the repository. The second and largest group is the Judge Advocate General, Record Group 153. This collection of about 800 boxes covers both the German and the Japanese war crimes trials. About 340 of the boxes deal with the Japanese. Access to specific documents in both record groups is through research assistants at the Washington National Record Center. The records can, in most cases, be accessed by the name of an individual or geographical location though RG 331 is not as completely catalogued as RG 153.

Some of the basic information on POW camps was drawn from the Provost Marshal General, American POW Information Bureau, Liaison and Research Branch, "POW Camps in Japan and Japanese Controlled Areas as Taken from Reports of Interned Prisoners." A set of these reports is found in the National Archives, Washington, D.C.

Other valuable official sources not noted elsewhere were: the Naval Historical Center, Washington, D.C., for copies of the operational records of air, surface, and submarine units of the U.S. Navy; the

National Archives and the Defense Audio-Visual Agency, both in Washington, D.C., for photographs; and the Association of Graduates, West Point, N.Y., for information on POWs who were graduates of this institution.

OTHER SOURCES

Published materials by the following organizations were used as sources as indicated in the Chapter Notes: American Red Cross, Washington, D.C., *Prisoners of War Bulletin, Vols. I, II, III* and *Far Eastern Prisoners of War Bulletin,* Vol. I, No. 1; American Ex-Prisoners of War, 700 W. Wabash Street, Olathe, Kansas, issues of the *Ex-POW Bulletin;* American Defenders of Bataan and Corregidor, 18 Warbler Drive, McKees Rock, Pennsylvania, issues of *The Quan;* Defenders of Wake Island, 2225 S. Overton, Independence, Missouri, issues of the *Wig-Wag;* Lost Battalion Association, 1617 Carls Street, Ft. Worth, Texas, "Roster of the Lost Battalion Association"; the 37th Division Veterans Organization, 65 S. Front Street, Rm. 707, Columbus, Ohio, copies of the *37th Division Veterans News.*

APPENDIX A

The 1929 Geneva Convention Relative to the
Treatment of Prisoners of War

Those provisions which had the most influence on the lives and ultimate fate of American POWs of the Japanese are set forth below:

GENERAL

ARTICLE 2

Prisoners of war are in the power of the hostile Power, but not of the individuals or corps who have captured them.

They must at all times be humanely treated and protected, particularly against acts of violence, insults and public curiosity.

Measures of reprisal against them are prohibited.

ARTICLE 7

Prisoners of war shall be evacuated within the shortest possible period after their capture, to depots located in a region far enough from the zone of combat for them to be out of danger.

Only prisoners who, because of wounds or sickness, would run greater risks by being evacuated than by remaining where they are may be temporarily kept in a dangerous zone.

Prisoners shall not be needlessly exposed to danger while awaiting their evacuation from the combat zone.

Evacuation of prisoners on foot may normally be effected only by stages

Source: U.S. Department of State, *Multilateral Agreements, 1918–1930,* pp. 938–957.

of 20 kilometers a day, unless the necessity of reaching water and food depots requires longer stages.

CAMPS

ARTICLE 9

Prisoners of war may be interned in a town, fortress, or other place, and bound not to go beyond certain fixed limits. They may also be interned in enclosed camps; they may not be confined or imprisoned except as an indispensable measure of safety or sanitation, and only while the circumstances which necessitate the measure continue to exist.

Prisoners captured in unhealthful regions or where the climate is injurious for persons coming from temperate regions, shall be transported, as soon as possible, to a more favorable climate.

Belligerents shall, so far as possible, avoid assembling in a single camp prisoners of different races or nationalities.

No prisoner may, at any time, be sent into a region where he might be exposed to the fire of the combat zone, nor used to give protection from bombardment to certain points or certain regions by his presence.

ARTICLE 11

The food ration of prisoners of war shall be equal in quantity and quality to that of troops at base camps.

Furthermore, prisoners shall receive facilities for preparing, themselves, additional food which they might have.

A sufficiency of potable water shall be furnished them. The use of tobacco shall be permitted. Prisoners may be employed in the kitchens.

All collective disciplinary measures affecting the food are prohibited.

ARTICLE 12

Clothing, linen and footwear shall be furnished prisoners of war by the detaining Power. Replacement and repairing of these effects must be assured regularly. In addition, laborers must receive work clothes wherever the nature of the work requires it.

Canteens shall be installed in all camps where prisoners may obtain, at the local market price, food products and ordinary objects.

Profits made by the canteens for camp administrations shall be used for the benefit of prisoners.

ARTICLE 13

Belligerents shall be bound to take all sanitary measures necessary to assure the cleanliness and healthfulness of camps and to prevent epidemics.

Prisoners of war shall have at their disposal, day and night, installations conforming to sanitary rules and constantly maintained in a state of cleanliness.

Furthermore, and without prejudice to baths and showers with which the camp shall be as well provided as possible, prisoners shall be furnished a sufficient quantity of water for the care of their own bodily cleanliness.

It shall be possible for them to take physical exercise and enjoy the open air.

ARTICLE 18

Officers who are prisoners of war are bound to salute only officers of a higher or equal rank of that Power.

LABOR

ARTICLE 30

The length of the day's work of prisoners of war, including therein the trip going and returning, shall not be excessive and must not, in any case, exceed that allowed for the civil workers in the region employed at the same work. Every prisoner shall be allowed a rest of twenty-four consecutive hours every week, preferably on Sunday.

ARTICLE 31

Labor furnished by prisoners of war shall have no direct relation with war operations. It is especially prohibited to use prisoners for manufacturing and transporting arms or munitions of any kind, or for transporting material intended for combatant units.

In case of violation of the provisions of the preceding paragraph, prisoners, after executing or beginning to execute the order, shall be free to have their protests presented through the mediation of the agents whose functions are set forth in Articles 43 and 44, or, in the absence of an agent, through the mediation of representatives of the protecting Power.

ARTICLE 32

It is forbidden to use prisoners of war at unhealthful or dangerous work.

Any aggravation of the conditions of labor by disciplinary measures is forbidden.

EXTERNAL RELATIONS

ARTICLE 40

Censorship of correspondence must be effected within the shortest possible time. Furthermore, inspection of parcels post must be effected under proper conditions to guarantee the preservation of the products which they may contain and, if possible, in the presence of the addressee or an agent duly recognized by him.

Prohibitions of correspondence promulgated by the belligerents for military or political reasons must be transient in character and as short as possible.

ARTICLE 42

Prisoners of war shall have the right to inform the military authorities in whose power they are of their requests with regard to the conditions of captivity to which they are subjected.

They shall also have the right to address themselves to representatives of the protecting Powers to indicate to them the points on which they have complaints to formulate with regard to the conditions of captivity.

These requests and complaints must be transmitted immediately.

Even if they are recognized to be unfounded, they may not occasion any punishment.

DISCIPLINARY PUNISHMENT

ARTICLE 45

Prisoners of war shall be subject to the laws, regulations, and orders in force in the armies of the detaining Power.

An act of insubordination shall justify the adoption towards them of the measures provided by such laws, regulations and orders.

The provisions of the present chapter, however, are reserved.

ARTICLE 46

Punishments other than those provided for the same acts for soldiers of the national armies may not be imposed upon prisoners of war by the military authorities and courts of the detaining Power.

Rank being identical, officers, noncommissioned officers or soldiers who are prisoners of war undergoing a disciplinary punishment shall not be subject to less favorable treatment than that provided in the armies of the detaining Power with regard to the same punishment.

Any corporal punishment, any imprisonment in quarters without daylight and, in general, any form of cruelty, is forbidden.

Collective punishment for individual acts is also forbidden.

ARTICLE 47

Acts constituting an offense against discipline, and particularly attempted escape, shall be verified immediately; for all prisoners of war, commissioned or not, preventive arrest shall be reduced to the absolute minimum.

Judicial proceedings against prisoners of war shall be conducted as rapidly as the circumstances permit; preventive imprisonment shall be limited as much as possible.

In all cases, the duration of preventive imprisonment shall be deducted from the disciplinary or judicial punishment inflicted, provided that this deduction is allowed for national soldiers.

ARTICLE 51

Attempted escape, even if it is a repetition of the offense, shall not be considered as an aggravating circumstance in case the prisoner of war should be given over to the courts on account of crimes or offenses against persons or property committed in the course of that attempt.

After an attempted or accomplished escape, the comrades of the person escaping who assisted in the escape may incur only disciplinary punishment on this account.

ARTICLE 54

Arrest is the most severe disciplinary punishment which may be imposed on a prisoner of war.

The duration of a single punishment may not exceed thirty days.

This maximum of thirty days may not, further, be exceeded in the case of several acts for which the prisoner has to undergo discipline at the time when it is ordered for him, whether or not these acts are connected.

When, during or after the end of a period of arrest, a prisoner shall have a new disciplinary punishment imposed upon him, a space of at least three days shall separate each of the periods of arrest, if one of them is ten days or more.

ARTICLE 56

In no case may prisoners of war be transferred to penitentiary establishments (prisons, penitentiaries, convict prisons, etc.) there to undergo disciplinary punishment.

The quarters in which they undergo disciplinary punishment shall conform to sanitary requirements.

Prisoners punished shall be enabled to keep themselves in a state of cleanliness.

These prisoners shall every day be allowed to exercise or to stay in the open air at least two hours.

JUDICIAL PUNISHMENT

ARTICLE 60

At the opening of a judicial proceeding directed against a prisoner of war, the detaining Power shall advise the representative of the protecting Power thereof as soon as possible, and always before the date set for the opening of the trial. . . .

ARTICLE 65

Sentences pronounced against prisoners of war shall be communicated to the protecting Power immediately.

ARTICLE 66

If the death penalty is pronounced against a prisoner of war, a communication setting forth in detail the nature and circumstances of the offense shall be sent as soon as possible to the representative of the protecting Power, for transmission to the Power in whose armies the prisoner served.

The sentence shall not be executed before the expiration of a period of at least three months after this communication.

INFORMATION

ARTICLE 77

Upon the outbreak of hostilities, each of the belligerent Powers, as well as the neutral Powers which have received belligerents, shall institute an official information bureau for prisoners of war who are within their territory.

Within the shortest possible period, each of the belligerent Powers shall inform its information bureau of every capture of prisoners effected by its armies, giving it all the information regarding identity which it has, allowing it quickly to advise the families concerned, and informing it of the official addresses to which families may write to prisoners.

The information bureau shall immediately forward all this information to the interested Powers, through the intervention, on one hand, of the protecting Powers and, on the other, of the central agency provided for in Article 79.

APPENDIX B

Japanese Army Regulations
for Handling Prisoners of War

The regulations reproduced below were originally issued in February 1904 as Army Instruction No. 22 and with some revisions thereafter were in force at the beginning of World War II.

Regulations for the handling of prisoners of war shall be as follows:

CHAPTER I
General Rules

Article 1. The term prisoner(s) of war as used in these regulations shall refer to combatants of enemy nationality or to those who by treaty or custom are entitled to treatment as prisoners of war.

Article 2. Prisoners of war shall be treated with a spirit of goodwill and shall never be subjected to cruelties or humiliation.

Article 3. Prisoners of war shall be given suitable treatment in accordance with their position and rank. However, those who fail to reply with sincerity and truth to questions regarding name and rank, and violators of other rules, shall not be included in this.

Article 4. Prisoners of war shall be required to conform to the discipline and regulations of the Imperial Army. Beyond this, their persons shall not be subjected to unwarranted restriction.

Article 5. Insofar as military discipline and moral standards are not affected, prisoners of war shall have freedom of religion and shall be permitted to attend worship in accordance with their respective sects.

Source: Stanley Falk: *Bataan: The March of Death,* Appendix A.

Article 6. In case of disobedience it shall be permissible to hold a prisoner of war in confinement or detention or to subject him to other necessary disciplinary action. In case a prisoner of war attempts to escape, he may be stopped by armed force and if necessary killed or wounded.

Article 7. When a prisoner of war not under oath is captured in attempted escape, he shall be subjected to disciplinary action.

When such a prisoner of war, after successful escape, is again made prisoner of war, no punishment shall be inflicted for the previous escape.

Article 8. The methods of disciplining prisoners of war shall, besides following the foregoing articles, be in accordance with the provisions of the army regulation for minor punishments. Criminal acts of prisoners of war shall be tried by army court-martial.

CHAPTER II

Capture and Transportation to the Rear of Prisoners of War

Article 9. When a person to be treated as a prisoner of war is captured, his personal belongings shall be immediately inspected, and weapons, ammunition and other articles which may be put to military use shall be confiscated. Other belongings shall either be held in deposit or shall be left in his possession as circumstances require.

Article 10. When, among the prisoners of war mentioned in the foregoing article, there are officers who should be treated with special honor, an army commander or independent divisional commander may permit them to carry their own swords.

In such cases the names of the prisoners of war together with the reasons shall be reported to Imperial General Headquarters, from whence due notice shall be transmitted to the Ministry of War. The weapons which had been carried shall be held in deposit in the prisoners of war camp.

Article 11. Commanders of armies and of independent divisions shall, upon negotiations with the enemy forces after combat, be permitted to return or exchange captured sick and wounded prisoners of war who swear on oath not to take part in combat during the remainder of the same war.

In such case, names, total number and reasons shall be reported to Imperial General Headquarters from whence the Ministry of War shall be duly notified.

Article 12. Each unit capturing prisoners shall duly interrogate said prisoners, prepare a roster containing the name, age, rank, home address, home unit and place and date of wounding; a prisoner of war diary; and inventories of articles confiscated or held in deposit in accordance with the provisions of Article 9.

When, as provided for in the next foregoing article, the return, exchange or release on oath of prisoners of war are effected, the fact shall be noted on the prisoner of war roster.

Article 13. Prisoners of war shall be divided into officers and warrant officers and under and shall be transported under guard to the nearest line of communications command or transport and communications organization.

When this is done, the articles held in deposit, prisoner of war rosters, prisoner of war diaries and inventories shall be forwarded together with the captured personnel.

Article 14. Army units, line of communications commands or transport and communications organizations may, upon conference on the handing over of PW's by a naval commanding officer, receive into custody those prisoners of war together with deposited articles, rosters, diaries, and inventories.

Article 15. Commanders of armies or independent divisions shall promptly report to Imperial General Headquarters the number of prisoners of war they desire to send to the rear. Imperial General Headquarters shall inform the Ministry of War thereof.

Article 16. When the Ministry of War is in receipt of the information mentioned in the foregoing Article 15, it shall report to the Imperial General Headquarters the post or other location where the reception of prisoners of war will be effected. Imperial General Headquarters shall inform the Ministry of War regarding the expected date of arrival at the designated point.

The same procedure shall be followed when the Ministry of War has been informed regarding the reception of prisoners taken by the Navy.

Article 17. Line of communications commands and transport and communications organizations which in accordance with Articles 13 and 14 have accepted prisoners of war shall transport said prisoners of war under guard to the location(s) mentioned in the foregoing article and shall there transfer said PW's together with deposited articles, PW rosters, PW diaries and inventories to the custody of the officer of the War Ministry charged with reception.

Article 18. When no Imperial General Headquarters is established, "Imperial General Headquarters" in this chapter shall be taken to read "General Staff Headquarters."

CHAPTER III
Accommodation and Control
of Prisoners of War

Article 19. (Rescinded)

Article 20. For prisoners of war accommodations, army establishments, temples or other buildings which suffice to prevent escape and are not detrimental to the health and honor of the prisoners shall be utilized.

Article 21. The army commander or garrison area commander under whose jurisdiction comes the administration of Prisoner of War camps (hereinafter to be referred to as the High Administrator of PW camps) shall determine

338 SURRENDER AND SURVIVAL

"regulations concerning PW camp duties" and shall make a report thereof to the Minister of War and duly inform the Director General of the PW Information Bureau.

Article 22. (Rescinded)

Article 23. (Rescinded)

Article 24. (Rescinded)

Article 25. (Rescinded)

Article 26. Insofar as mail sent and received by prisoners of war is, by international treaty, exempted from postage dues, the High Administrator of PW camps shall confer with the Post Office in the vicinity of the PW accommodations and shall determine a suitable procedure for the handling of postal matters.

Article 27. Rules and regulations concerning control within PW camps shall be determined by the High Administrator.

CHAPTER IV
Miscellaneous Rules

Article 28. Those enemy sick and wounded who, after medical treatment at dressing stations or hospitals, are considered incapable of military service shall, after due promise not to serve in the same war, be returned to their homes. However, those who have important relations with the conduct of the war are not included in this.

Article 29. Articles belonging to the prisoners of war and held in deposit by Imperial Government offices shall be restored to their possession at the time of their release.

Article 30. In case of the death of a prisoner of war, the money and possessions of the deceased shall be sent to the Prisoner of War Information Bureau by the unit, organization, hospital or dressing station concerned. When the belongings are of a perishable nature, such shall be sold and the proceeds of the sale shall be forwarded instead.

Article 31. The last will and testament of a deceased prisoner of war shall be handled in the same way as that of Japanese military personnel by the unit, organization, hospital or dressing station concerned, and shall be duly forwarded to the Prisoner of War Information Bureau.

Article 32. (Rescinded)

Article 33. Direct welfare activities for the benefit of prisoners of war by organizations legally established for charitable purposes may be permitted on submittal of a written pledge to the effect that no infractions or violations of the rules and regulations concerning prisoners will be made.

APPENDIX C

American POWs of the Japanese 1941–1945

Estimated Number Captured, Died, Returned to U.S. Control

I. American military personnel captured by the Japanese in the Pacific Ocean area:

The Philippines	22,000
Wake Island	1,555
Java	890
Japan and elsewhere	300
Celebes	255
Guam	400
China	200
	25,600

II. American military personnel killed or died after capture by the Japanese:

The Philippines	5,135
On prison ships	3,840
Japan	1,200
Manchuria	175
Burma	130
Wake Island	100
Korea	70
	10,650

III. American military personnel liberated by or rejoining U.S. forces:

Japan	11,400
The Philippines	1,500
Manchuria	1,200
Burma–Thailand	480
Celebes	200
Korea	150
China	20
	14,950

Sources Used in Estimation

1. Philippine Department, U.S. Army, Machine Records Unit—Station Strength and Miscellaneous, November 1941; Philippine Harbor Defense report of operations; *Operations in the Pacific in World War II, The Rising Sun in the Pacific* by S. E. Morison; Records of the Lost Battalion Association; United States POWs, Provost Marshal General estimate, December 20, 1944; Japanese report on American POWs, June 1946.

2. Official records of deaths, Cabanatuan and Camp O'Donnell; records, diaries, and postwar statements and writings pertaining to Manchuria and Korea; records of the Lost Battalion Association; Japanese testimony during Allied war crimes trials pertaining to downed American flyers.

3. U.S. Army reports of recovered U.S. personnel; postwar statements and writings of survivors.

INDEX

12/85

DATE DUE